Exile and Tradition

Dalhousie African Studies Series

General Editor: John Flint

Exile and Tradition

Studies in African and Caribbean Literature

Edited by Rowland Smith

Africana Publishing Company
A Division of Holmes & Meier Publishers
New York
Dalhousie University Press

First published in the United States of America 1976 by
Africana Publishing Company
a division of
Holmes & Meier Publishers, Inc.
101 Fifth Avenue
New York, New York 10003

© Longman Group Ltd 1976

First published 1976

Library of Congress Cataloging in Publication Data
Main entry under title:

Exile and tradition: studies in African and
    Caribbean literature.

    (Dalhousie African studies series)
    1.   African literature—History and criticism—
Addresses, essays, lectures. 2.   Negro literature—
History and criticism—Addresses, essays, lectures.
I.   Smith, Rowland, 1938–   II.   Series.
PL8010.E9   1976   896   76-2379

ISBN 0-8419-0263-1
ISBN 0-8419-0264-x pbk.

Printed in Great Britain

Contents

Acknowledgements

We are grateful to the following for permission to reproduce copyright material:

A. D. Donker Ltd for the poems 'Ode to a Still-Born Child' and 'The Pension of Jiveass' by Mandelenkoso Langa, 'Two Buckets' by Stanley Mogoba, 'I Hid My Love' by Njabulo S. Ndebele and 'Gumba, Gumba, Gumba' by M. Pascal Gwala from *To Whom It May Concern* edited by Robert Royston, published by A. D. Donker, 1973; Raven Press (Pty) Ltd for the poems 'To Label My Utterings Poetry', 'Valley of Plenty is What it is Called', 'They Speak so Sorrowfully . . .', 'Liberal Student Crap!', 'Can the White Man Speak for Me?', 'Say, Percy Dad', 'My Sister has Become a Schemer', 'Democracy has been turned into a Whore', 'Two Little Black Boys', 'Fall To-morrow', copyright James Matthews and Gladys Thomas, 1972, from *Cry Rage!*, 1972; Oxford University Press and The Third Press for the poems 'An Abandoned Bundle', 'The Moulting County Bird', 'The Detribalized', 'The Chauffeur Shuffle', 'Always a Suspect', 'Boy on a Swing', 'This Kid is No Goat' and 'Ride Upon the Death Chariot' from *Sounds of a Cowhide Drum* by Oswald Mbuyiseni Mtshali, published by Oxford University Press © Oswald Joseph Mtshali 1971, reprinted by permission of the publisher; Présence Africaine for the poems 'Return' from *Présence Africaine* 1971 and 'Against our love which asked for nothing more' from *Névralgies* in *Présence Africaine* 1965; Renoster Press for the poems 'City Johannesburg', 'Ofay-Watcher Throbs-Phase', 'Ofay-Watcher Looks Back', 'What's In This Black Shit?', 'Black Bells' and 'That's Not my Wish' by Mongane Wally Serote from *Yakhal'Inkomo*, Renoster Books, 1972, copyright © 1972; the author for his poem 'Five Letters to M.M.M.' by Njabulo S. Ndebele.

We regret that we have been unable to trace the copyright holders of the following and would appreciate any information that would enable us to do so:

The poem 'Raving Mad' from *Cadastre* published by Editions Du Seuil; the poems 'This Side of Town' and 'You Never Know' by Mike Dues.

Rowland Smith

Introduction

The similarity of concern among these essays is remarkable. Although they deal with the literature of areas separated from one another by geography, politics, and even language, the authors return repeatedly to two basic issues. These are the traditions peculiar to African cultures and the sense of alienation which has so frequently resulted from the imposition of western codes on those formerly organic cultures. The unique quality of specific African views or situations is a theme common to most essays in this collection. Kofi Awoonor and Wole Soyinka write theoretically about the differences between western and African aesthetic assumptions. Nadine Gordimer describes the work of South Africa's new black poets struggling to capture in their writing the nightmare reality of their day-to-day world. Chinua Achebe insists on a 'local and particular' vision. And D. Ibe Nwoga analyses the critical consequences of the peculiar fusion of traditions underlying modern African writing.

This basic obsession with the differences between indigenous reality and the imposed values of Africa's white conquerors is to be found in all the essays. It manifests itself in Daniel Kunene's discussion of the literature of Lesotho as it emerged in missionary-dominated literacy during the nineteenth century. The cultural schism between the Sesotho writer trained to revere 'European' literacy and his indigenous audience is mirrored in Isaac Yetiv's essay on an identical schizophrenia found at the opposite end of the continent among French-educated North African writers. And Peter Okeh's picture of 'authentic' Africa (that 'natural' Africa of pre-colonial times) revealed in Camara Laye's writing leads into his discussion of the perversion of these values—by the French colonial regime—as seen in Oyono's work. Even the more specific cases of alienation dealt with in G. D. Killam's essay on *Arrow of God,* and in the essay on 'The Johannesburg *Genre*', are aspects of the central theme of this collection.

Emile Snyder's chapter on Césaire and Max Dorsinville's chapter on Senghor share the legacy of common terminology and assumptions bequeathed by the French proponents of Negritude. In addition they deal with the concept of exiled consciousness which French black writers have discussed so evocatively. In the Caribbean the cultural exile of the African under European domination was matched by a physical exile. As a result, Caribbean literary traditions offer a fascinating perspective on Africa. And Maximilien Laroche's essay on the African origins of the Haitian zombi myth involves the whole question of cultural adaptation to slavery and exile which runs through most chapters in this volume.

All these essays were originally read as papers at two conferences held at Dalhousie University in Halifax, Nova Scotia. Those by Chinua Achebe, Kofi Awoonor, Nadine Gordimer, Daniel Kunene, D. Ibe Nwoga and Emile Snyder were read at the Dalhousie/Mount Saint Vincent Conference on African Writing in May 1973. Donald Stuart, of Memorial University of Newfoundland, played a vital role in the organising of this first conference, the proceedings of which were published in the Winter 1973–4 issue of the *Dalhousie Review*. The remaining essays were read in the literature section of the annual conference of the Canadian Association of African Studies held at Dalhousie in February–March 1974.

Max Dorsinville and Peter Okeh translated their own papers from the French in which they were originally delivered. Those by Maximilien Laroche and Isaac Yetiv, also originally read in French, were translated by Edward Messinger.

Both conferences were exciting and vital. The heady quality of the meetings and the electricity in the proceedings are difficult to recapture in print, depending as they did on the presence of many extraordinary people. But the quality of the essays themselves is of more durable stuff, as the readers of this volume will no doubt judge for themselves.

Notes on the Contributors

Chinua Achebe was born in Eastern Nigeria in 1930. He has been Head of Talks with the Nigerian Broadcasting Corporation and Director of External Broadcasting. He was founding editor of the Heinemann African Writers' Series, and has been Senior Research Fellow at the University of Nigeria in Nsukka. His four published novels are *Things Fall Apart, No Longer at Ease, Arrow of God*, which won the first Jock Campbell Award, and *A Man of the People*. He has also published a collection of short stories, *Girls at War and Other Stories*, and his volume of poems, *Beware Soul Brother*, won the first Commonwealth Poetry Prize. At present he is a Professor in the English Department at the University of Massachusetts in Amherst, and editor of *Okike*, an African journal of new writing.

Donatus Ibe Nwoga was born in Nigeria in 1933 and educated at Queen's University, Belfast, and University College, London. He is especially interested in the traditional literature of Africa, and in particular that of the Igbo of Nigeria. He is editor of the anthology, *West African Verse* (1967), and joint compiler of *Igbo Traditional Verse* (1973). Since 1962, he has lectured at the University of Nigeria at Nsukka and is now Head of the Department of English.

Emile Snyder was born in Paris in 1925, of a French mother and American father. He holds an MA in comparative literature from Harvard University and a PhD in French literature from the University of California, Los Angeles. After holding appointments at the Universities of Washington, Wisconsin, Dar es Salaam and Chicago, he is now Professor in the French/Italian Department, Comparative Literature Department and African Studies Program at the University of Indiana. He has published a volume of poetry *Faux-Papiers* (Paris, 1973) and bilingual editions of Aimé Césaire's *Return to my Native Land* and *Cadastre*, as well as numerous articles, translations and criticisms.

Maximilien Laroche, born in Cap-Haitien, Haiti, in 1937, studied law in Haiti and literature in Montreal and France, where he completed a doctorate in comparative literature. He is now associate professor at Université Laval, Quebec, where his special fields of interest are seventeenth-century French drama and West Indian French literature. He has published many articles and four books: *Haïti et sa littérature, Portrait de l'Haïtien, Marcel Dubé* and *Le miracle et la métamorphose, essai sur les littératures du Québec et d'Haïti.* He is currently working on Haitian mythology and literature in Creole and on Quebec drama from 1940 to 1960.

Max Dorsinville was born in Haiti and educated in Canada and the United States (Ph.D 1972, Comparative Literature, City University of New York). A professor of English and Comparative Literature at McGill University, Montreal, he is the author of *Caliban Without Prospero: Essay on Quebec and Black Literature* (Press Porcepic, Erin, Ontario, 1974) and of several articles on Renaissance fiction, Quebec and black literature published in *PMLA, Canadian Literature, Livres et Autres Québecois* and other journals. Max Dorsinville is currently at work on a comparative study of the figure of 'The Outsider' in Quebec and African fiction.

Peter Igbonekwu Okeh, born at Ebe in Nigeria and educated at St Charles' College, Onitsha, and the University of Nigeria, Nsukka, holds a doctorate in French from Université Laval, Quebec. Since 1969 he has been on the staff of the Université de Moncton where he is a professor of French and African literature. His publications (all in French) include: 'African writers and the search for a better Africa, the odyssey of the African scholar as seen in African literature', '*Trente Arpents* and *Arrow of God*: testimony of a changing society'; 'Self-inquest: one explanation of Camara Laye's "enracinement" '; 'The Beginnings and Growth of African Literature' and 'African dynamics in African literature'.

Isaac Yetiv, born in Tunisia in 1929, graduated from the Ecole Normale in Tunis and studied mathematics and physics in Tunis and Paris. From 1950 to 1967 he lived in Israel, teaching maths, physics and languages. After taking a BA in French and Political Science at the Hebrew University in Jerusalem, he came to the University of Wisconsin as a graduate student working towards a PhD in French, which he was awarded in 1970. Since then he has taught French and Hebrew Languages and Literature at the University of Hartford and has published several articles dealing with French North African literature and Franco-Jewish literature, as well as three books: *The Theme of Alienation in the North African Novel of French expression, 1952–1956*, *Lmad Ivrit* (a comprehensive course in modern Hebrew) and *Dijhada*, a novel in Hebrew. In September 1975 he became Head of the Department of Modern Languages at the University of Akron, Ohio.

Daniel P. Kunene, born in South Africa in 1923, took MA and PhD degrees at the University of Cape Town and taught African languages and literature at the same university and later at the University of California, Los Angeles. Since 1970 he has been associate professor of African languages and literature at the University of Wisconsin, where he has been chairman of the Afro-American Studies Department. His publications include: *Heroic Poetry of the Basotho* (Oxford 1971); *The Beginnings of South African Vernacular Literature* (with Randal A. Kirsch), U.C.L.A. 1967, 'The Works of Thomas Mofolo', U.C.L.A. African Studies Center Occasional Paper, 1967; 'The Ideophone in Southern Sotho', *Journal of African Languages*, v, 4, part 1, 1965; 'A Preliminary Study of Downstepping in Southern Sotho', *African Studies*, 31, 1, 1972. His poems have also been published in various magazines and he is currently researching on the Sesotho prose style of Thomas Mofolo with special emphasis on his involvement with character and event.

Rowland Smith is a naturalised Canadian who was born in Johannesburg in 1938. He was educated at St John's College, Johannesburg, the University of Natal, and Lincoln College, Oxford. He has held teaching positions at the University of Natal and the University of the Witwatersrand where he was Assistant Editor of *English Studies in Africa*. Since 1967 he has been a member of the English Department at Dalhousie University in Halifax, Nova Scotia, where he is an Associate Professor. He is the author of *Lyric and Polemic: The Literary Personality of Roy Campbell*, McGill-Queen's University Press, 1972.

Nadine Gordimer was born in Springs, South Africa, in 1923. She has travelled in Africa, Europe, North America and Australia, and has lectured in all four continents, but has always lived in South Africa. She has published short stories, novels and collections of short stories. These include: *The Soft Voice of the Serpent, The Lying Days, Six Feet of the Country,*

A World of Strangers, *Friday's Footprint*, which won the W. H. Smith Award, *Occasion for Loving*, *Not For Publication*, *The Late Bourgeois World*, *A Guest of Honour*, which won the James Tait Black Memorial Prize, *Livingstone's Companions*, and *The Conservationist*, which won the Booker Prize. She has also won the French award, Le Grand Aigle d'or.

G. D. Killam is Professor and Head of the Department of English at Acadia University, Canada. He has held the Chair of Literature in the University of Dar es Salaam and taught at Fourah Bay College in Sierra Leone and at the Universities of Ibadan and Lagos. He has published *Africa in English fiction*, *The Novels of Chinua Achebe* and *African Writers on African Writing*, contributed chapters to *Introduction to Nigerian Literature* and *Literatures of the World in English*, as well as various articles. He is currently writing a biography, *Odeziaku: the Iniquitous Coaster of Onitsha*, and revising his book on Achebe's writings.

Kofi Awoonor was born in Wheta, Ghana, in 1935 and educated at the University of Ghana, the University of London, and the State University of New York. His publications include: *Rediscovery*, *Messages*, *Ride Me Memory*, *This Earth, My Brother*, *The Breast of the Earth* and *Guardians of the Sacred Word*. He is Professor of English and Comparative Literature at the State University of New York at Stony Brook, and Senior Lecturer at the University of Cape Coast, Ghana.

Wole Soyinka, born in 1934 at Abeokuta, Nigeria, and educated at University College, Ibadan, and the University of Leeds, has published a large number of essays, plays and poems, as well as two novels and a volume of autobiography, *The Man Died*, based on notes he made in prison. A former head of the Department of Theatre Arts at the University of Ibadan and Professor in Dramatic Literature at the University of Ife, he has also been Visiting Professor at the Universities of Sheffield and Dakar and Fellow of Churchill College, Cambridge. He is editor of *Transition* magazine.

Chinua Achebe

Thoughts on the African Novel

When I was first invited to the Dalhousie Conference on African writing I was asked to speak about the African writer and the English language. I fired back a flat *No!* Then I was asked to say what I should prefer to talk about. I said nothing; I had no idea what I wanted to talk about. Finally I was confronted with a *fait accompli* in the form of a printed programme in which *The African Novel* was put down against my name. I had then to accept, having twice already proved unco-operative and ungracious.

But, as it happened, I had just about this time resolved not to make any further pronouncements on the African novel or African literature or any of these large topics unless I dreamt up something really novel and spectacular to say. But perhaps the day-to-day thoughts and worries are just as important, being always with us. So I give them to you.

Many years ago at a writers' conference in Makerere, Uganda, I attempted (not very successfully) to get my colleagues to defer a definition of African literature which was causing us a lot of trouble. I suggested that the task might become easier when more of our produce had entered the market. That was ten years ago. I was saying in effect that African literature would define itself in action; so why not leave it alone? I still think it was excellent advice, even if it carried a hint of evasiveness or even superstition.

I do admit to certain residual superstitions; and one of the strongest is the fear of names, of hurrying to a conclusion when the issue is still wide open. If I may paraphrase a proverb which seems to me appropriate: *Do not underrate a day while an hour of light remains.* In other words, be careful, for one hour is enough to do a man in.

Edogo's mind was in pain over the child. Some people were already saying that perhaps he was none other than the first one. But Edogo and Amoge never talked about it; the woman especially was afraid. Since utterance had power to change fear into living truth they dared not speak before they had to.

The world of the creative artist is like that. It is not the world of the taxonomist whose first impulse on seeing a new plant or animal is to define, classify and file away. Nor is it the world of the taxidermist who plies an even less desirable trade.

But I am never fully consistent, not even in my superstitions. I always find thoughts antagonistic to my secure position floating dangerously around it. It is these floating thoughts I wish to put into words.

The first is that the African novel has to be about Africa. A pretty severe restriction, I am told. But Africa is not only a geographical expression; it is also a metaphysical landscape—it is in fact a view of the world and of the whole cosmos perceived from a particular position. This is as close to the brink of chaos as I dare proceed. As for who an African novelist is, it is partly a matter of passports, of individual volition and particularly of seeing from that perspective I have just touched with the timidity of a snail's horn. Being an African, like being a Jew, carries certain penalties—as well as benefits, of course. But perhaps more penalties than benefits. Ben Gurion once said: 'If somebody wants to be a Jew, that's enough for me.' We could say the same for being an African. So it is futile to argue whether Conrad's *Heart of Darkness* is African literature. As far as I know Joseph Conrad never even considered the possibility. In spite of all temptations he remained a European. And it is not even a matter of colour. For we have Nadine Gordimer, Doris Lessing and others.

And then language. As you know, there has been an impassioned controversy about an African literature in non-African languages. But what is a non-African language? English and French certainly. But what about Arabic? What about Swahili even? Is it then a question of how long the language has been present on African soil? If so, how many years should constitute *effective occupation*? For me it is again a pragmatic matter. A language spoken by Africans on African soil, a language in which Africans write, justifies itself.

I fully realise that I am beginning to sound like a bad dictionary—the type you take a strange word to and it defines it with a stranger word; you look *that* up and it gives you back your original strange word; so you end up with two mysteries instead of one! But that is the reality of our situation, and it is surely more useful to begin to deal with its complexity than propose catchy but impossible simplifications.

At the root of all these strange and untidy thoughts lies a monumental historical fact, Europe—a presence which has obsessed us from Equiano to Ekwensi. For Equiano a preoccupation with Europe was pretty inevitable. After all, he had only just recently freed himself from actual enslavement to Europeans. He lived in Europe and was married to a European. His ancestral Igboland had become a fragmented memory.

In our own time a preoccupation with Europe has seemed almost equally inevitable despite the passage of nearly two hundred years. In the colonial period and its aftermath our preoccupation with Europe took the form of protest. Then a bunch of bright ones came along and said: 'We are through with intoning the colonial litany. We hereby repudiate the crippling legacy of a Europe-oriented protest. We are tough-minded. We absolve Europe of all guilt. Don't you worry, Europe, we were bound to violence long before you came to our shores!' Naturally, Europe, which was beginning to believe the worst about itself, is greatly relieved and impressed by the mental emancipation, objectivity and sophistication of these newcomers. As if any intelligent writer of protest had ever taken a starry-eyed view of Africa or doubted the reality of evil in Africa, the new anti-protest, broad-minded writer will now endorse the racist theory that Africa *is* evil, *is* the heart of darkness.

It is this illusion of objectivity, this grotesque considerateness, this perverse charitableness which asks a man to cut his own throat for the comfort and good opinion of another that I must now address myself to.

Quite often the malady (for it is indeed a sickness) shows fairly mild symptoms and is widespread; at other times it comes in its virulent forms. But mild or severe it manifests itself as self-disgust and an obscene eagerness to please our adversary.

There is a Nigerian academic who went to study in Britain in the late 1920s and decided to become an Englishman. So he settled down in Britain after his studies, married and raised a family and by all accounts was perfectly happy. Forty years later, as a result of an unhappy conjunction of events, he found himself appointed to an administrative position in a Nigerian university. To his first press interviewer he boasted that he spoke no Nigerian language. He cannot recognise Nigerian food, let alone eat it. Given a chance he will appoint a European over a Nigerian to teach at his university; his argument: a university, as the name implies, is a universal institution.

But fortunately, this man is not a writer. For wouldn't it be awful if writers—those bright hopes of our society—should become afflicted with such a warped vision; a vision which creates a false polarity between an object and its abstraction and places its focus on the abstraction? Personally I am no longer entirely optimistic. Let me present two short passages of the kind that has been causing me great discomfort:

> This is the confrontation which *The Interpreters* presents. It is not an 'African' problem. Events all over the world have shown in the new generation a similar dissatisfaction. . . . Thus Soyinka, using a Nigerian setting, has portrayed a universal problem. This is what makes both this novel and the whole corpus of Soyinka's work universally valid.
>
> (*Eldred Jones—'The Essential Soyinka'*)

Before I go on, let me make two points. First, I am not in disagreement with Professor Eldred Jones' evaluation of Soyinka but with the terms he has chosen for that evaluation. The second point is that I regard Eldred Jones as our finest literary scholar, a man of great sensitivity and perception whom I should have much preferred not to disagree with. But the dogma of universality which he presents here (I believe, absent-mindedly) is so patently false and dangerous and yet so attractive that it ought not to go unchallenged. For supposing 'events all over the world' have *not* shown 'in the new generation a similar dissatisfaction . . .', would it truly be invalid for a Nigerian writer seeing a dissatisfaction in *his* society to write about it? Am I being told, for Christ's sake, that before I write about any problem I must first verify whether they have it too in New York and London and Paris?

What Professor Eldred Jones is proposing is that I renounce my vision which (since I do not work with the radio telescope at Jodrell Bank) is necessarily local and particular. Not so long ago a similar proposition was made to me, an attempt to discredit my vision and the absolute validity of my experience. But it came from 'expected quarters'. At the end of the war in Nigeria (in which, you may know, I was on the wrong side) I had an invitation to visit New Guinea and Australia. But some official or officials in Lagos saw to it that I did not get a passport. When I protested to the Commissioner for External Affairs he wrote me a nice, intriguing letter with words to this effect:

> Dear Achebe,
> Thank you for your letter in which you complained about difficulties which you thought you had with my officials . . .

You can see, can't you, the close kinship between that letter and the proposition by Eldred Jones? They are both telling me to be careful in defining 'difficulties'. Because other people may not agree, I had better check my vision with them before saying what I see. Such a proposition is dangerous and totally unacceptable, for once you agree to 'clear' your vision with other people you are truly in trouble. Now let us look at another short extract from the same essay by Eldred Jones in a book called *Introduction to Nigerian Literature*:

When Wole Soyinka writes like this his audience is not a local one; it is a universal one. Indeed at this point he widens his immediate range of reference by making the Court Historian invoke the precedent of the Trojan War.

Thus in the first extract Eldred Jones praises Wole Soyinka for not writing about an African problem but a universal one; and in the second for not writing for a local but a universal audience! Surely, African criticism must be the only one in the whole world (or perhaps universe) where literary merit is predicated on such outlandish criteria. But as I said earlier I don't really believe that Eldred Jones thought seriously about this. He has simply and uncritically accepted the norms of some of the prevailing colonialist criticism, which I must say is most unlike him. Perhaps I should point out in fairness also that in the first extract he did put *African* in quotes, although it is not clear to me what exactly the quotes are supposed to do. Perhaps they hint at a distinction between *real* and *so-called* African problems. This may redeem the situation somewhat, but not very much. For *real* and *so-called* Africa can and do become metaphysical retreats for all kinds of prejudice. Thus a certain critic many years ago said of Ekwensi's *Burning Grass*: 'At last Ekwensi has drawn real Nigerian characters . . .' without saying what unreal Nigerian characters looked like. But one sensed that an African from Lagos or Nairobi might be deemed less real than a Masai or a Tuareg, surely a matter of social taste and not of literary criticism!

I shall look at one last aspect of the same problem. Professor Emile Snyder has reminded us that politics are always present in literature, giving examples ranging from Dante to Eliot. Why, he asked, do we get so worked up about it in discussing African literature? Of course, the reason is that we are late starters. I mean really late—after the prizes are all given out and the track judges have packed up their things and gone home. Such late starters are generally very conscientious. Though no one is looking, they will cut no corners.

That is why, for instance, we must now have our own debate on art for art's sake; why we must have pundits decreeing to us what is or is not appropriate to literature; what genres are for us and what we may only touch at our peril; why literary legislators pass laws telling us what social and political roles artists may (but more usually, may not) perform.

Thus in a curious novel entitled *The Trial of Christopher Okigbo* Ali Mazrui has a poet tried in the hereafter for throwing away his life on the battlefield like any common tribesman. There is no condemnation of war as such, only of poets getting involved—for 'some lives are more sacred than others'. In the words of one of the novel's leading characters (an African Perry Mason clearly admired by Mazrui):

> a great artist was first of all an individualist, secondly a universalist, and only thirdly a social collectivist.

Since these roles and attributes are not known instinctively by the artist in question (otherwise how would Okigbo not know what was legitimate activity for him?) it stands to reason that he requires some one like Mazrui to tell him (a) the precise moment when he crosses the threshold of mere artist and becomes a great artist and (b) how to juggle with his three marbles of individualism, universalism and social collectivism.

What I am saying really boils down to a simple plea for the African novel. Don't fence me in.

I dare not close without a word of recognition for that small and proprietary school of critics who assure me that the African novel does not exist. Reason: the novel was invented in England. For the same kind of reason I shouldn't know how to drive a car because I am no descendant of Henry Ford. But every visitor to Nigeria will tell you that we are among the world's most creative drivers!

Only fifteen years ago a bright, sceptical academic at a Nigerian university could raise a laugh by saying: 'That would be the day when English literature is taught from Chaucer to Achebe.' Today, I much regret to say, that same academic makes a living teaching African literature in some cosy corner of the globe, presumably teaching more Achebe than Chaucer. Na so dis worl' be.

In conclusion, all these prescriptions and proscriptions, all these dogmas about the universal and the eternal verities, all this proselytising for European literary fashions, even dead ones; all this hankering after definitions may in the end prove worse than futile by creating needless anxieties. For as everybody knows, anxiety can hinder creative performance from sex to science.

I have no doubt at all about the existence of the African novel. This form of fiction has seized the imagination of many African writers and they will use it according to their differing abilities, sensibilities and visions without seeking any one's permission. I believe it will grow and prosper. I believe it has a great future.

Recently one of my students pointed to a phrase on the cover of Camara Laye's *The Radiance of the King* and said 'Do you agree with that?' It was a comment credited to my good friend, Ezekiel Mphahlele, to the effect that this was 'the great African novel'. I told the student that I had nothing to say because I had an interest in the matter; and I'm glad to say, the joke was well taken. Actually, I admire *The Radiance of the King* quite a lot; still, I do hope that the great African novel will not be about a disreputable European.

D. Ibe Nwoga

The Limitations of Universal Critical Criteria

The subtitle for this paper is: The Case for an Aesthetics of African Literature. The question it tries to explore is whether, now that a comparatively extensive body of African literature has been published, some conventions have been established, awareness of which is necessary for fruitful criticism of that literature. Has anything emerged which could be identified as a specific method for assessing the meaning, expertise and direction of African literature? The title of the paper was suggested by reaction to the beginning of a review of the plays of Wole Soyinka and J. P. Clark in 1963 by Martin Esslin in which he wrote:

> I must, at the very outset, disclaim any special knowledge of the social and cultural background from which these plays spring. Indeed, I presume that must have been the reason I was asked to review them in these pages—to provide, for once, the corrective of a change of perspective, as it were; of focus, of viewpoint; to submit them, like organisms in a laboratory, to a survival test *in vacuo* by seeing how they appear to someone who, in the course of his professional work, has to read an endless succession of plays from totally different backgrounds and who will therefore, almost automatically, apply to them the same general yardstick; who will judge them not as African plays but as plays pure and simple.[1]

His review of the plays was a corrective on the concept, but the presumptions of universal critical criteria which he stated have been quite strong in the criticism of African literature.

The search for an aesthetics of African literature is not as chauvinistic as it might sound. What emerges might not be exclusively African. All literatures—either of different places or different times for the same literature—have had their conventions, but these may, in fact, consist of elements or stages of other literatures. Moreover, the validity of the question is not in any prescriptive effect in the sense that one can say that 'This writer does not write in this way, therefore he is not an African writer'. The resulting answer would be descriptive of assumptions and technical elements behind the literature, hence, a statement on the proper or adequate critical tools which would constitute a means of getting at meaning and appreciating the felicities of our literature. Variations are bound to exist between one writer and another, but there must be some core of creative direction within a contemporaneous cultural milieu and it is this tradition that it is fruitful to start from.

Reactions to Western Critics

Critical attention began to be paid to African writing in the late fifties and early sixties and much of this came from European critics. It was presumed that since this literature was written in European languages, it had to be assessed in terms of the traditions of the literature of those languages. Much of the discussions at the 1963 Freetown Conference on African Literature and the Universities tended towards a conclusion that African literature written in English should be considered as English literature, that this literature was 'extending the boundaries of English literature',[2] and that 'we don't want to have a special paper on African literature'.[3] African writers themselves resented a tendency to lower standards when assessing their writings. In 1962, Wole Soyinka, for example, was complaining that 'European foreign critics are not helping by being Eurocentrically condescending, applying a different standard for writing'.[4]

Stringency of critical standards is, however, not the same thing as an adequate or fruitful approach to criticism, and it was clear to most African writers that significant criticism of their work was not emerging from people of different interests, tradition and background. The expression of this awareness was violent in 1962 when J. P. Clark displayed the various ways in which he thought European critics were trying to impede African writers through their criticism;[5] and Chinua Achebe described three types of European critics of African writers, accusing even the best of them of a cocksureness based on ethnocentrically conceived certainties of aesthetic truth, concluding with an assertion that 'No man can understand another whose language he does not speak' and adding in parenthesis that 'language here does not mean simply words but a man's entire world-view'.[6] As late as 1967 the same matter was brought up in an interview with Ama Ata Aidoo of Ghana, who declared:

> I do not see that there is any validity in having someone who does not belong to the society from which the literature itself springs, telling you how to write. I'm sure you've heard every African writer say this, but I do not see how it can work. What I mean is, if the writing is from a certain background, it's only the people who are from the background who can tell the world, 'This is good', and then the world takes it. To me it is so simple one doesn't have to talk about it. You know, nobody else but the English critical world could say that John Osborne is a good playwright. Now when you get England recognising Osborne as good or bad, at any rate controversial, then other people become interested. See what I mean?'[7]

Perhaps the most virulent personal expression of the rejection of non-indigenous criticism is J. P. Clark's reference to Gerald Moore as 'Old John Bull . . . alias Mr I-know-my-Africa'.[8]

The basis for these rejections of external criticism have been varied: some European critics have resented the tone of African writers in their criticism of European culture and European imperialism and have reacted by injecting into the criticism the extraneous factor of the supposed ingratitude of these African writers as biting the hands that fed them; others, in the surprise that these primitives have actually written, and more, have used English to write, have tended to give condescending praise, often leading to championing the cause of a naive African literature and exhibiting a hungry acceptance of a quaintness and exoticism irrelevant to the real achievement of a literature; others still, more serious as critics, and determined to apply the same stringent standards of literary criticism, have nevertheless presumed on an understanding of Africa which they did not have. The summation of these opinions, I think, is the expectation of the writers that valid criticism of their work can only come from an understanding of their background and a recognition of the fact that they are trying to do something new and authentic to that background, both in the historical fact of their society and the independence of a literary tradition. It is perhaps this that makes the writers impatient with criticism which tends towards the identification of the sources and inspiration of their writing in Greek drama and English poetry.

The Problem for the African Critic

If this sounds like racial prejudice against non-African critics, it must be seen in its historical context that the early critical atmosphere of African literature was dominated by western critics. Though there was the presumption that the African critic would be better placed than the European to get at the root of the African's achievement, such an eventuality was not automatic. A recent editorial in *Présence Africaine* brings this out:

> It is important to associate the people with the interpretation of their cultural life and not to leave its interpretation and animation exclusively in the hands of an elite which is culturally dependent on the West and can be more easily manipulated and conditioned by the latter than an entire nation. On the whole the situation of such an elite, which is culturally cut off from its people and lives outside its own civilisation, promotes the ascendancy of Westerners (whether Africanists, or members of the University, or politicians) over the administration of our cultural affairs. Seen and written about through the eyes of a foreign culture, our people can only be the objects—and not the creative subjects—of their history.[9]

What is said here applies both to the writers and the critics: we have been to the same schools and through the same cultural exile. But my interest here is with the critic. The African critic of my generation has to warn himself continually that his study of literature and literary criticism has been in a different tradition and that his preliminary aesthetic tendencies and certainties might have been directed outside himself and his genuine authentic reactions. He has to study to shed those elements which no longer prove congenial to his sensibility and try to establish an approach which, though not completely divorced from the learnt criteria, nevertheless might have a different centre. This accounts for the deliberately negative title of this paper. It can be a constant effort, trying to identify the limitations of the so-called 'universal' criteria—which really mean the principles and processes learnt in University study of English literature (and in this context, universal is the same thing as western)—and trying to recognise the manner of reaction of literature more homogeneous with African tradition and the modern literature of Africa.

The African who is a critic is not therefore automatically an African critic. He does not automatically offer the African writer the atmosphere of understanding which he craves, and some of what the writers have said about western critics could equally well apply to Africans. The effort which I have described above is necessary for the critic, African or non-African, to fulfil the role which the present state of our literary tradition and the nature of our literature impose on him.

What I intend to do in the rest of this paper is to suggest the nature of shared concerns and outlook which operate among the writers, critics and the society; to describe what might, at least for the moment, be called a characteristic mode of African aesthetic perception; limiting myself to poetry, to illustrate how this can lead to a poetry demanding a particular method of appreciation; and finally, to suggest the function of criticism in the African context. My approach will be positive, and what 'limitations of universal critical criteria' there are will only emerge by inference.

The Socio-Historical Context of African Literature

The facts of the recent history of Africa are well known to any student of African affairs. Diachronically, there are the external events of the slave trade, economic exploitation, colonial domination, the struggle for and achievement of independence and the present management of African affairs by African civilians and soldiers with some neo-colonial intrusion. Synchronically, the situation is a little more complex: we have the contemporaneous existence of various types of acculturated states ranging from the relatively traditional modes of life to the totally westernised modes of life; there are the realities arising from contact with the outside world, both through the colonial experience and through the incredibly expanded media of international communication (I doubt that there is any village in Africa in which a radio is not to be found)— factors which have not only created new patterns of economic, political and religious expectations and desires, but have also disrupted or confused the homogeneity of the traditional value system and sanctions among the general populace; there is, finally, in this overabbreviated and overgeneralised catalogue, the fact of the manner in which government by Africans is operating in Africa—the fact of the people's generated expectations from their people in power and how these expectations are being fulfilled or not fulfilled.

I have not elaborated on these facts because that is not the point. What is important is that out of these experiences there arise certain expectations which influence the nature of the writers' work and thereby demand a certain critical direction. Put crudely, this critical direction is the demand we make of our writers to tell us what to do with ourselves; the insistence found in many of the comments by African readers that the writers show positive commitment to the contemporary issues in Africa.

One aspect of the events referred to above is that they are public, communal events. Their predominating impact on the minds and attention of the intellectual elite to which the writers and their audience belong makes for an audience-oriented literature. If one sought a period of English literature to which to relate this orientation, it would be found more in the literature of the period from Dryden to Johnson than in modern English literature. Events of traumatic nature to the whole community have taken place and are taking place. There are concerns felt, not so much by the individual in his personal capacity, but shared by the generality of the people. There is a sense of participation, albeit reducing in intensity recently, in the total movement of people in the organisation of their affairs and their world. There is still a measure of faith in the perfectibility of human societies, that people have only to know what is right for them and their society and they will struggle together to achieve those aims.

The African writer is operating within this context, varying in intensity of facts in different parts of Africa, but still demanding that he use his art in pursuit of public ends. Some conferences on African Literature have specifically emphasised this context, especially the African-Scandinavian Writers' Conference in Stockholm 1967,[10] the series of talks and discussions in Africa Centre in London in 1968 under the title 'Protest and Conflict in African Literature',[11] and a conference held at the University of Nigeria, Nsukka, in 1973 under the title 'Literature and Modern West African Culture'.[12] The discussion has gone beyond the level of whether the writer should be committed, to a discussion of the nature of that commitment—to some it is necessary to have a definite ideological commitment, preferably to a Marxist ideal. Though some writers may feel it unbearable 'that people are creating for the writer an almost superstitious role . . . as if he were a special kind of human being who has certain duties, functions, privileges mystically set apart from other human beings',[13] the role is there. And this explains the tone of Wole Soyinka's bitter tirade against the writers of Africa when he claimed that 'In the movement towards chaos in modern Africa, the writer did not anticipate. . . . He was content to turn his eye backward in time and prospect in archaic fields for forgotten gems which would dazzle and distract the present. But never inward, never truly into the present, never into the obvious symptoms of the niggling, warning, predictable present from which alone lay the salvation of ideals.' Admitting that the writings might have genuine literary value, still he is distressed that 'the present philosophy, the present direction of modern Africa was created by politicians, not writers', and asks, 'is this not a contradiction in a society whose great declaration of uniqueness to the outside world is that of a superabundant humanism?'[14]

Partly resulting from the above, and partly derived from African tradition is another aspect of the context, that of a greater emphasis on community than on persons. Where the individual (character in a novel, persona/poet in poetry) is emphasised, the dimensions of his individuality are undercut by the fact that he is a representative, a paradigm of states of being which extend through the community.

Moreover, the individual is part of a community which is supposed to bear his burdens and whose burdens, depending on his position, he certainly bears. An interesting sidelight with regard to the artists' circumstances is thrown on this by a statement in an article by Cyprian Ekwensi:

> All my life has been built round the formula that a writer has first of all to eat, to pay his rent, support a family. In our society a man does not run away from his responsibilities because of what *he* wishes to do. He weighs the consequences of his actions on his dependants, then adjusts this actions to the situation, sometimes to his own disadvantage. This spirit of selflessness has suppressed many of genius. At the same time it has kept family life going. If I had my way I would run away from everybody, shut myself up in a room in some strange land and go on writing. This is what many of the great writers have done. It tends to sharpen one's recollection.[15]

The strains and joys of this wider responsibility of the individual not only affect the freedom of the writer as a person; they can also influence the tone of his writing when he writes on that society. They offer an area of thematic interest, and can influence the development of the content of the literary piece.

Perhaps the most intrinsic result of the described socio-historical context is the nature of the literature under discussion, in that it is a literature of mixed traditions. Most of modern African literature is written in the language, not of the people, but of the former colonial masters. The literary traditions of the masters came along with the language, the literary traditions indigenous to the people are still strong and viable, and so we have a literature straddling two conventions with more or less comfort. These facts present to the writers crucial problems of choice. But this is a widely explored area, and I will end it by referring to a significant statement which Gerald Moore made in 1963:

> This encounter (of the African poet with the English language) presents problems which are not being faced by any European writer, and which haven't been faced by the European writer for a long time. . . . Since the emergence of the vernaculars in the, Middle Ages, I don't think we have had any corresponding experience of making this fundamental choice.[16]

Within this context then, modern African literature was born and has grown to its present stage of maturity. The writer and his audience live within the environment of these realities and ideas and to the extent to which the context influences the writing, to that extent does an awareness of the context determine adequate understanding and direct the critic's functioning.

The Mode of Aesthetic Perception

For some years there has been a rather consistent critical rejection of Negritude for a variety of reasons. One is that it refers one back, especially in much of its poetry, to a glorious African past—innocent, brave, harmonious—which the colonial demons came and destroyed. This is of course an overstatement and a myth, or rather is not the whole truth. But I think the attack on it has been largely exaggerated too. Most peoples have had to build up a myth of their past, a myth which holds them from too violent a dislocation of tradition, a pillar onto which they can anchor their sense of continuity and meaningful progress. If it is a lie, it is a useful lie, as many a widow knows who has tried to bring up her children with the memory of a brave and immaculate father, much to her chagrin if she had had a rough marriage. And it is not such a lie after all, for Africa had its measure of innocence, of bravery, of communal harmony, and it did suffer its measure of external intrusion, oppression, exploitation and domination, and no-body can deny it. Not one of the complaining writers has failed to refer at least once to the facts and their repercussions. All the same, it is a myth that could be dangerous by reinforcing what the Guyanese novelist Wilson Harris calls 'victim stasis' and 'victor stasis'—psychological fixations which perpetuate themselves by constant projections outwards—'victim projecting out of himself the making of monster/victor, victor projecting out of himself the making of monstrous victim'.[17]

What is more crucial and relevant, however, is the discussion on Senghor's concept of the difference of African man from western man of the twentieth century and the accompanying claim that Africa has something to give to world civilisation. With regard to the second part, I think it is pusillanimous to think that Africa has nothing specific to contribute to world culture, but this again is an overworked topic which can only provide diversionary interest here. There are sufficient internal problems to concern us, and as Soyinka says, especially later in this passage:

> The myth of irrational nobility, of a racial essence that must come to the rescue of the white depravity, has run its full course. . . . The movement which began with the war cry of cultural separatism. . . has found a latter-day modification in a call to be the bridge, to bring about the salvation of the world by a marriage of abstractions. It is a remarkable fact that the European writer who had both the leisure and the long history of introspection to ascertain his spiritual needs has not yet sent out a call to the black writer for rescue.[18]

So we are not better than other people, and, in any case they have not asked us to come and get them out of their desiccated mechanical world. But are we in any way different? Or rather, were we different in any way which could be important for the proper understanding of both the themes and conventions of our literature?

I am halted in the middle of an intended tirade by the realisation that the matter is suddenly too simple. There are no people who are not peculiar in the sum of their cultural values—English, Canadian, American, Chinese, Russian, African, etc.; there is no society in which there has not developed a way in which its people relate themselves to the world and to their fellows. Perhaps it is the overstressing of the peculiarity that is culpable. Perhaps also the definition of this peculiarity could be misguided. But, especially in the context of literature written within one culture in the language of another, it is essential to grasp some points of this difference polemically, to clarify any peculiarities of expression or form in that literature.

Senghor, writing about the African philosophy of being, speaks of the African ontology as follows:

> Far back as one may go into his past, from the northern Sudanese to the southern Bantu, the African has always and everywhere presented a concept of the world which is diametrically opposed to the traditional philosophy of Europe. The latter is essentially *static objective, dichotomic*, it is, in fact, dualistic, in that it makes an absolute distinction between body and soul, matter and spirit. It is founded on separation and opposition: on analysis and conflict. The African on the other hand, conceives the world, beyond the diversity of its forms, as a fundamentally mobile, yet unique, reality that seeks synthesis.[19]

A basic theme is expressed here, capable of being developed in a variety of ways. Senghor directs it, in his quest for what Africa can give to the world, into a higher *morality in action* so that 'for the African, living according to the moral law means living according to his nature, composed as it is of contradictory elements but complementary life forces. Thus he gives stuff to the stuff of the universe and tightens the threads of the tissue of life' (p. 186), and to a theory of art in which he claims that it is 'rhythm—the main virtue, in fact, of negritude—that gives the work of art its beauty' explaining rhythm as 'simply the movement of attraction or repulsion that expresses the life of the cosmic forces; symmetry and asymmetry, repetition or opposition: in short, the lines of force that link the meaningful signs that shapes and colours, timbre and tones, are' (pp. 191–2).

These are developments of the idea worth debating. But what is of greater interest here is the suggestion of the relationship between the general statement and what Senghor calls 'the mystic civilisations of the senses' (which incidentally he also saw in the Slav and Germanic peoples of the late nineteenth century). My understanding of the issue is related to a distinction between modes of knowing—that whereas traditional western man has evolved a more detached, analytical mode of understanding of his world, environment and aspects of human functioning, traditional African man retained a more holistic, instinctive mode of understanding. I try various expressions to describe this mode—spiritual absorption, instinctive perception of whole meaning, sensitive interaction—but these are words that have their meaning in the language of a cultural mode of perception which is particular and rationalistic. The total of these expressions, however, comes close to what I mean, for which the word rapport may be used.

The reduction of these modes of knowing to a dichotomy of 'emotion' and 'reason', (Kofi Awoonor, for example, presumes that Senghor says that 'the African is only emotion and not reason'),[20] some attempts to reproduce this phenomenon in works of art, have led to the emotional rejection which has attended the idea. The danger is that in the hustle and bustle of rhetoric there is the tendency to throw away the core of truth with the bulk of nonsense. If the 'purity and innocence of Africa' is not the truth; if the 'girl soaping her body and laughing in the rain' is not the symbol of the African reality, does it automatically become true that 'the educated African from abroad . . . who walks about with his mouth open . . . startled by . . . the black man's heightened sensitivity' has come back to recolonise us; that he is repeating 'the damnable old *cliché* that we have come to associate with the colonial or the European who comes to Africa with that back-to-the-womb expression on his face'?[21]

In Achebe's poem, 'Vultures', an illustration is taken from the facts of the Second World War:

> . . . Thus the Commandant at Belsen
> Camp going home for
> the day with fumes of
> human roast clinging
> rebelliously to his hairy
> nostrils will stop
> at the wayside sweet-shop
> and pick up a chocolate
> for his tender offspring
> waiting at home for Daddy's
> return. . . .

The bitterness of the irony here derives from the fact that both activities are real, none pretended, by the commandant of Belsen. The commandant did commit the atrocities of the camp. The commandant did love his family. Perhaps what is wrong with the current discussion of the Africa personality or negritude is illustrated by the conclusion of Achebe's poem:

> Praise bounteous
> providence if you will
> that grants even an ogre
> a tiny glow-worm
> tenderness encapsulated
> in icy caverns of a cruel
> heart or else despair
> for in the very germ
> of that kindred love is
> lodged the perpetuity
> of evil.[22]

Both the praising of providence and the despair are static reactions as against a dynamic reaction. The point is that any attempt at 'correcting' the commandant at Belsen camp would have to be by dynamic interplay of one factor of the reality of his personality against the other. This dynamic principle is taken into account in another of Achebe's poems 'Beware, Soul Brother'. Irony is intended in the opening lines but it is an irony of judgement rather than of fact:

> We are the men of soul
> men of song we measure out
> our joys and agonies
> too, our long, long passion week
> in paces of the dance . . .

He reminds us of the parallel truth:

> Our ancestors, soul brother, were wiser
> than is often made out. Remember
> they gave Ala, great goddess
> of their earth, sovereignty too over
> their arts for they understood
> so well those hard- headed
> men of departed dance where a man's
> foot must return whatever beauties
> it may weave in air, where
> it must return for safety
> and renewal of strength.

And so he warns,

> But beware soul brother
> of the lures of ascension day

for others there will be that day
lying in wait leaden-footed, tone-deaf
passionate only for the deep entrails
of our soil. . . .
Take care
then, mother's son, lest you become
a dancer disinherited in mid-dance
hanging a lame foot in air like the hen
in a strange unfamiliar compound.[23]

The point I have been making is that the acceptance of a different mode of knowing is not a denial of wisdom; that the statement about intuitive knowledge or 'heightened sensitivity' does not automatically become a 'myth of irrational nobility' or a rejection of a sense of practicality in the management of day-to-day affairs.

One may digress a little further into wider fields and insist that there is not only one way of arriving at truth. I found the following passage in an exhilarating book *Mathematics and the Imagination* and I will quote it at length:

The problems of the infinite have challenged man's mind and have fired his imagination as no other single problem in the history of thought. The infinite appears both strange and familiar, at times beyond our grasp, at times natural and easy to understand. In conquering it, man broke the fetters that bound him to earth. All his faculties were required for this conquest—his reasoning powers, his poetic fancy, his desire to know.

To establish the science of the infinite involves the principle of *mathematical induction*. This principle affirms the power of reasoning by recurrence. It typifies almost all mathematical thinking, all that we do when we construct complex aggregates out of simple elements. It is, as Poincaré remarked, 'at once necessary to the mathematician and irreducible to logic' . . . mathematical induction is not derived from experience, rather it is an inherent, intuitive almost instinctive property of the mind. . . .

. . . Without any sense of discontinuity, without transgressing the canons of logic, the mathematician and philosopher have bridged in one stroke the gulf between the finite and the infinite. The mathematics of the infinite is a sheer affirmation of the inherent power of reasoning by recurrence.[24]

One is reminded that Plato joined mathematics to music and poetry as the 'arts of philosophy' by which Plato meant, as the Canadian Northrop Frye says, 'the identifying of the soul of man with the forms and ideas of the world'.[25] The point of the long quotation is to emphasise the validity and value of a type of knowledge which 'without trangressing the canons of logic' comes in 'an inherent, intuitive and almost instinctive' manner. My argument is that if it should be the case that for a variety of reasons, including the homogeneity of a closed society which breeds a proliferation of instinctively held archetypes of intellect and emotion, the African should be found to have a predominating tendency towards this type of knowledge, then it should be recognised, not indeed as exclusive, but as characteristic.

Now to return more specifically to our topic—the mode of aesthetic perception. Wole Soyinka, talking in 1962 about the audience response to his play *A Dance of the Forests*, revealed a preference for non-rationalised perception of meaning:

> But what I found personally gratifying and what I considered the validity of my work, was that the so-called illiterate group of the community, the stewards, the drivers—the really uneducated non-academic world—they were coming to see the play every night. . . . If you allowed them, they always felt the thing through all the way, and they came night after night and enjoyed it tremendously. I never asked them what they made of it, you know. . . . The only time when they become quite frankly lazy is when they find that their instincts to reject what seems strange are supported by a columnist in the paper, they suddenly feel, 'Oh! yes, we thought that you know, I mean what's all this nonsense', but left to themselves, and given the proper guidance, I have no doubt at all that we have one of the most interested audiences, in any event, in any cultural event, here in Nigeria.[26]

The crucial words here are: 'they always felt the thing through all the way . . . I never asked them what they made of it'. I think what is excluded here is a specifically analytical understanding. By 'felt' here I don't think either that Soyinka is talking about emotional or sensuous response in their western connotations. Perhaps rapport is the word, the direct interaction between the observed art object and the as yet unverbalised archetypes of the subject's spirit or soul or imagination or sensitivity or totality of person. Soyinka's appeal for 'the proper guidance' is for the critic to identify and verbalise these archetypes to give support to the rapport—and Kofi Awoonor has suggested one guiding principle when he said he could quite easily understand *A Dance of the Forests* because 'in one aspect it's simply a kind of cycle of events cutting through the history of a people; and this makes a lot of meaning to me if you see some of the traditional performances of any society in West Africa'.[27]

The same mode of perception is presupposed in Christopher Okigbo's reply to an interviewer who asked him why his poetry was so hard to understand:

> Well, because what we call, understanding . . . passes through a process of analysis, if you like, of the intellectual—there is an intellectual effort which one makes before one arrives at what one calls the meaning. Now I think it is possible to arrive at a response without passing through that process of intellectual analysis, and I think that if a poem can elicit a response, either in physical or emotional terms for an audience, the poem has succeeded. . . .[28]

'Physical' and 'emotional' here are attempts to give some definition to a generalised non-intellectual response. In another interview Okigbo talked of girls in a secondary school in Northern Nigeria crying when he read some of his poems to them—though they could not explain why.[29]

More recently, Kofi Awoonor, talking about his strange haunting novel *This Earth, My Brother . . .*, acknowledges that he was inviting the reader to share in the protagonist, Amamu's vision, adding

> There is an invitation to participate in the festival of the senses. I think if we go back to the festival of the senses, our destruction of things and people will cease.[30]

Perhaps I don't quite understand what is implied here by 'the festival of the senses' but it sounds very close to Senghor's 'the mystic civilisation of the senses' especially when Awoonor continues to say that Amamu's long journey in the novel is both on a realistic and a mythical level.

Let me conclude this section then by stating that there is strong evidence to suggest that the characteristic mode of African aesthetic perception is non-analytic or non-intellectual, relying essentially on the achievement of rapport with the art object. This response can be analysed and Robert Plant Armstrong's *The Affecting Presence* (University of Illinois Press, 1971) is a very interesting analysis of this phenomenon. Senghor's analysis in terms of cosmic vision and the interplay of life forces is also interesting. I would myself suggest a more prosaic explanation in terms of the abundance of uninhibited archetypes and sensitivity to which the work of art relates in the subject. All these can be debated. But the phenomenon itself is a reality—the response itself is non-analytical.

The Nature of Poetic Expression

The implications of this mode of perception in literary expression I will discuss only from the poetic genre for purposes of meaningful limitation.

A principal effect is that it would give rise to a poetry which, in some crucial manner, would have an emphasis on the individual phrase or what has been called a 'lyric total' in spite of, or helpful to, the total expression. Let me illustrate briefly how this has worked in traditional poetry. It should be borne in mind that traditional poetry is of various forms and is to be seen in a variety of media. Some poems are, for example, to be found in the context of dance in which their contribution is only a partial element in the total effect. In these contexts we find an emphasis on simplicity of language and paucity of images so that the senses are liberated to participate in the other elements of song and dance. Where imagery of the symbolic kind enters, it is limited mainly to the chorus which might just be a statement of intense meaning repeated after each solo statement, a statement moreover which is of such popular circulation that though its import continues to retain its impact, its meaning is quite clear. In a dirge dance, for example, the statement 'mgbala ezeele'—'the fence has collapsed'—will be repeated interminably by the chorus of dancers while the solo cantor will weave in, at will, and perhaps without the dancers listening, a description of the dead person and his qualities. In a war dance the chorus will be repeating 'mbaogu okweere nwoko'—'the boast of bravery befits a man'— while the soloist describes the prowess of the community of fighters and the cowardice of the enemy.

At the other extreme is the poetry which relies on its verbal content and quality for its effect (in addition, of course, to unreproducable elements like visual [facial and body] movements and tonal timbre of the reciter). This is the peak of poetic expression and is unaccompanied or minimally accompanied by musical instruments. This is adult poetry, found in various contexts—religious incantation, praise of kings and warriors, dirges—but sharing in the formal quality I have mentioned and on which I will now try to expand.

Without prejudice to what Ali Mazrui calls 'versified intelligibilities', simple poetry in which personal moments of experience are communicated with beauty and ease,[31] the tendency in much African verbal art is to catch a moment or a whole experience once and for all in an expression of intense sharpness. This tendency, incidentally, features in other areas of aesthetic representation—in the motifs of painting, sculpture, music, dance, masquerade. The idea is to re-create an idea or an experience by representing it in a diversity of such expressions rather than to state the reality or to analyse it. A dirge from Nsukka will illustrate the point:

> A great tree has crashed down
> > the birds are scattered in the forest
> Your name gave us passage in strange lands
> > this then is what has happened?
> When danger struck like lightning you led the attack
> > is this then the end of your journey?
> What you had you gave to the people,
> > is your store now empty?
> Alas! Alas!
> > Earth's path has been dammed.
> Hand stronger than hand has broken the hand
> > a trap has caught the tiger
> Tree at the gate that blunted the matchet's edge
> > this then is what has happened?[32]

The discussions on the relative contributions of traditional African literature and modern European traditions have already taken place. This, in addition, is no study of traditional African poetry. But I need to restate some factors which have to be taken into account in achieving understanding for criticism of the new tradition. The dirge above centres on one central perception of the misfortune of losing a strong support of a family line. More importantly, it creates this sense of loss through a concatenation of individual expressive categorical images drawn from a variety of levels of existence, drawing equivalences between one and another at a symbolic level. Quite a few of the images are separable as praise names addressed to the dead person.

Of what importance is this for the understanding of our modern poets? One of the functions of the critic in modern Africa is to create

an atmosphere of understanding for our artists in such a way that presumed difficulty will not obstruct the growth of a literary audience.
And one of the biggest stumbling blocks at the moment is the presumed
obscurity of the poets.[33] The question then is whether the pattern of
poetic expression I have described has enough influence on the poets
so that a realisation of the fact can help an insight into their method and
release the reader to their significance.

In Sunday Anozie's challenging book on Christopher Okigbo I find
the following comment:

This recognition [of an idea in a section of Okigbo's *Silences*] is not
at all the result of any attempt to probe logically the poet's mind,
since in fact this is quite impossible, especially in a movement
whose dialectic is obscure. Rather than a logical recognition, a
sympathetic response is here attempted to the ambitions of a
poetic art still struggling to find its feet and which throughout the
poem, *Silences* I, is mainly concerned with cross-breeding visionary
and aesthetic symbols or images with rhythmical variations in a
frail reaching after a musical and dramatic suggestiveness.[34]

Without agreeing with the particular interpretation of meaning, one
notices certain factors here which relate to the tradition discussed
earlier—the non-necessity of a logical process of understanding, the
approach from sympathetic response arising from a poetic method of
'cross-breeding visionary and aesthetic symbols or images'. Okigbo was
to mature from his early poetry in which these symbols and images had
a rather complicated structure of dialectics, to the prophetic declama-
tory poetry of 'Path of Thunder'. The pattern of combination was to
ease out, but the poems were still to rely on the heavily symbolic units
of imagery.

Soyinka's poetry, different in point of view and emphasis, shows the
same dependence on units of imagery. Without Okigbo's encyclo-
paedic vastness of areas of reference, but with an intensity of knowledge
of the resources of Yoruba mythology and literary traditions, Soyinka
still constructs his poems from a sensibility which in one event sees the
event's cosmic equivalents and repercussions and recreates the experience in terms of affective units of imagery. A very enlightening study
of *Idanre* by Femi Fatoba in a recent issue of *Nigeria Magazine* brings this
out. Fatoba is flamboyant in his expressions but the two following
passages make one point.

Something else which came to my mind was that I was brought up (and that very badly) on Western Literature and had failed all along to realise the death of WORDS in the West. By WORDS, I mean words in the sense of vehicles of magic and magic in the sense of creations of sensations and phenomena which are beyond human verbal explanation. We refuse to bring WORD back to life because the trouble of raising it from death demands belief in those ancient codes of life, like ordinary human trust and moral uprightness; and most important of all, the absorption of the good in the old into the best of the scientific present and future. A total rejection of the past is one of the main ingredients in the poison which killed WORD. We then prop up its shadow and paint it in loud colours as if that would seal the gangrene in the letters which go to make up words.

And later,

One image attracts the other and they all shock one with a bloody and magnetic force which pulls one out of the dark exclusives of the mind into a reality which stings the eyes and the conscience and pricks the flesh like sharp hot nails.[35]

Again the mythic, mystic vision which sees in each event its parallels and meaning at various levels of existence and the magic recreative power of symbolic images as the source of meaning rather than through the dialectical logic of development. For time past, present and future are subsumed in the single moment of epiphanic understanding. This is the peak to which African poetry, traditional and modern, aims.

Briefly, in the context of this paper, I will mention two other points. One is that a poetry that relies so heavily on the use of images must require in the reader or critic a depth of understanding of the mythology, traditions and imaginative literature of the community from which the writers come. The cultural significance of the images becomes essentials of meaning as Anozie aptly brings out in contrasting Paul Theroux's interpretation of the rainbow image in Okigbo's *Heavensgate* and the real significance of the rainbow to Okigbo and the Igbo.[36] And there is not much of Soyinka that can be understood without a deep knowledge of Yoruba mythology and oral traditional literature.

Secondly, this poetry, even when it is most abstruse and mythical is still public and man/society oriented. Of his *Silences*, which are perhaps his most obscure after *Distances*, Okigbo says in his Introduction to *Labyrinths*: 'Both parts of *Silences* were inspired by events of the day:

Lament of the Silent Sisters, by the Western Nigeria Crisis of 1962, and the death of Patrice Lumumba, *Lament of the Drums,* by the imprisonment of Obafemi Awolowo, and the tragic death of his eldest son.'[37] Soyinka was later to say of *Idanre*:

> *Idanre* lost its mystification early enough. As events gathered pace and unreason around me I recognised it as part of a pattern of awareness which began when I wrote *A Dance of the Forests.* In detail, in the human context of my society, *Idanre* has made abundant sense. . . . And since then the bloody origin of Ogun's pilgrimage has been, in true cyclic manner, most bloodily re-enacted.[38]

In both it is the fate of a people and their hopes that is the theme rather than the fate of individuals, in both the mythical cycle of chaos and regeneration is seen in terms of the society. A sociological awareness of the ontology and mentality of a people will help prevent the interpretation of their symbols in terms outside the orbit of their poet's possible meaning. Pessimism, for example, is not cosmic in the poetry but related to specific situations; and the apocalyptic poet of Africa still has a strong faith in the awakening of the storm into a harvest season, of the night into a dawn of sunlight. So, Soyinka at the end of 'deluge':

> And no one speaks of secrets in this land
> Only, that the skin be bared to welcome rain
> And earth prepare, that seeds may swell
> And roots take flesh within her, and men
> Wake naked into harvest-tide;[39]

and Christopher Okigbo's last lines of poetry, some of it borrowed from the Spanish, proclaim

> beyond our crumbling towers—
> Beyond the iron path careering along the same beaten track
> The glimpse of a dream lies smouldering in a cave,
> together with the mortally wounded birds.
> Earth, unbind me; let me be the prodigal; let this be
> the ram's ultimate prayer to the tether . . .
> An old star departs, leaves us here on the shore
> Gazing heavenward for a new star approaching;
> The new star appears, foreshadows its going
> Before a going and coming that goes on forever . . .[40]

The Function of Criticism

I have dealt with my topic by indirection because I believe that the reality of a different tradition establishes the need for a different approach, and the areas of this difference will determine the areas of changed perspective. So I will conclude briefly.

From what I have said so far it may be deduced that the critic in Africa is called upon to be more of a literary citizen than a literary scholar. For one thing, the writer and his 'midwife' the critic are operating in a context of a literate community in which, when books have served their specific role for studies and the acquisition of skills, they are not much regarded (except thrillers) and aesthetic pleasure is mainly derived from oral situations. An interested and participating audience for the writers has still to be created. Secondly, a greater percentage of this audience has a limited comprehension of the language in which modern African literature is written. More importantly, we are dealing with a new literature the traditions of which have been in the formative stage. Most educated Africans have been brought up on the English tradition, while the most creative of African writers have been forging a tradition for themselves more congenial to their environment and sensibilities. The critic therefore has to gather the threads of this new tradition and communicate it to his people to open the literature to them.

The manner of critical awareness which this calls for is not dominated by any dogmatic knowledge of systems. Aesthetic certainties derived from any established traditions will only jeopardise the chances of full response. And this matter is complicated for the African critic by the dual need to encourage the writers and yet offer them the full depth of searching criticism necessary for the valid growth of our literature. But another Nigerian critic, Dr Abiola Irele, has presented these specific problems in greater breadth, and I will conclude with his words:

> The double relationship of this literature to two imaginative traditions, with the particular forms of human universe which lie behind each of them, calls for a special orientation of criticism in dealing with it, an orientation which is sociological by implication. It involves a process whereby the very differentiation that marks the two frames of reference of this literature imposes upon the critical function important adjustments of those principles worked out in the Western tradition, to the peculiar modes of sensibility

which feature in the African works, and which derive from the African background, of which the uses of language, both conditioned by and conditioning the traditional modes of feeling and apprehension, constitute a distinct social reality.[41]

Notes

1 'Two Nigerian Playwrights', reprinted in *Introduction to African Literature*, ed. Ulli Beier, London, Longman, 1964, pp. 255–62.

2 Gerald Moore in *African Literature and the Universities*, ed. Gerald Moore, Ibadan University Press, 1965, p. 85.

3 Ezekiel Mphahlele, *African Literature and the Universities*, p. 87.

4 'Interview with Lewis Nkoski', reprinted in *African Writers Talking*, ed. Dennis Duerden and Cosmo Pieterse, Heinemann, 1972, p. 176.

5 'Our Literary Critics', *Nigeria Magazine*, 74, September 1962, pp. 78–82.

6 'Where Angels Fear to Tread', *Nigeria Magazine*, 75, December 1962, pp. 61–2.

7 'Interview with Maxine McGregor', reprinted in *African Writers Talking*, p. 25.

8 'Interview with J. P. Clark' in *Palaver, Interviews with Five African Writers*, Texas, 1972, p. 16.

9 'The African Critic and His People', *Présence Africaine*, 83, 3rd Quarterly, 1972, p. 7.

10 *The Writer in Modern Africa*, ed. Per Hastberg, Scandinavian Institute of African Studies, 1968.

11 *Protest and Conflict in African Literature*, eds. Cosmo Pieterse and Donald Munro, Heinemann, 1969.

12 *Literature and Modern West African Culture*, ed. D. I. Nwoga, soon to be published by Ethiope, Benin, Nigeria.

13 J. P. Clark in *Palaver*, p. 20.

14 'The Failure of the Writer in Africa', reprinted in *The African Reader*, eds. Wilfred Cartey and Martin Kilson, Vintage, 1970, p. 138.

15 'The Power and the Penury', *Drum*, Nigeria edition, April 1973 (p. 19—for some unknown reason, the pages of *Drum* are not numbered).

16 'The Language of Poetry', *African Literature and the Universities*, p. 96.

17 *Kas-Kas: Interviews with Three Caribbean Writers in Texas*, University of Texas, 1972, pp. 46–7.

18 'The Failure of the Writer in Africa', p. 141.

19 'Negritude: A Humanism of the Twentieth Century', *The African Reader*, p. 184.
20 *Palaver*, p. 62.
21 Ezekiel Mphahlele, discussing *The African* by William Conton in *The African Image*, 1962, pp. 22–3.
22 *Beware, Soul Brother*, Nwamife 1971, pp. 39–40 (where Commandant is misprinted 'Commandment'); *Christmas in Biafra and other Poems*, Doubleday, 1973, pp. 58–9.
23 *Beware, Soul Brother*, pp. 29–30; *Christmas in Biafra . . .*, pp. 46–7.
24 Edward Kasner and James Newman, *Mathematics and the Imagination*. Harmondsworth, Penguin, 1968, pp. 42–3.
25 *The Stubborn Structures*, London, Methuen, 1970, pp. 7–8.
26 *African Writers Talking*, p. 177.
27 *Ibid.*, p. 34.
28 *Ibid.*, pp. 143–4.
29 Marjory Whitelaw, 'Interview with Christopher Okigbo', *Journal of Commonwealth Literature*, 8, 1969, pp. 28–37.
30 *Palaver*, p. 60.
31 'Abstract Verse and African Tradition', *Zuka* I, September 1967, pp. 47–9.
32 Unpublished. But what is said of the poem can be seen in a variety of publications—*Yoruba Poetry*, ed. Ulli Beier, *Igbo Traditional Verse*, eds. Egudu and Nwoga from Nigeria and collections of the poetry of other areas of Africa.
33 I have done a study of this issue of obscurity in 'Obscurity and Commitment in Modern African Poetry', *African Literature Today*, 6, 1973, pp. 26–45.
34 Sunday Anozie, *Christopher Okigbo: Creative Rhetoric*, Evans, 1972, p. 118.
35 '*Idanre*—An appreciation', *Nigeria Magazine*, Nos 107–9, December–August 1971 (actually came out in 1973), pp. 101 and 106.
36 Anozie, *Christopher Okigbo*, pp. 43–6.
37 *Labyrinths*, Heinemann A.W.S., 1971, p. xii.
38 *Idanre and Other Poems*, Methuen, 1967, p. 58.
39 *Ibid.*, p. 62.
40 *Labyrinths*, p. 72.
41 'The Criticism of Modern African Literature', *Perspectives on African Literature*, p. 20.

Emile Snyder

Aimé Césaire: The Reclaiming of the Land

Take a cruise to the French-speaking Caribbean, a cruise skilfully organised by your local travel agency so that what you will see there will match the expectations of the travel folders. You will stay at a Hilton-type hotel and be entertained at night by local musicians; you will go on a guided tour in the interior and drive so fast that the memories you retain of the people will be images of colourful bandannas wrapped around the heads of women, shapes moving gracefully in the sunlight, a waving of hands and the smiles of children. And you will return home rhapsodising to your friends about the paradise which is Martinique. Surely—you will be inclined to say—all this nonsense about colonialism and neocolonialism must be insidious propaganda propounded by misguided radicals. And not even once will you have guessed at the reality of life in Martinique: the physical and mental misery of the people, their sense of despair at an unchanging situation, their loss, over the years, of pride, of colour, of self.

This bleaker image of Martinique—the other side of the advertised coin—faced Aimé Césaire from his birth, undermining his childhood, festering during his adolescence, and bursting open like a neglected sore just as he was about to depart from Martinique 'with rapture'. But in the most closeted chambers of his consciousness memories awaited, restless for the poems which would deliver them and exorcise them.

Beginning with *Return to my Native Land* (*Cahier d'un retour au pays natal*, 1939) that long epic, dramatic and lyrical poem which André Breton called 'nothing less than the greatest lyric monument of the epoch', the painful memories began to emerge. Césaire recalled his mother working late at night to improve the family earnings:

> . . . I am even awakened at night by
> those tireless limbs which pedal the night, by the
> bitter puncture in the soft flesh of the night

made by a Singer machine my mother pedals,
pedals for our hunger.[1]

Césaire evoked his island:

At the end of the dawn, flowered with frail
creeks, the hungry West Indies, pitted with
smallpox, dynamited with alcohol, stranded in
the mud of this bay, in the dirt of this city
sinisterly stranded.

And the apparent passivity of his Martinique brothers:

In this inert city, this brawling crowd which
so astonishingly by-passes its cry, its motion,
its meaning, calm, passive to its true cry, the
only cry you want to hear for it is all the city can
say, because the sound inhabits some refuge of
shadow and pride in this inert city, going by its
cry of hunger, of grief, of revolt, of hate, this
crowd so strangely blabbing and mute.

And in prose Césaire ridiculed his secondary school friends, the sons of
the mulatto bourgeoisie, aping the white world, and fuelled by what
Frantz Fanon called the drive for 'lactification':

I was literally choking amid these Blacks
who thought of themselves as white.

Already by 1939 Césaire was instinctively fusing with the history of the
race the more immediate, existential conditions of his own life.

How do you accept, act upon, and transform such a past if not by
speaking against it, if not by trying to raise 'the good drunken cry of
revolt'? How do you validate your existence, record for yourself and for
your posterity a plot of land in the world register (*cadastre*), if not by
trudging back along the ancestral path to return to the source—Africa,
the matrix, the point of embarkation for the black diaspora and the
irreversible moment of parturition? You must sail back to the 'homeland', the family names, the genealogies which almost dissolved in the
wake of the slavers' ships.

For Césaire the Orphic voyage was to pass through Paris. It was there,
as a student at the Ecole Normale, that he met Léopold Sédar Senghor
from Senegal (and later he was to say that the first time he met Senghor

he began to think of himself as an African), that he befriended the poet Léon Damas from French Guiana, and that he merged with the African and Caribbean students attending the classrooms of the Sorbonne and sharing thoughts while sitting at the cafés on the Boulevard Saint Michel. An elite group? Yes indeed, but what poet, what novelist, what intellectual has not willingly or unwillingly at some point been co-opted into the intelligentsia class, by reason of his education and the privilege of having to till the stacks of a library rather than the furrows of an impoverished land? An elite group, yes, but one intent upon denouncing the mystifications of the colonial reality (including the ambiguity of its own situation as an acculturated class), and asserting something of its own specificity as black men among men.

The 'Negritude' movement was launched, Césaire coining the word for the first time in *Return to my Native Land,* Senghor refining the theory, Alioune Diop providing with his review *Présence Africaine* (furthering the pioneering work of *Légitime Défense* and *L'étudiant Noir*) the voice or vehicle for keeping alive the palaver among black men, for defining 'the originality of African culture', for promoting 'its insertion into the future concert of nations'.

Césaire's contribution, over the years, took many forms. As a polemicist, in *Discours sur le colonialisme* (1950) he attacked the arrogant premises on which western intellectuals asserted the so-called superiority of western culture; as an historian, in *Toussaint Louverture* (1961), he rehabilitated the historical figure of the great Haitian patriot; as a playwright, he embarked upon a dramatic trilogy centred on black heroes in the world because, as Césaire once said to Lylian Kesteloot 'we need heroes of our own'. His first real play, *La tragédie du roi Christophe* (1963), focused upon the forceful figure of the Haitian ruler, Henri Christophe. *Une saison au Congo* (1967) depicted the martyrdom of Patrice Lumumba and the rape of the Congo by foreign powers. To close the trilogy Césaire is said to be projecting a play on Malcolm X. In addition to his literary career, Césaire entered Martinique's politics, serving for years as mayor of Fort-de-France. He also joined the French Communist Party to which he adhered for over a decade, resigning from it in 1956 and putting forth the reasons for his defection in a brilliant letter addressed to Maurice Thorez, the then titular head of the party.[12]

But poetry has remained for Césaire the most cherished, the most exacting, and the most intimate way to conciliate his anger with his love, his despair with his dreams, his sense of his own blackness with his yearning for an anonymous and universal presence in a future fraternal world. Poetry has always been for Césaire the 'miraculous weapons', *les Armes Miraculeuses,* as the title of his volume of 1964 announced.

Refusing the facile exoticism of the previous generation of black poets writing in French (despite the fact that his vocabulary drives the reader to a variety of dictionaries), eschewing the simple statement (for Césaire once said that there was a world of difference between a political pamphlet and a poem), Césaire adopted the nightmarish visions of a Lautréamont or Rimbaud, the convoluted syntactical subtleties of a Mallarmé, and followed the hermetic plunges of the Surrealists into the reservoir of the unconscious.

But for him so much of Surrealism was only a matter of technique. For Césaire's visions coagulated into precise images of the indignities and tortures suffered under the colonial system, and into counter-images of anticipated liberation which would bring about the flowering of love and the reconciliation of man with the universe. Moreover, the syntactical meanders of Césaire's poems do not stem from a *précieux* mind. They reflect his intentions to record the tortuous labour of memory grappling with lost landmarks. They, at the same time, underline the dialectic project which is political in nature and often stated at the onset by the very titles of the poems. Thus Césaire, although technically heir to the Surrealist tradition, stands ideologically poles apart from it. Nothing in his poetry is gratuitous. The imagination is not allowed to wander aimlessly for self-gratification. Each poem is in itself a project, a praxis—in the Sartrian sense of the word—carefully mapped out by a sense of urgency and of responsibility. The dialectic moves from the awareness of a tragic racial past to the lucid recognition of the present horror, compelling the poet forward to revolt in the name of a desired transcendence. The movement is from awareness to revolt and to love.

Let us trace this dialectic in 'Raving Mad', one of the most poignant poems from his early volume, *Soleil Cou Coupé* (1948) salvaged in the recapitulative text of *Cadastre* (1961).[3]

Raving Mad

Greetings to you birds slicing through and scattering the circle of
                                    herons
and the genuflexion of their resigned heads
in a sheath of white down

Greetings to you birds who peck open the true belly of the swamp
and the chieftain's chest of the setting sun

Greetings to you raucous cry
  resinous torch
  in which mingle the trails
  of rain ticks and white mice

Raving mad I greet you with my ravings whiter than death

Simple open sea
I welcome my future hour
when each word each gesture will liven
your face like that of a blond goat
foraging in the intoxicating vat of my hand

>   And then then
>   my good leech
>   then the beginning of time
>   then the end of time
>   and the erect majesty of the original eye.

It is twilight. The poet imprisoned in his anger, contemplates a circle
of herons. They stand there, outlined in the sunset, on one leg, the other
leg doubled back under the knee, and their heads lowered into their
bodies. And the poet perceives in this attitude of the herons a symbol of
the resignation of his black brothers under colonial subjugation. This
resignation is expressed ironically—for Césaire's poetry is frankly anti-
Christian—through the image of penitents in genuflexion before the
altar:

>   and the genuflexion of their resigned heads
>   in a sheath of white down.

But all of a sudden a flock of small birds traverse the circle of herons and
the herons, frightened, take flight. All the birds (small birds joined by
the herons) taking off towards sunset are for Césaire messengers of hope.
In Césaire's bestiary almost all birds are symbols of liberation on the
way.

The poet greets three times these harbingers of freedom, anticipating
his own freedom. He follows the birds as far as his eyes can see. They
ose themselves in the swamp. But, by poetic transposition, this swamp,
his dusk, now become the mediation for a psychic plunge into the

past, into Césaire's collective past which he relates to Africa by the war-like personification of nature: 'and the chieftain's chest of the setting sun'.

And it is no longer the 'raucous cry' of the birds which the poet greets but his own recovered voice now asserting itself. For he is now going to be able to 'raise with stiffness the great black cry so that the foundations of the world will be shaken' ('d'une telle raideur le grand cri nègre que les assises du monde en seront ébranlées'), a project he will set for himself in his dramatic monologue *Et les chiens se taisaient* (1956). The imagination of the poet carries him into the most secret recesses of the bush—(and of the past)—; it is there that life pulses with real intensity: 'rain ticks and white mice'.

Césaire begins to feel free at last from his psychic torture. Having recovered a sense of his roots, he also recovers his personal and collective voice which he now uses to vilify his oppressors: 'Raving mad I greet you with my ravings whiter than death!' Note that for Césaire, as for Damas, the colour white always has a negative connotation, being synonymous with physical death, spiritual atrophy, and cultural decadence: manichaean principle in French black poetry (not always adhered to by Senghor!) which tends to counter-balance the opposite manichaeanism of western poetry where the colour white has been associated for centuries with notions of virginity, purity, spirituality and strength: 'Raving mad I greet you with my ravings whiter than death.'

Moment of supreme arrogance, of supreme liberation when the poet's whole being coheres with his anger. Now Césaire can go beyond his anger, surpass it, and channel it towards a higher synthesis:

> I welcome my future hour
> when each word each gesture will liven
> your face like that of a blond goat
> foraging in the intoxicating vat of my hand.

The last movement of the poem, an oceanic movement (for Césaire is an oceanic poet always conscious of the presence of the ocean lapping his small island: he once referred to Martinique as a 'dandruff speck on the surface of the ocean') prefigures universal fraternity. But this leap toward the 'future hour' of freedom is also a return to a primal unity: return to simplicity ('simple open sea'), and to the harmony of man with the universe. Freedom will express itself through the now possible gestures of love between man and women, the sensual communication:

> When each word each gesture will liven
> your face like that of a blond goat
> foraging in the intoxicating vat of my hand.

Beautiful image, that of a woman whose angular face, bathed in the golden colour of sunset, is being intimately, almost domestically, caressed by the loving hand of the poet!

Without freedom there cannot be, for Césaire, any possibility of loving. But with the advent of freedom the cycle is completed, the 'beginning of time' and 'the end of time' fuse into a myth of fertility, the frankly phallic image of the triumphant sun, the old Egyptian symbol of power and fecundity: 'the erect majesty of the original eye'.

Critics have often remarked upon the tone of violence in the poetry of Césaire. It should be seen, however, that violence for Césaire is only the second term of the dialectic, the moment of negativity in the Hegelian sense. True, by comparison with his manifested anger, Césaire's final leap into love and tenderness is verbalised quietly—a muted lyricism—in the poems. Often a single verse reveals it, as if the poet overwhelmed by his newly discovered treasure finds himself too shy to share it with the rest of the world. In *Return to my Native Land*, referring to his pregnant wife but without naming her or his child precisely, he simply wrote:

> and you, O star, will draw lemuridae from
> your foundation with the unfathomable sperm
> of man
>   *the not dared form* (my italics)

In Césaire's poetry images of renaissance through love counterbalance images of violence and destruction. Examples abound in the volume *Cadastre*. In 'Millibars of the storm' he wrote:

> Dream let's not yield
> among the hooves of frenzied horses
> a tearful noise groping towards the immense wing
>   of your eyelid.

In 'Chevelure', at the conclusion of the poem, he invoked the loving woman:

> and you
> abode of my insolence of my tombs of my whirlwinds
> mane bundle of lianas fervent hope of shipwrecks

> sleep softly on the meticulous trunk of my embrace my
> woman
> my fortress.

In 'The Wheel', after having recalled ancestral miseries:

> but you minutes will you not wind onto your spool of life
> the lapped up blood
> the art of suffering sharpened like tree stumps by
>   the knives
> of winter,

he prophesised the rebirth of nature enhanced by the loving face of his woman:

> the doe drunk with thirst
> bringing to my unexpected wellstones your
> face of an unmasted schooner
> your face
> like a village asleep in the depth of a lake
> and which is reborn to the realm of green and
> to the fruitful year.

A rebirth 'to the realm of green and to the fruitful year', that is the key to Césaire's most private obsession. His anthropomorphisation of nature which he carries to a near *frisson* of eroticism reflects his desire to reintegrate himself into the very minute manifestations of the vegetable mineral and animal world. There is, in his poetry, a rich catalogue—indeed an encyclopaedia—of flora and fauna. A brief repertoire of his images should include plants, shrubs, flowers, such as a 'silphium-lascinatum' cassia, monk's hood ('aconit napel'), solandra, albizzia, umbel and terrebela—to name only a few—and trees such as a ceiba, kaelcedra, cassia, manchineel, baobab, and flamboyant. Césaire reflects the preoccupation of the botanist, bent as he is to avoid the 'vulgar' terms in preference for the Latin names which embody the genus of the species.

His bestiary is just as impressive. It not only includes known birds, fishes and insects, such as a toucan, macaw, aras, gekko (lizard), scollopendra (centipede), remora (sucking fish), medusa-aurelia (jelly-fish), shark, dolphin, but it also includes fossilated forms of life and mythical ones: the lailape, a gigantic fossil carnivorous dinosaur, the amphisbaena, a serpent in classical mythology, and the griffin, half-animal, half-human creature said to have kept watch over the tombs of the Egyptians. Finally the poems seem embedded into the earth, drawing their strength from the mineral eternity; numerous are the references to clay, laterite, dacite, chromium, mercury, and so on.

This constant obsession with the botanical, zoological, and geophysical world (overwhelming by far the human *personae* of his poems) might lead us to think that Césaire has spent his formative years with his head buried in specialised scientific dictionaries. The documentation alone is shattering. Are we dealing here with a poet conceitedly flashing his esoteric erudition? Jacqueline Sieger, in an interview with Césaire in *Afrique* (No. 5, October 1961), asked him about this seemingly *recherché* aspect of his poetry:

One feels that you are searching for the erudite word and soon this gives to your poetry an impression of esoterism;

to which Césaire answered:

It is true that the language of my poems is very precise; it is because I have wanted, above all, to *name* things. If I want to speak of a certain tree, I say a palm tree, of a certain flower, an hibiscus. And why not? The French poet, in his turn, does not speak of flowers but of the rose or of the violet.

(my own translation)

Césaire's precise nomination of the natural world has a political implication—political because racism attempts to *disfranchise* a man from his geographical roots, indeed perhaps from the earth itself. In *Antisemite and the Jew*, J. P. Sartre, considering the situation of the Jew in France, remarked that anti-semitism aimed at questioning the very legitimacy of the Jew's presence on French soil and within the context of French history. Are not his roots—hence his biology, his culture and his allegiance—in Odessa or in some other extra-territorial places, would the racist say? Thus racism (all forms of racism) attempts to *deterritorialise* its victim who becomes reduced to beg acceptance as an alien or to seek to assimilate in the hope of disappearing from this monstrous illegitimacy fostered upon him.

Similarly Césaire, the son of uprooted African slaves, is first compelled to react against this curse. Naming the world in its totality is one way of claiming for himself an unchallenged plot (a *cadastre*) from which he cannot be disfranchised. Africa, the Africa which Césaire evokes at times in idealised terms (and which is not the Africa of Africans but the Africa of a Caribbean grandchild), is but a passage to a more lasting—Moses-like—homeland which is the universe itself! Naming the Nile, the Niger, the cities of Timbuktu or Uagadougou, is for Césaire like setting road signs along the homeward journey. But in the final analysis Africa is not enough for Césaire, for the centuries of colonialism have *disfranchised* him from that original homeland. In *Return to my Native Land* he wrote:

> No, we have never been amazons of the king of Dahomey, nor the princes of Ghana with eight hundred camels, nor wise men of Timbuktu under Askia the Great; nor architects in Djene, nor *mahdis* nor warriors. Under our armpits, we do not feel the itch of those who bore the lance. And since I have sworn to hide nothing of our history (I who admire nothing so much as the lamb chewing his afternoon shadow), I want to declare that we were from the very first quite pitiful dishwashers, shoeshiners without scope and, at best, rather conscientious sorcerers whose only incontestable achievement has been the endurance record under the lash.

Hence, nothing short of the whole undifferentiated earth can be his homeland; but Césaire feels that even that birthplace has been vitiated by racism, by human stupidity and hatred. It is therefore necessary to restructure poetically this ideal birthplace of man, beginning with an apocalyptic disaster (one of his poems is entitled 'Tangible Disaster') and followed by a loving reconstruction. Césaire, a sort of self-appointed Noah figure, gathers lovingly all the beasts, birds, insects, saps, to shelter them from moral deluge. And then, having done so, Noah becomes Thor, the god of thunder and lightning, raining retribution upon the wicked. And the sky and the sun remain the only witness to this apocalypse which is a genesis in reverse. Césaire's poetry abounds with 'convulsive sky', 'exploded stars', 'splitting craters', 'braziers of flames', and 'primal debris'. Purification through fire from which even extinct volcanoes find renewed strength. The poem 'Crusades of Silence' ends with the terrifying vision of Chimborazo, the volcanic mountain in the Andes, awakening once more to its original potential: 'Chimborazo though extinct still devours the world'.

In this poetic destruction of the universe there is a refusal to accept the world as handed down from an official version of Genesis because, to Césaire, those who may have written it as well as those who pretend to derive moral commandments from it, are immoral people. Genesis, and the natural reproductive cycle which Césaire loves so much, and to which he returns constantly through the images of water, ovaries, tadpoles, seeds in germination, *should* in his mind have led to the full blossoming of man in a fraternal world. However, already in the official Genesis Césaire finds himself and his black brothers cast out. That is why he said with irony 'Don't mind me, I am of before Adam', meaning not only that ideally he wishes to antedate a creation which has gone foul, but that in that Christian version of creation, starting with Adam, his own black forefathers had already been damned.

Léon Damas, the French Guiana poet, has expressed a similar attitude in a bitter poem entitled 'Against our love which asked for nothing more':[4]

> Against our love
> which dreamed of living in a free space
> which dreamed of living its own life
> of living a life
> which would be
> neither
> shameful
> nor leprous
> nor faked
> nor partitioned
> nor haunted
> they have invoked NOAH
> and NOAH called upon SHEM
> and SHEM called upon JAPHET
> and JAPHET referred it to NOAH
> and NOAH called upon METHUSELAH
> and METHUSELAH once again took out of the arsenal
> all the tinsel rags
> all the taboos
> all the warning lights of prohibitions
>
> Beware
> Now dangerous
> Detour
> Game-preserves
> Private property
> Guarded domain
> No trespassing
> Dogs and Niggers forbidden on the lawn
> (my own translation).

Politics and metaphysics are inseparable for Césaire. For the imbalance in human rapports (racism) has upset the innate balance of the universe. Nature henceforth re-enacts, in the poet's mind, the drama of human beings enslaved through hatred and stupidity. In an early poem, 'Les Pur-Sangs', from *Les Armes Miraculeuses*, Césaire paralleled man's enslavement with the deterioration of the harmonised forces of the universe:

> the earth no longer makes love with the sun
> the earth no longer rubs its cheek against the stars' clusters;

but as the poet finds a way to free himself from the yoke of servitude, as he begins to grow

> . . . like a plant
> without remorse and without stumbling
> toward the loosened hours of the day,

the earth too begins to regain its original composure:

> And the earth began to breathe beneath the gauze of mists
> And the earth stretched. A loosening came
> upon its knotted shoulders. In its veins
> a crackling of fire

Cosmic eroticism (and Sartre wrote in *Orphée Noire* that Césaire 'vegetalises, animalises sea and sky and stone') is his disguised love for the earth; it is at the same time the expression of his anguish at feeling *disfranchised* from it through centuries of racism. Tree-forms, lateriteforms, fossilated and organic forms become the only tenable *cadastre* of a man whose very race has been uprooted. In the already mentioned interview with Jacqueline Sieger, Césaire clarified his position:

But I am an African poet! I feel very deeply the uprooting of my people. Critics have remarked upon the recurrence of certain themes in my works, in particular plant symbols. I am in fact obsessed by vegetation, by the flower, by the root. There is nothing gratuitous in that, it is linked with my situation, that of a black man exiled from his native soil. It is a psychological phenomenon from which I have never freed myself and which I feel to the point of nausea. It is as if I was hearing, in the most intimate part of my sensibility, the echoes of the lapping of the waves, the tossing which the slaves felt in the holds of the slave ships. The tree, profoundly rooted in the soil, is for me the symbol of man who is self-rooted, the nostalgia of a lost paradise. (My own translation)

Césaire's *cri de coeur* is first directed to his black brothers, but it does not stop there. It extends itself to all men who, in some ways, have been humiliated, have suffered injustices, are seeking for redress and for peace. André Breton, perhaps the first to have understood the universal impact of Césaire's indignation, summarises it in this manner:

What to my mind makes this indignation priceless, is that it transcends at every moment the anguish felt by a Negro because of the fate of Negroes in modern society and, indistinguishable from that felt by all poets, artists and true thinkers, while furnishing Césaire with a special fund of verbal genius, embraces the more generally determined condition of man today, in all its intolerable and also infinitely improvable aspects.

The dialectic of Césaire's poetry, in short, synthetises the potentially *précieux* aesthetics of Surrealism with the political thrust of humanistic and existential ideology, the past and present with the future, and the experience of a unique individual with the universal condition of man.

Notes

1 The quotations from *Return to my Native Land* are from my own translations in the bilingual edition, *Return to my Native Land*, Paris, Présence Africaine, 1971.
2 *Lettre à Maurice Thorez*, Présence Africaine, 1956.
3 *Cadastre*, Edition du Seuil, 1961.
4 Léon Damas, 'Névralgies', *Présence Africaine*, 1965.

Maximilien Laroche

The Myth of the Zombi

If the problem of the transformation of African myths in the Americas, and more particularly in the Antilles, is to be dealt with in a satisfactory manner, it should become the object of a comparative study of African and Caribbean mythologies. By examining examples from the oral literature, religions, the carnival, or folklore, it would be possible to observe in what way the people of the Antilles transformed their African heritage, the procedures they followed and the direction they took.

The figure of the zombi seems to me to provide a particularly significant illustration of the changes that these beliefs, customs, legends and stories brought by the slaves to the New World underwent in the Antilles. It can, above all, help us to understand the way in which, in Haiti at least, these beliefs, customs, legends, stories or practices were adapted to the new geographical, political, and social situation the African slaves and their descendants had to face.

To speak of the character of the Haitian zombi, therefore, is to speak of the evolution of African myth into Haitian myth, of a process by which the African, as he became a Haitian, was able to retain the essential nature of his heritage and at the same time renew it. Or rather, adapt it, for although he held on to his ancestral myths he nevertheless gave them a new application, a new meaning, one not different from the old but one capable of serving a similar function within the framework of a new situation.

What is a Haitian Myth?

It may seem idle to pose such a question. The literature on myths and mythology is so abundant that, as Robert Ackerman has ironically noted, it no longer seems possible to do anything but comment on the commentaries of the myth.[1] To answer my question, I would seemingly need only to go back to the etymology of the word I am using: myth, 'muthos', narrative. But I must be careful when I attempt to define something which is particularly Haitian (the Haitian myth of the zombi) using a word which is Greek in origin. What I am asking is this: What is a *Haitian* myth? Or if one prefers: What is a Haitian narrative? And to this question a reply immediately presents itself: this narrative is of an oral not a written kind, and the particular oral tradition of which it is a product is that of the African Negro.

In fact, Creole (which is the language of Haitian narratives, at least of the popular ones) is not only a still unwritten language, but one which finds its syntactic and, to an even greater extent, its semantic roots in Africa.

If I must define the Haitian myth, therefore, it will not be to the Greeks nor even to the structuralists like Lévi-Strauss or Greimas that I will first turn, but rather to those who have commented on African myths. In this regard, Léon-Vincent Thomas has made a number of remarks which are also applicable to Haitian myths. While admitting that the African myth possesses the traditional form of a narrative, Thomas points out that this narrative is not just a simple story, a relation of past events, but a 'system and mode of knowledge which can become, and indeed usually does become, the model which determines the structure of the plot'.[2] 'For myth in an oral culture, before being a narrative fixed by writing, is the spoken word, the facial expression, the gesture which defines the event within the individual heart.'[3] Myth, then, is not simply narrative, something static and fixed, but action. Thus it unites 'the sacred and the historic'—for it is necessary 'to view the black African myth from three different angles: as a narrative; as something which expresses a world order and is situated in a religious framework; not to mention its possible basis in actual fact' (p. 134). 'Black African myth possesses a situational character (it is a socio-economic product, an ideological superstructure inseparable from its social structure in the Marxist sense of the term)' (p. 139). 'It ties together the everyday, the ephemeral, to the atemporal, the meta-physical. It is a fixed account but also a recounting; a network of words, or rather symbols—words, that is, which act' (p. 142). And this remains true in spite of the fact that the individual recounting may present the basic myth in a fragmented form (p. 137). A narrative, to be sure, is always the narration of one specific sequence of events and because of this cannot help but be limited in its connotations despite the symbolic significance of these events. These events, therefore, must be seen in connection with events in other narratives. A myth, in other words, is always an integral part of an entire mythology.

This is illustrated clearly by the Haitian myth of the zombi which can be directly traced to certain African beliefs and which, to all appearances, is closely linked to the purely Haitian myth of the 'kanzo' and the figure of the horned Shrove Tuesday. The network of cross-references which it is necessary to establish between the characters of Haitian narratives can only lead, therefore, to a clearer picture of the Haitian mythology we are discussing.

One of the fundamental traits of the Haitian mythology, as also of African mythologies, resides in its non-Promethean character, as is evidenced in René Dépestre's remark that the zombi is a stealer not of fire but of salt. This trait can perhaps be explained by L.-V. Thomas's observation that African religions including Haitian voodoo are religions of life forces, of participation. Man, in his relation to God, is in the position of someone who wishes not to steal or to appropriate the divine life force but to participate in it. This fundamental clarification also sheds light on the following remark of Geoffrey Parrinder. The comment refers to African mythologies but is perfectly valid for those of Haiti as well: 'We find here the typically African view according to which death is never natural but occurs as the result of some human misdeed.'[4]

In Haiti, as in Africa, it is not God who brings about man's death. He at least does not wish men to die. If they do die it is always through the fault of another man. There is, in other words, no such thing as a natural death. Death is always artificial. This is all the more true in that, strictly speaking, the deceased is never really separated from his relations. In a certain sense, he continues to live on earth.

The African 'Living-Dead' and the Haitian Zombi

This idea of the 'living-dead'—which is, as we know, another name for the dead yet living zombi who continues to inhabit the earth and visit the living—is found in the popular Haitian religion, voodoo, as well as in African religions. John M'biti, in his book on African religions and philosophies, has given us, in the chapter entitled 'Spiritual Beings, Spirits and the Living-Dead', an excellent description of the situation of the living-dead:

The departed of up to five generations are in a different category from that of ordinary spirits. . . . They are in the state of personal immortality and their process of dying is not yet complete. We have called them the living-dead . . . these are the 'spirits' with which African peoples are most concerned. . . . They are still part of their human families. . . . The living-dead are still 'people'. . . . They return to their human families from time to time, and share meals with them, however symbolically.[5]

Jean-Baptiste Roumain, in his chapter devoted to the concept of death found among the Haitian peasants, describes in a similar manner the fate of the soul after death. We see here that the purpose of the Haitian voodoo funerary rites is to maintain good relations between the living and the deceased (or rather his soul), for if the appropriate 'services and honours' have not been rendered to his spirit, he can prove to be a harmful irritant to the relatives who have survived him. Without these funerary rites, the deceased can never quit his body and the place he has lived in peace. An initial ceremony, called the *dégradation*, consists, then, of forcing the soul to forsake the body; a second ceremony, the *casser-canari*, celebrated at a later time, seeks to liberate the soul of the deceased completely, or rather to drive it away—or, if the need should arise, to transform it from a harmful into a benevolent influence for the living.

For the deceased, or rather his soul, continues not only to dwell upon the earth, visit the places he has inhabited, and maintain relations with those who have survived him, but he can either serve or injure the living, be useful or harmful to them. And indeed, it is from this presence of the dead and their power over the living that the myth of the zombi is born. '. . . The soul, which has just been liberated from its physical home, can be controlled by means of rituals known to the initiated and used again, for numerous purposes, in the form of a "zombi".'[6] Since the dead do not truly die, since death is almost always artificial, the will not of God but of another man, the transformation of a live man into a dead one may reflect a specific decision on someone's part to metamorphose a living being into a dead one in order to use to his own best advantage the power this dead being will have over the living.

Zombi Narratives

The myth of the zombi sprang from this belief—shared by Africans and

Haitians—in the absence of a real barrier between life and death. This myth is the subject of numerous popular Creole narratives which have been recounted by French-speaking Haitian writers.

Among the latter, it is Magloire St.-Aude, in his *Veillée* [Vigil], who has most strikingly described this phenomenon:

Je me trouvai assis dans un fauteuil, dans une sorte de couloir-galerie, contigu à la chambre de la morte, juste à la porte de l'appartement d'icelle, en sorte que je faisais vis-à-vis à la défunte.

En toilette blanche, comme une communiante, rehaussée, aux seins, de brouillons de dentelles, Thérèse, en son immobilité éternelle, n'était pas lugubre. Elle n'avait pas de mentonnière, et sa jupe-cloche, toute droite, ne godait guère.

Les lèvres esquissaient un sourire, imperceptiblement nuancé d'espièglerie. Les cheveux, d'un noir corbeau, noyaient le front. Mais, en examinant de près le visage (en étendant le bras, je touchais le cadavre), une particularité me fit frissonner: les yeux n'étaient pas hermétiquement fermés, et, entre ses paupières, la morte semblait me regarder . . . et me regardait, en effet, avec une fixité qui m'affolait d'angoisse. J'essayai de bouger, mais une crampe intolérable paralysait mes mouvements. Je voulus parler, mais j'étais aphone. Et Thérèse me regardait toujours.

Moi seul.

Et mon regard, comme aimanté, ne parvenait pas à se détacher de ces yeux d'autre-monde.[7]

[I found myself seated in an armchair, in a kind of hall-like gallery next to the dead woman's room, right at her apartment door, so that I was facing her.

Clad in white, like a communicant, with frothy lace at her breast, Therese, in her eternal immobility, was not mournful. She wore no chin-band and her hoop-skirt was straight and unsagging. An imperceptible smile, touched with mischief, hovered about her lips. Her hair, pitch black, totally covered her forehead.

But, examining her face closely (by stretching out my arm, I could touch the body), I noticed something which made me shiver: her eyes were not tightly shut and, from between her eyelids, the dead woman seemed to be watching me . . . and in fact was watching me, with a fixed stare which petrified me with fear. I tried to move but an intolerable cramp paralysed my movements.

I wanted to speak but couldn't.

And Therese kept watching me.

Me alone.
And my own eyes, as if magnetised, were unable to tear themselves
away from those eyes from another world.]

The zombi that Magloire St-Aude describes in this extract was only
at the start of her career. For the zombi, or living-dead, dies only in
appearance and is resurrected by those who have created the illusion of
his death. Ordinarily, that is according to the most widely held beliefs,
a spell is cast on someone who then 'dies' and is buried. But in the night
following his burial, the one who has cast the spell goes to the cemetery
and there, with the aid of the appropriate incantations brings back to
life, albeit a lethargic one, the dead man who is not dead but simply
lost in sleep. And from this point on, this dead man who has returned
to life, but to a life without any real autonomy, to a larval existence, is
the property of the person who has killed him. He is thus chained to this
master and forced to work for him.

In a story of an hallucinatory nature entitled 'Chronique d'un faux
amour'[8] [Chronicle of a False Love], a story inspired by some widely
known and widely believed—if not necessarily true—facts, Jacques-
Stephen Alexis has the original thought of presenting the zombi to us
from the inside rather than from the outside, of pulling us into the
mind of the living-dead who watches his own life go by as if he were a
'stranger' to it:

> . . .*Un cisaillement crève les heures.* . . . *On me tire, on m'attire* . . . *Un
> tambour hoquette de peur.* . . . *Les vis grincent et hurlent.* . . . *La bière est
> ouverte!* . . . *On me glisse une cuiller entre les dents.* . . . *La vie coule.* . . .
> *Elle pénètre mon gosier qui s'entrouve.* . . . *Elle fuse dans mes bras, elle me
> parcourt le ventre.* . . . *Mon sexe revit et se remet à palpiter.* . . . *Mes
> jambes.* . . . *Voilà mon coeur qui repart, forcené, délirant.* . . .*On m'arrache!*
> . . . *Le tambour fait rafales, cloches et cymbales à mes oreilles.* . . . *Je suis
> debout!* . . . *Je crie* . . . *Ils me frappent, ils me fouettent, ils me battent, ils
> me poussent.* . . . *Je marche* . . . *Je marche à travers le cimetière, ville lilli-
> putienne qui s'éloigne.* . . . *Voici les lueurs de Port-au-Prince, épanouie
> comme une fleur de rêve* . . . *Je hurle* . . . *Ils me fouettent! Je me débats,
> je me bats, je mords, je griffe, mais ne peux m'échapper! Ils m'attachent.
> Le tambour ronfle parmi les cris de mes geôliers et les sifflets des cravaches.* . . .

[. . . The hours are sheared away. . . . I am pulled and lured. . . . A
drum hiccups with fear. . . . The screws grate and shriek. . . . The
coffin is opened! . . . A spoon is slid between my teeth. . . . Life

flows in. . . . It reaches my throat which begins to open. . . . It fuses through my arms and spreads through my vitals. . . . My member is revitalised and begins to palpitate once again. . . . My legs. . . . And there goes my heart, frantic, delirious. . . . I am pulled out! . . . The drum goes wild, bells and cymbals in my ears. . . . I am on my feet! . . . I scream. . . . They hit me, beat me, whip me, push me . . . I walk . . . I walk through the cemetery, a Lilliputian city which disappears behind me. . . . There are the lights of Port-au-Prince, glowing like a flower in a dream. . . . I cry out. . . . They whip me! I struggle and fight, bite and scratch, but I can't escape! They bind me! The drum pounds among the shouts of my jailers and the hiss of the riding-whips. . . .]

How does a zombi appear, *in vivo*, in the reality of his new existence? Here is how Alfred Métraux describes him in his book on Haitian voodoo:[9]

L'étincelle de vie que le sorcier réveille dans le cadavre ne le rend pas entièrement à la société des hommes. Le zombi demeure dans cette zone brumeuse qui sépare la vie de la mort. Il se meut, mange, entend, parle même, mais n'a pas de souvenir et n'est pas conscient de son état. Le zombi est une bête de somme que son maître exploite sans merci, le forçant à travailler dans ses champs, l'accablant de besogne, ne lui ménageant pas les coups de fouet et ne le nourrissant que d'aliments insipides. L'existence des zombi vaut, sur le plan mythique, celle des anciens esclaves de Saint-Domingue. Le houngan ne se contentant pas du labeur quotidien de ses morts, les emploie à des tâches malhonnêtes, comme de voler les récoltes des voisins. Il existerait une classe spéciale de zombi, dits zombi-graine, dressés à dérober les fleurs de caféier et à les greffer sur les arbres de leurs maîtres.

On reconnaît les zombi à leur air absent, à leurs yeux éteints, presque vitreux, et, surtout, à l'intonation nasale de leur voix, particularité également propre aux Guédé, génies de la mort. Leur docilité est absolue à la seule condition qu'on ne leur donne pas de sel. Si, par inadvertance, ils goûtent d'un plat contenant, ne serait-ce qu'un grain de sel, le brouillard qui enveloppe leur cerveau se dissipe d'un coup et ils deviennent subitement conscients de leur affreuse servitude. Cette découverte réveille en eux une immense colère et un incoercible besoin de vengeance. Ils se précipitent sur leur maître, le tuent et ravagent ses biens, puis prennent la route à la recherche de leur tombeau.

[The spark of life that the sorcerer awakens in the corpse does not return him entirely to the society of men. The zombi remains in that grey area separating life and death. He moves, eats, hears, even speaks, but has no memory and is not aware of his condition. The zombi is a beast of burden exploited mercilessly by his master who forces him to toil in his fields, crushes him with work, and whips him at the slightest pretext, while feeding him on the blandest of diets. The life of the zombi, on the mythical level, is similar to that of the old slaves of Santo Domingo. The 'houngan' is not satisfied with the everyday tasks performed by his dead slaves, but uses them for dishonest acts such as raiding his neighbours' crops. There supposedly exists a special class of zombi, known as the grain zombi, who is trained to steal the buds of the coffee-plant and graft them onto his master's trees.

Zombis can be recognised by their vague look, their dull almost glazed eyes, and above all by the nasality of their voice, a trait also characteristic of the 'Guédé', the spirits of the dead. Their docility is absolute as long as they are given no salt. If they inadvertently eat any food containing even a single grain of salt, the fog enveloping their minds is immediately dispelled and they become suddenly aware of their enslavement. This discovery arouses in them an immense anger and an uncontrollable desire for revenge. They hurl themselves on their master, kill him and ravage his goods, then go off in search of their graves.]

Do zombis really exist? Ordinarily we are shown people who, we are told, were zombis, and we are given to understand that they did not die a natural death but rather were 'zombified'. It is very rare, on the other hand, that anyone has testified to having known someone before, during and after his zombification—unless he was the one who cast the spell!

This is why we must use the term 'mythology' and speak of a belief which is basically subjective. Just as the belief the Greeks may have had in Zeus has nothing to do with the actual existence of Zeus, the belief the Haitians may have in the existence of the zombi has nothing to do with the actual existence of such a being. We accept Graeco-Roman mythology as a body of beliefs with their own independent existence and it is less important to verify them than to examine their symbolic value. This is the position adopted by André Bonnard in his books on Ancient Greek civilisation. And it is by taking this point of view that an ethnologist like Alfred Métraux can, in his book on Haitian voodoo, compare Haitian mythology with that of Ancient Greece.

The Symbolic Value

Various authors, among them L.-V. Thomas, have emphasised the symbolic value of myths. But in this regard, it is Jean Rudhart who has most convincingly explained the intelligibility of myths:

> *Pour comprendre le mythe, il faut se mettre en état de l'écouter et de le vivre. Il faut reconstituer dans son propre esprit l'ensemble du système, tous les souvenirs et les structures mentales qui conditionnent l'expérience dont le mythe est solidaire et laisser agir sur soi les images, les schèmes, les structures symboliques, tels qu'ils se définissent dans cette vaste ordonnance. Un mythe ne peut être compris que mythiquement.*[10]

[To understand myth, one must dispose himself to listen to it and live it. One must re-create in his own mind the totality of the system, all the memories and mental structures conditioning the experiences underlying the myth, and open oneself up to the symbolic structures, images and designs as they manifest themselves within this vast order. A myth can only be understood mythically.]

We must look therefore to the African religions to find the original form of the zombi. The Haitians are former Africans: Africans transported to America by slave-traders and forced to work for masters from whom, by proclaiming their independence, they finally liberated themselves. But what I summarise here in a single sentence took more than three hundred years to accomplish. Between the sixteenth century, when the Spaniards brought the first Africans to Haiti, and 1804, the year the Haitian rebels proclaimed their independence from the French colonisers, there were so very many struggles, there were so very many constraints to be endured, that as a result the African was metamorphosed into a Haitian. In other words, a new man was born, forced to adapt his beliefs to a new situation, forced to create for himself a new soul. In this way, the African religions gave birth to voodoo in which one finds African elements adapted to the new situation in Haiti. The figure of the zombi may allow us to understand this metamorphosis.

African religions are characterised, as we know, by a remote God. God, in the religions of Africa, is the Creator who at one time lived on earth in the midst of men but who one day, for various reasons depending on the particular religion, decided to abandon man and earth. From that moment, he has remained remote from men. Geoffrey

Parrinder[11] points out, in this context, how close this idea of the separation of man and God is to the story of Adam and Eve driven from the Earthly Paradise. But this is rather a parallelism of contrast—a contrast which becomes clear if we consider how the idea of death must change depending on whether we see it from the point of view of an African religion according to which God has abandoned the earth and left man alone and free to exercise his will, or from the Judao-Christian viewpoint according to which man is continually striving to regain a lost paradise.

In the popular Haitian religion, the concept of God seems clearly the same as in the African religions: that of a remote God who has abandoned the earth:

Le mot 'Dieu' revient constamment dans la bouche des paysans haïtiens, mais il serait faux d'en conclure qu'ils le craignent ou même qu'ils s'en soucient beaucoup. Le 'bon Dieu' est un Deus otiosus, s'il en fut. Il n'évoque à l'esprit aucune image précise et il est trop lointain pour qu'il y ait avantage à s'adresser à lui. 'C'est un bon papa débonnaire, incapable de se fâcher et de se faire craindre, et avec qui on saura se débrouiller lorsqu'il faudra lui rendre compte de sa vie. Il n'est donc pas besoin de s'astreindre à le servir.[12]

[The word 'God' is constantly on the lips of the Haitian peasants, but it would be wrong to conclude from this that they fear him or are even particularly concerned with him. This 'good God' is a *Deus otiosus* if there ever was one. His name brings no clear image to mind and he is too remote to be worth calling to. He is like a nice, easygoing daddy, who never gets angry or scares you and who won't make it too hard for you when the time comes for you to give an account of your life. There is no need, therefore, to bother taking the trouble to serve him.]

This comment by Alfred Métraux is by and large true but betrays perhaps too clearly the author's scepticism and does not take sufficiently into account the ambiguous position of the Haitian who continues to be a Christian even as he practises voodoo, and for whom God may appear either remote or accessible depending on whether he is considered, at any given moment, in his African or his Christian aspect. Métraux's comment, above all, does not take into account the fact that the African or Haitian God, even a remote one, is not a God to whom one remains indifferent. For the African or the Haitian does not place himself in a position of Promethean hostility in relation to God. Jean-Baptiste Roumain is more discriminating and comes closer to defining the actual faith of the Haitian peasants when he says this about God: ' "The Great Master" created the "loas" as intermediary spirits when, for reasons now forgotten in Haiti, he abandoned earth'.[13] God in Haiti is remote, but not for exactly the same reasons as in Africa or, to put it a different way, because the religion brought from Africa has become Haitian. What better proof of this than that the African explanations for God's abandonment have been lost to memory?

The same is true of the African concept of death which has become Haitianised. The two views show strong similarities, however, in comparison with the Judao-Christian attitude towards death. Since, for both African and Haitian, the true centre of existence remains decidedly the earth from which God has become remote but not, in point of fact, totally separate, death can only be a moving away—life in a different form, man's way of keeping his distance in imitation of God. Death, therefore, is not a break, a separation, a sundering, but a metamorphosis, a transformation—life in a different form.

This view of death is found as well in Haitian voodoo which some consider to be a religion of ancestor worship like the African religions and which is without question, in certain of its rites, a cult of the dead.

Haitian Voodoo: Religion and Politics

The Haitian is a former African or, more specifically, an individual who was forced to turn from metaphysical to political considerations because of the constraints imposed on him by colonisation. And voodoo, a religion of African origins, is Haitian precisely because of the political dimensions which have been added to its religious beliefs. By political dimensions we mean, of course, economic and social ones.

We know that the Haitian War of Independence began with a voodoo ceremony: the oath of Bois-Caiman sworn by slaves who were determined to gain their freedom or die, and who pledged therefore to fight the colonisers to the death. Indeed, it is this scorn for death which inspired the song which often rose in the Haitian ranks as they made their attack on the French troops:

Grenadier a laso	*Grenadiers à l'assaut*
Sa ki mouri zafe a yo	*Qu'importe la mort*
Nan pouin manman	*Il n'y a pas de mère*

nan pouin pitit   *Ni d'enfant*
Sa ki mouri zafe a yo   *Qu'importe la mort*

[Grenadiers to the assault
What is death?
We have no mother
No child
What is death?]

The figure of the zombi represents the African view of death as it was transformed within the Haitian context. He is the symbol of the slave, the alienated man robbed of his will, reduced to slavery, forced to work for a master. This explains his double economic and religious significance. A man becomes a zombi when, as a result of certain ritualistic practices, a spell is cast over him by an individual possessing supernatural powers. But the reasons for transforming a man into a zombi appear natural indeed to the individual who casts the spell: he wants to possess a being who will serve him, work his fields and constitute a truly low-cost work force. To put it bluntly, he wants cheap labour.

As we can see, the zombi is not first and foremost an exclusively religious figure. The persistence of the Haitian belief in the zombi can only be explained by the double role it plays—which is to transform African beliefs into political concepts which can be applied either defensively or offensively to the situation as it exists in Haiti.

We have already indicated the importance of voodoo's defensive role in our discussion of the War of Independence. The religious beliefs brought from Africa constituted the bonds unifying the blacks in their war against the French armies. They were a defensive weapon in so far as they could provide the Haitians with hope, courage and the will to fight. They were, so to speak, a kind of ideological, emotional, and spiritual armour for the people of Haiti.

But the voodoo's role as weapon, purely defensive in the anticolonialist period, became double, defensive and offensive, in the neocolonialist period following independence. In effect, in so far as it was able to establish itself as an autonomous religion, in so far as, at a later date, it had to serve men who were no longer involved in a struggle against their masters but in struggles among themselves, voodoo has taken on a two-fold aspect, at times offensive, at times defensive. The Haitian practitioner of voodoo, after having used his faith as a protection against outsiders, came to use it as both a defensive shield and an arm of aggression in his dealings with his compatriots.

Voodoo, in other words, has created both a heaven and hell for itself. But a heaven and hell within man's reach, on earth, with a view of death in conformity with the African belief in a simple transformation of life, in a metamorphosis which is therefore reversible. This is why the zombi's condition is not a permanent one. It can change. When the zombi, who has received only the most tasteless of foods, manages to eat some salt, this salt revitalises him and jerks him out of the state of mindlessness in which he is buried. Salt is the agent which renews the awareness of life, the antidote to the spell which brought on the state of zombification. It is similar to divine fire in that it gives back the breath of life and reawakens the mind. The zombi's state is a symbolic one for it is at the centre of a network of symbols concerned with life and death.

An essentially religious figure but playing an economic role, the zombi is the symbol of a condition brought about in an unknown way but reversible by human will. We must therefore resituate this figure within the context of all the beliefs and legends which make up the mythology of Haitian voodoo. The symbol of sudden death, he has as his counterpart the 'kanzo', the initiated one who has withstood trial by fire or undergone the ordeal of a sojourn beneath the waters and who can now challenge death. At the height of the earlier civil wars a person of this kind was considered invulnerable to bullets. And certain generals of former times led the assault on the enemy troops, brandishing their red, fire-coloured scarves, paying no heed to the rain of bullets that fell about them.

And even today, what stories cannot be heard . . . ?

Death, in Haiti, a momentary and reversible transformation of life, takes on a menacing form in the character of the zombi who is, in reality, the legendary, mythic symbol of alienation: of a spiritual as well as physical alienation; of the dispossession of self through the reduction of the self to a mere source of labour. Every curse, every turn of fate represents a threat of zombification. The zombi is the incarnation of the only truly feared death. This explains the fascination the character of the zombi holds for Haitian writers. They see in him the image of a fearful destiny which they must combat; a destiny which is at once collective and individual. The attitude of the writer Magloire St. Aude toward the dead woman in *Veillée* thus takes on a new meaning: this zombified woman is the writer's double. Killing her is paradoxically an act of rebirth for the poet since he enables himself once again to grasp hold of life by warding off his fate, by removing the threat which weighed upon him in the dead woman's unbearable stare.

Perhaps not enough attention has been paid to the fact that Jacques Roumain's *Gouverneurs de la rosée*[14] [Masters of the Dew], the most optimistic novel in Haitian literature, begins with these words: 'We must all die'. The death he describes, the slow death of a community, an economic as well as spiritual death, is nothing other than a zombification. A feared but not unconquerable death. Not unconquerable, that is, for the Haitian, who is not a fatalist if we make this term synonymous with despair; for when he exclaims 'Good God', he is in effect giving utterance to his deep-seated hope. The zombi is the incarnation of fate. Of a fate which is reversible and thus transitory. Indeed, one of the characters of Jacques Roumain's novel declares, to everyone's agreement: 'Life is life; it's useless to take short-cuts or go the long way round; life is an eternal return. It is said that the dead come back to Guinea and that death itself is only another name for life.'

The Zombi as Character of a Secondary Mythology

In *Le Miracle et la métamorphose*[15] [The Miracle and the Metamorphosis], I proposed a distinction between primary and secondary mythologies, a distinction based not on the originality or unoriginality of a mythology, but on the fact that certain mythologies are built on persistent myths but develop in a different direction from already existing mythologies. The impact of colonisation on African myths is pointed out very clearly by L. V. Thomas. And one can easily understand that the Africans transported to the Americas had of necessity to adapt their ancestral myths to their new situation.

The Haitian voodoo, the Cuban 'santéria', and the Brazilian 'candomblé' can serve to demonstrate this transformation of elements of African culture in the Americas. The Haitian zombi illustrates a particular form of this transformation. The character of the 'living-dead' of which M'Biti speaks is a religious being, not the social being that the Haitian zombi represents. That person who belongs to the African 'living-dead' is an individual who finds himself midway between the gods and mankind, in a halfway-house where he remains before detaching himself completely from the earth and men and returning permanently to the spirit world. This condition is normal, reflecting a normal state in man's relationship to God and thus to the universe as well.

We are dealing here, then, with a natural state through which each man must pass after death, a state, therefore, which is neither good nor bad in itself since it is within the nature of things. The situation is completely different in the case of the Haitian zombi, the living-dead who is reduced to this condition by evil spells and as the result of human actions. If the African living-dead is the image of a particular situation in which man finds himself in the universe, the Haitian zombi is rather a particular image of man's situation among other men, of the relationship of all men among themselves.

The African figure and the Haitian figure are symbols of two types of reality. In the first case, of a metaphysical and religious reality, in the second, of a reality which is political and social. Should we consider, with the Austrian philosopher Kurt Fisher, that this second reality is the only true one? 'The relationships of men among themselves are, in the final analysis, the only decisive ones.' Let us propose rather that we are dealing here with a particular facet of reality—a social and human facet which complements the metaphysical one—and that therefore the principle distinguishing primary and secondary mythologies does not represent a value judgement of one over the other but rather establishes its specific orientation, the special way in which the myth fuses together the real and the divine. Starting out with a shared vision of the world, successive generations translate their different experiences, their different desires, through a different disposition of the same myths: a disposition which, by developing a new facet of the myth, allows us to grasp it in all its complexity.

Indeed, it is possible here to find a similarity between this concept of primary and secondary mythologies and the notion of 'subjectivised' and 'objectivised' speech proposed by the linguist Gustave Guillaume. If objectivised speech is one which permits the speaker to establish relationships not simply among abstract language concepts but among these concepts as they are fixed by specific thoughts, mythologies too become objectivised through the experience of a people. And it was apparently the trauma of slavery, transportation from Africa to Haiti, the experience of colonial oppression, which led the Africans who had suddenly become Haitians to make an adjustment in their conception of the living-dead, to see him no longer simply in the metaphysical perspective which was theirs in Africa, but from the economic, social and political point of view which was thenceforth to be that of the Haitians. René Dépestre is more explicit in regard to the meaning of the myth of the zombi:

Ce n'est pas par hasard qu'il existe en Haïti le mythe du zombi, c'est-à-dire le mort-vivant, l'homme à qui l'on a volé son esprit et sa raison, en lui laissant sa seule force de travail. Selon le mythe, il était interdit de mettre du sel dans les aliments du zombi, car cela pouvait réveiller ses facultés créatrices. L'histoire de la colonisation est celle d'un processus de zombification généralisée de l'homme. C'est aussi l'histoire de la quête d'un sel revitalisant, capable de restituer à l'homme l'usage de son imagination et de sa culture.[16]

[It is not by chance that there exists in Haiti the myth of the zombi, that is, of the living-dead, the man whose mind and soul have been stolen and who has been left only the ability to work. According to the myth, it was forbidden to put salt in the zombi's food since this could revitalise his spiritual energies. The history of colonisation is the process of man's general zombification. It is also the quest for a revitalising salt capable of restoring to man the use of his imagination and his culture.]

Dépestre's remarks serve as an excellent complement to the following comment, made by an historian, concerning the failure of the French colonisation of Haiti:

C'est là vraiment la fin du premier empire colonial de la France, celui qu'avaient commencé Richelieu et Colbert.[17]

[This is really the end of the first French colonial empire, the one inaugurated by Richelieu and Colbert.]

These words, with which the editor of the *Letters of General Leclerc* begins his introduction to these letters, give cause for reflection. The revolution in Haiti marks a turning-point in the History of France: the point at which ends the first colonial empire, the one Richelieu and Colbert had attempted to establish in the Americas; the starting point as well—here at the turn of the nineteenth century—of the African colonial empire, an empire which France would begin to build in earnest the moment the 'bourgeois king' Louis-Philippe stepped onto the throne.

But in the overall African perspective, which cannot be separated from events in Haiti, the Haitian revolution marks the Europeans' first setback in their attempt to subdue Africa. After having tried to colonise Africans in the Americas, the Europeans set out to attempt the same experiment in Africa itself.

The victory of Dessalines was not simply a defeat for Napoleon; since Haiti's declaration of independence brought the automatic abolition of the Black Code, this victory also represented the defeat of Louis XIV who promulgated the code as well as the death of the dream of Richelieu and Colbert. At the junction of this defeat and this victory there lies the New World, that mythical region where the new Adam dreamed of by Europe was to be born and where there sprang up instead the Haitian of 1804. America, crossroads of myths, is thus the land to which came European and African mythologies, some to die and others to be reborn.

The myth of the zombi—the stealer of salt who, as Dépestre tells us, replaces the stealer of fire—is that element of a secondary mythology comparable with the 'American Adam', an aspect of the American Dream in the United States which is simply the modern version of the dream of the Pilgrim Fathers, the Puritans fleeing the England of Cromwell and the Restoration. Birth, death and rebirth of myths: there is a history of man's dreams to be written inside this dialogue between peoples, races and continents.

Notes

1 Robert Ackerman, 'Writing about writing about myth', *Journal of the History of Ideas*, January–March 1973, xxxiv, 1, pp. 147–55.

2 Léon-Vincent Thomas, 'Pour une sémiologie de la mort africaine', *Ethnopsychologie*, revue de psychologie des peuples, 27e année, juin–septembre 1972, p. 158.

3 Léon-Vincent Thomas, 'Réflexions sans titre au sujet des mythes africains', *Cahier des religions africaines*, vi, 12, 6e année, juillet 1972, p. 135.

4 Geoffrey Parrinder, *Mythologies africaines*, Paris, Odège, 1969, p. 63.

5 John M'biti, *African religions and philosophy*, London, Heinemann, 1970, p. 82.

6 Jean-Baptiste Roumain, *Quelques moeurs et coutumes des paysans haïtiens*, Port-au-Prince, Imprimerie de l'état, 1959, p. 155.

7 Magloire St-Aude, *Veillée*, Port-au-Prince, 1956.

8 Jacques-Stephen Alexis, *Chronique d'un faux-amour*.

9 Alfred Métraux, *Le vaudou haïtien*, Nrf, Paris, Gallimard, 1957, pp. 250–1.

10 Jean Rudhart, 'Cohérence et incohérence de la structure mythique: sa fonction symbolique', *Diogène*, No. 77, janvier–mars 1972, p. 47.

11 Geoffrey Parrinder, *Mythologies africaines*, p. 34.

12 Alfred Métraux, *Le vaudou haïtien*, p. 72.

13 Jean-Baptiste Roumain, *Quelques moeurs et coutumes des paysans haïtiens*, p. 155.

14 Jacques Roumain, *Gouverneurs de la rosée*, Paris, éditeurs français réunis, 1950.

15 Maximilien Laroche, *Le miracle et la métamorphose*, Montréal, Éditions du Jour, 1970.

16 René Dépestre, *Change*, Violence II, No. 9, Paris, Seuil, 1971, p. 20.

17 Charles Victor Emmanuel Leclerc, *Lettres du général Leclerc*, commandant en chef de l'armée de Saint-Domingue, publiées par Paul Roussier, Paris, Société de l'Histoire des Colonies Françaises, p. 7.

Max Dorsinville

Senghor or the Song of Exile

(for Ann de Casseres)

To imagine the concept of exile in Senghor's work, one must first consider the historical contingency so well dramatised by Chinua Achebe in his novel, *Things Fall Apart*: the moment when a traditional, self-sufficient culture disintegrates, either because its values are deemed aberrant or problematical—when the sacred becomes the object of scepticism—or because of the intrusion of a foreign culture. Above all one must recognise that the world which is falling apart is Africa and the Third World in general: societies turned upside down, condemned henceforth to a state of exile within which they are to redefine themselves. One can imagine the profound trauma at the origin of the Third World: the break-up of the circle of collective understanding, the increasing split affecting various levels in the society, the presence of the Other at the heart of relationships between husbands and wives, fathers and sons, villages, clans and tribes.

Georges Lukacs wrote:

Bienheureux les temps qui peuvent lire dans le ciel étoilé la carte des voies qui leur sont ouvertes et qu'ils ont à suivre! Bienheureux les temps dont les voies sont éclairées par la lumière des étoiles! Pour eux tout est neuf et pourtant familier: tout signifie aventure et pourtant tout leur appartient. Le monde est vaste et cependant ils s'y trouvent à l'aise, car le feu qui brûle dans leur âme est de même nature que les étoiles. Le monde et le moi, la lumière et le feu se distinguent nettement et jamais néanmoins ils ne deviennent définitivement étrangers l'un à l'autre, car le feu est l'âme de toute lumière et tout feu se vêt de lumière. Ainsi il n'est aucun acte de l'âme qui ne prenne pleine signification et ne s'achève en cette dualité: parfait dans son sens et parfait pour les sens: parfait parce que son agir se détache d'elle et que, devenu autonome, il trouve son propre sens et le trace comme un cercle autour de lui.[1]

[Blessed are the times which can read in the starlight sky the map of roads that are opened to them and that they must follow! Blessed are the times whose roads are lighted by the light of stars! For them everything is new and yet familiar; everything signifies adventure and yet everything belongs to them. The world is vast and yet they are at ease, for the fire that burns in their soul is the same as the stars! The world and the I, the light and the fire are clearly distinguished but nonetheless they never become definitely foreign to each other; for fire is the soul of all light and fire is clothed with light. Thus there is no action of the soul that does not achieve full significance and end in this duality; perfect in its meaning and perfect for the senses; perfect because its action is detached from the soul and, once autonomous, this action finds its own meaning and this meaning draws itself like a circle around the action.]

Far from thinking about the Third World, Georges Lukacs accurately evokes the sense of the lost native land whose spellbinding power acts as an archetype in its literature. To place the breaking point at the origin of the imagination of the colonised man, think of Senghor. He is the little boy leaving behind the ancestral region of Joal, the games of innocence, to enter the white man's school and be exposed to values unknown to the age of innocence. Here is the first realisation of exile: the concrete and evocative world of Joal juxtaposed to the abstract world of book knowledge dispensed by the outsider. Here too is the first temptation: that of Senghor, but also that of Nwoye, Oduche, Obi Okonkwo, Achebe's characters, Hamidou Kane's Samba Diallo, Césaire's narrator in *Return to my Native Land*, Naipaul's characters, Lamming's and many others. The values of the white world glittering with promises perceived through the prism of desire: to possess them is to become the Other. The boy feels the pull of a religious calling and dreams of wearing the white cassock associated with light and civilisation. Deflected from that vocation, he identifies the true source of light. The young man leaves for Paris, following in the footsteps of generations of other colonials. Paris, or it might be London, Madrid, Amsterdam. The big cities. No doubt the desire to lose oneself in the world is understandable: a naive faith that this is the way to escape the feeling of exile. Fanon analysed this phenomenon, which is now commonplace. That metropolis and its treasures so desperately desired are still denied to the exile from the colonies. The evidence is forceful:

the chasm between everyday life in the West and the world of thought. It was Fanon, again, who illustrated the trauma: 'Look Mum, a darkie, I'm frightened!'² Surprise, recoil, chagrin, desolation. The colonised man cannot escape this feeling of isolation entering through all the pores of his skin.

Take Paris, in 1930. Here were gathered Senghor, Damas, Césaire; earlier Léro, Roumain, Achille, Sajuste had lived there, just as, later on, Diop, Glissant, Laye and others were to do so. They met and discovered the inevitable. Comparisons were made, parallels drawn, similarities startled; differences hitherto emphasised disappeared in the shock of discovery. Their common history bore witness: they were confronted by a denial of their own culture. But also there was a feeling of belonging to a common culture relegated to the depths of a deliberately forgetful consciousness in an everyday existence officially sealed by the look of the Other, and the growing awareness that the world was once theirs. This is the exile of the 'Negroes of sad season',³ an exile which became part of their consciousness. Negroes from the West Indies torn away from Africa, estranged from themselves, involved in a colonial society where caste ruled supreme, dissociated from their brethren by the class system, now found themselves in the metropolis, far away from their native land. But also there were Negroes from Africa, Negroes from the United States, invariably scattered, dispossessed, reduced to being mere public clowns. One can imagine Senghor and his friends seized with the shock of realising their own ignorance, an ignorance deliberately instilled and enforced. They are intoxicated by jazz but also by furious reading. Over in Harlem there had been a Negro renaissance in the twenties. They identify with Langston Hughes, Alain Locke, Countee Cullen. The distant Haiti and Toussaint l'Ouverture have to be claimed as part of their newly found cultural past. But nearer at hand there were Frobenius, Griaule, Delafosse, Gide and other good men lifting the conspiratorial veil of silence that shrouded Africa. They reveal not the Africa of 'Shoo good eatin' ' and 'Yassir', an Africa one loathes, but the Africa of the Songhai, Malian and Sudanese empires; of civilisations flourishing with heroism, courtesy, elegance; civilisations of whole men. Africa did exist; it had endured after all. Hence, there could be only one logical attitude: the return to the sources, the affirmation of the cultural values of the black world, and—why not?—Negritude would dare to be.

The word would become flesh. Black consciousness would emerge— in the light of history—from its neglect and obscurity. 1934-5 was a watershed if ever there was one. 1804, to be sure. 1927 and other important milestones of a Negritude standing up before its time. But these are the events of Haiti or Black America walled in by the silence of black isolation; a diaspora without name or consciousness. There one finds black isolation; but also the illusion of living still within the circle of the warm and reassuring world of African authenticity. That simple world of authentic, pre-colonial Africa, condemned to tragic surprise in the face of each invader's sudden arrival, gun in hand, with a mouthful of sweet and sour words. The world of the good folk, gossipy and pleasure-loving, quiet and unassuming.

But how is the exile in the metropolis to circumscribe, sing, translate that authentic world which he feels instinctively and wishes to measure and appraise? How is he to describe and set it within an historical condition which has been understood? It is memory which must break through the walls of black isolation. The black present is one of non-acceptance. The black past must therefore colour the present and re-affirm the exile's own identity. In childhood there had been a world of one's own. In memory it still exists: Joal, the ancestors, the presence of women, and above all the singing at night, gathered around the camp-fire, when the community renews itself by remembering its past. It has endured through time and space. And its collective memory has endured. The word of that collective memory—the speech of the griot— ancestors and spirits, all bear witness to a deeply felt self. One *was* part of a world of warmth. Did it ever exist? For the colonial in the metropolis it is a world already invaded and surrounded by the Other. Exile has already forced him to rely on memories. It is therefore an inner world; it is a dream distilled from the essence of reality. The poet sifts and resifts his memories. These are the seeds of Senghor's poetry: the native land is lauded with an intensity exactly proportional to the distance imposed by exile.

The diptych is forever accepted. Alienation? Schizophrenia? Split personality? Its articulation in poetry reconciles opposites; a deep sense of self co-exists with the tactical retreat of the group facing the invader. When explored, this inner world discloses that exile can be a kingdom. One thinks of Senghor's black woman, 'sombre raptures of dark wine'.[4] She is Noliwe surrendering to Chaka so that from the union of the revolutionary and his betrothed the children of the new dawn are born. The warrior, laid low by the armed struggle, surrenders to the harsh daylight of exile so that the procreative union may occur. One might say this is Negritude transcending the contingency, identified through memory and actualised in the dance of being. Negritude 'thrusting its roots into the red flesh of the soil',[5] as Césaire says, an impetuous soil, vast and fertile. But it is also an affirmation of self rooted in the tension between opposites.

Being born into the world signifies exile and an obsession with the native land. One must assimilate but not be assimilated. Senghor has understood this. One must appropriate the *values of the Other* and transform them into the 'miraculous arms' of the decolonised consciousness. The French language will be shattered by the profound sensitivity of the rediscovered land; it will be loaded from within with images and symbols that will justify it to a colonised people. The foreign language, imposed like a straitjacket, a prison at first, will be transformed into savannahs with distant horizons, rivers sown with crocodiles. The same language will also be filled with the sounds and colours of a Harlem whose vitality crashes against the sterility of a concrete, industrialised Manhattan. 'A tidal wave of pus and lava over the felony of the world,'[6] cries Roumain. But that language must also dance in the corrida of the stars; the extinct volcano must leap up, as must 'that crowd [bypassing] its own cry.'[7]

Césaire says that the history of man is not over, that the 'pulsations of humanity [do not stop] at the doorstep of the niggertrash' (p. 99). The external world can be rebuffed. That world, stamped with the marks of not belonging, that closed world in which the Negro is denied, would resound with the poundings and stompings of men who reject the deafness brought on by 'the clamour of the day' (p. 116). The Senghorian night, dark, majestic, reassuring, bearer of wisdom, would cover the harsh day, and from it would come messengers of hope, bearers of humanism. In their exile, they would understand what was deafened by the world of the daylight clamour: that the exile of the colonised man is the striking symbol of the exile of man plunged into the modern world. Technology, the quest for material progress, the concrete Manhattans of civilisation, are nothing but a sham. The men with hard blue eyes, the men of technology, lied to others since they had already lied to themselves, through fear of the unknown, fear of the dark, fear of being alone. It is not surprising that in building his civilisation of light western man shattered the harmony of things, of vital pulsations, and yet tortured himself by imagining that the darkness was still a threat to him.

Flash of insight into the mythical arrangement of colonisation: the black man reflects the white man's self-negation. The exile that western man would not assume was foisted directly on the man of Dark Africa, the man of sorrows, the scapegoat, the good porter who would take on the white man's burden. Negritude became a modern humanism, indeed. As a result, the exiled condition of the black took its place at the confluence of contradictions in the culture of the coloniser. Naturally, links were established between myth, aesthetics, politics, history and culture, and a pattern emerged.

First, keep one's distance, refuse to take part in the headlong reckless course of a world severed from its moorings; then recognise that the acceptance of one's exile generally satisfies the initial prescription of the coloniser. On second thoughts, if the colonised man realises that from a state of exile the native land is better rediscovered, celebrated, espoused, he thereby resolves a problem that the coloniser debates in vain whenever he allows any debate at all. Exile then becomes a privileged situation. Once it is accepted as an inevitable consequence of modernity, exile would henceforth be seen as offering that sense of distance necessary for the emerging of the artistic, cultural and psychic authenticity of being in-the-world. [8]

To sum up: the multiple forms of exile for Senghor and for all colonised people are (1) the exile of the colonised man educated in a colonial context; (2) the exile of the colonised man in the metropolis; (3) the psychic exile of the colonised man wherever he may be; (4) the exile of being black in the world; (5) the exile of the artist; (6) the exile of being in the world of modernity.

There are critics of Senghor and Negritude who gleefully point out that such a weight of exile confirms the indictment that this type of poetry lacks reality. They are not only European intellectuals acting in bad faith but also the 'liberated' thinkers still backward in realising that the only true decolonisation is that of the mind. The charge is that Senghor and his comrades of the thirties spoke to others but not to their own kind; that Senghor became French while the Africa that existed before the twilight of the gods, with its passions and its tutelar roots, continued to exist unbeknown to him in the villages and the countryside, in the vernaculars and the beliefs lost to that prodigal son. All of which means only that Negritude is misunderstood; for it is not just Senghor's, Césaire's or Damas' but a common history and a sensitivity shared by Soyinka as well as by Achebe, Awoonor, Ouologuem and other artists of modern Africa.

A literature in the language of the coloniser is situated precisely at the crossroads. One path leads to exile; the other to the native land.

This is the aesthetic of the artist-prodigal son, whose inspiration comes from collective memory and recollection and who demonstrates that the Senghorian profile is that of any African writer. And, I would add, of any colonised writer, when one thinks of the Quebecers, Gaston Miron and Paul Chamberland, and other poets who sang the praises of Quebec during the sixties.

Awoonor seems to have been misunderstood when, at the Halifax conference in May 1973, he said[9] that Amamu, the central character in his novel *This Earth, My Brother*, dies so as to be reborn to himself and to his people; and that, moreover, it was the principle of recurrence germane to the vital cycle of Africa—where destruction is always accompanied by creation—that he aimed to convey. Amamu's odyssey does not culminate in failure. The Halifax audience expressed surprise, naturally, for one prefers spectacular clashes following which things fall apart. But Chinua Achebe himself knows that traditional Ibo society was already undergoing a process of transformation long before the coming of the white man. The defiant oppostion of an Okonkwo terminates in suicide, which is an act of atonement auguring the complete change of life among the Ibo and ultimately their adoption of the modern world. Okonkwo dies, but the clan survives and life goes on.

Indeed, Senghor and other masters of the new aesthetic are only recalling a destiny germane to the tradition of collective wisdom. Like Ezeulu in *Arrow of God* or the Most Royal Lady in *Ambiguous Adventure*, Africa has always known how to cushion the exile of its sons in the harmony of the vital cycle. There are no oppositions, no contraries, no crushing dichotomies with their weight of failure, but correlations, exercises in balance and equilibrium, rhythm of pulsating life. In its most intimate self, this Africa participates in the polarisation between exile and native land which is only tragic when the sense of values collapses in an alienated and impotent consciousness: that of the naive colonised man. A parade of defeated people, tragic heroes, victims sapped of willpower by ambiguous experiences: to some readers this sums up the contents of the African novel. Let us speak rather of cultures made wise by imponderables; cultures that do not crumble before the invader but effect strategic retreats—launching thereby the technique of guerrilla warfare—cultures that blend with the shadows, take over the new armaments of the enemy and turn them against those for whom Césaire pleads for indulgence: 'Mercy for our omniscient and naive conquerors.'[10] And Ouologuem may well add 'O Lord, a tear for the childlike good nature of the niggertrash! Have pity, O Lord!'[11]

Cultures in flight from slavery, full of guile, excel in irony and sarcasm when faced with the enemy; they are supple and flexible cultures but resilient as lianas. Here we have the inventive and industrious Ibo, there the Asante who sees you coming; a little further off the Yoruba with their spells and graces crossing the Atlantic to Africanise the New World. In Haiti it is Voodoo; in Cuba, Santéria; in Brazil, Candomblé. Here or there you give me a John the Baptist and I hand you back Shango. Call for James the Elder and I turn him into Baron Samedi. You lend me a Virgin and I offer you Erzulie. And I can supply you with Ogouns, Papas Loas, Zombis and Bocors to your heart's content. It is a question of syncretism, cultures which from the first contact with the Other have tactically redefined themselves. It is no coincidence that these phenomena of evil spirits and mischief-makers are all products of exile, an exile well understood in its strategic significance: as foundation stone granting the great leap forward to the native land. Ouologuem is absolutely right: the century-old rule of the Saifs is steeped in the abiding tradition of fleeing enslavement. People who see things coming and let them happen, but hit the target every time, 'playing the game of the world!'[12]

I said above that some people were critical of Senghor and other Negritude poets because of their exile. One has to place the indigenous tradition and the European import side by side in the Senghorian aesthetic. Césaire once said to Dépestre: 'Force them to escape, Dépestre, one must force them to flee their slavery!'[13] I can imagine Senghor smiling understandingly, eyes slanted behind glasses with French rims (naturally!) while his detractors speak of inauthenticity, assimilation, galloping francophilia and quote from his famous poem 'Prayer for Peace', dedicated to Georges and Claude Pompidou. Let us look a little closer. Senghor in his poem calls for the pardon of Europe and the celebration of peace restored at the end of the last world war. Pardon for what? For everything and nothing. And while he is on the subject, why should the poet not take the opportunity to thank France for its colonial empire which allowed him to discover and to fraternise with his brethren, red, yellow and brown? The Europe of the administrators and of the swift-footed *colons*, of the problem drinkers and the psychopaths, not to mention the torturers, but also the Europe of thought, generosity, tolerance, the humanist ideal—both are evoked. The real France—that goes without saying—is in the second category. And the poet goes on with unparalleled audacity, distributing pardons and praises up to the last verse, loudly proclaiming Christian love echoed by the brassy ring of the bells signalling the end of High Mass: 'Ite missa est!' This is Senghor at his most French, most supine, or at his most 'Uncle Tom', as they would say in the United States (not realising the capabilities of old Tom to escape his slavery). Not so. A Haitian knows that the last word of the verse is 'Bless you, Master!' The rhetoric of flight from slavery: evasions, disguises, equivocations are just a few of the poet's 'miraculous arms'. To put it differently: imagine Senghor, a smile playing around his lips, eyes half-shut behind glittering gold-rimmed glasses, declaiming these verses with a sing-song and syrup in his voice. All of Senghor is there: the shrewdness of the satirist tactician, the generosity of the moralist, but also the undeniable attachment to a native land, never more native than when extolled under cover of the Luxembourg gardens.

But this Senghorian exile is not to be reduced to just a poem or to the analysis of a series of poems. Senghor himself says that meaning is less dependent on discourse, analysis, linear thought, than on breath, rhythm, sensibility. It is a question of capturing in essence this quality of exile. It is in a flesh and blood product of multiculturalism and multilingualism, a product of an historical interbreeding. It is an exile which grasps the true meaning of the native land once the latter is perceived as being internally divorced from itself. See, for example, the dazzling imagery of the Antilles in the first part of Césaire's *Return*. A sentiment of exile profoundly rooted in a consciousness of the native land, a consciousness *more* native than the land itself entrapped by the ignorance of its own condition. Exile becomes imperative since it allows the native land to be remodelled, reshaped, reborn. Take the exile engraved on the inner world of the colonised thinker. A man exposed to temptations, to deceptive lures, a man who wears the white mask of complacency. But that thinking man decides one fine day to break through the mask which oppresses him and isolates him from his people. His people are perceived through the mirror of colonialism reflecting all men as wearers of masks, performing roles allotted by some stage director. This thinking man realises that his exile, hitherto determined by his social class and by his presence in the metropolis, is no different from that of his people. And he looks back once more at those who have never left the native land, the talkers, the dancers, the sensual ones foaming at the mouth with the dew of mornings greeted by a concert of cocoricos and the aroma of black coffee: the most native land. This is the authentic scene, whose abundance he, the exile, has lost. The merit of Senghor, Césaire and the Negritude poets lies in having focused on the native land and borne witness through their deeply evocative poetry that they are always aware of a dynamic tension between the imagined and the real landscape, a tension at the centre of which they assert their identity. The native land, paradoxically, may never have been like this. The evocation of childhood, or innocence, is wedded to the dream process of the imagination, which becomes the only way to identify the continued existence and landscape of the native land. This is an artistic vision, far from art for art's sake, or from unbridled romanticism. The world of this myth, of this dream, is one which inspires actions. That dream world embodies an attitude towards life which is relevant to the real world in which the colonised man is cut off by exile; and in which the coloniser too is a victim of the phenomenon of exile, but with the major difference that he is unaware of it. Senghor sings of the native land beyond spoliation and stabs in the back, and he puts out his hand to reconcile the flesh and the stone, the lion and the bull, technological man and sensuous man. He calls for an end to exile through recognition.

Successfully pursuing the goals of Breton and his friends, Senghor illustrates in the adaptability of a Negritude which all can experience that the real world can be compatible with the dream world, the native land unite with the land of exile without any feeling of imbalance or inequality. Since the Middle Ages that state of exile has been the lot of the western artist whose anguish at being deprived of an audience grows heavier in the twentieth century. It is both assumed and transcended in Senghor's elevated and resonant language echoing a world of correspondences vitally perceived—a world into which Baudelaire could only hope for insight. The state of exile allowing the realisation of a political, poetical and mythical design, can only be conceived as a starting point of promises and possibilities. Senghor emphasises, of course, the primacy of myth, culture, imagination over the bare bones of the so-called sociological reality of his critics. It is a matter of perspective, point of view, admittedly one closely linked to an understanding of aesthetics in the sense of the true as well as the beautiful.

Senghor's reply is that the African experience throughout the centuries is not indebted to a conception of man issued from eighteenth-century Europe. Africa can do without a definition of man predicated on a rational perspective, or in terms of a notion of material progress measured by quantitative science. The qualitative, the essence which above all lies beyond the parameters of scientific thought is here celebrated: rhythm, sensibility, tenderness. It is Noliwe, the black woman, 'firm-fleshed ripe fruit, mouth making lyrical my mouth'.[14] Or Senghor may sing of events imperceptible to the naked eye as the essence of African culture. In either case, one finds oneself once more in an imaginary landscape, a kingdom where exile and the native land are reconciled. Senghor salutes the black man and recognises in the black American in Harlem or in the ranks of the American army on V-Day, in the West Indian, Haitian, Martinican or Guyanan, the harbingers of spring, the features of a common human family and order responsive to the movement of the world itself. The voice of collective wisdom (the participant in the tug-of-war of antitheses assumed and fully lived) rises and asserts that just as a river flows from its spring, the world of day will be reconciled with the night-world, technological man with the man of the dance, the culture of learning with that of experience, just as the state of exile was always wedded to the native land, the consciousness of the deep self identified with the accidents of history and contingency.

Notes

1 Georges Lukacs, *La Théorie du Roman*, Paris, Gouthier, 1963, pp. 19–20. The translation that follows is my own.

2 Frantz Fanon, *Peau Noire Masques Blancs*, Paris, Seuil, 1962, p. 110. My own translation.

3 Réné Dépestre, 'On les Reconnaît', in *Black Poets in French*, ed. Marie Collins, New York, Scribner's, 1972, p. 69.

4 Léopold Senghor, 'Femme Noire' in *Senghor Prose and Poetry*, ed. John Reed, London, Oxford University Press, 1965, p. 105.

5 Aimé Césaire, *Cahier d'un Retour au Pays Natal*, Paris, Présence Africaine, 1971, p. 116.

6 Jacques Roumain, 'Bois d'Ebène', in *Black Poets in French*, p. 60.

7 Césaire, *Cahier d'un Retour au Pays Natal*, p. 33 (my own translation).

8 Jean-Paul Sartre, 'Orphée Noir', preface to *Anthologie de la Nouvelle Poésie Nègre et Malgache de Langue Française*, Léopold Senghor, Paris, P.U.F., 1969, pp. xv–xvi, xxix, xxx.

9 See Awoonor's essay, below, pp. 170-172

10 Césaire, *Cahier d'un Retour au Pays Natal*, p. 120.

11 Yambo Ouologuem, *Bound to Violence*, New York, Harcourt Brace, 1971, p. 95.

12 Césaire, *Cahier d'un Retour au Pays Natal*, p. 116.

13 Césaire, 'Réponse à Dépestre, Poète Haitien', *Présence Africaine*, Nos. 1–2, 1955, p. 144.

14 Senghor, 'Femme Noire', *Senghor Prose and Poetry*, p. 105.

Peter Igbonekwu Okeh

Two Ways of Explaining Africa:
An Insight into Camara Laye's
L'Enfant Noir and Ferdinand Oyono's
Le Vieux Nègre et la Médaille

Opinions vary about what the 'essential' elements in African literature should be. Some expect the African writer to produce literary works that are aesthetically impeccable; others want him above all to try to contribute to a better knowledge of the black world. Obviously any work claiming to be classed as literature must first of all be well written. But I am the last man to blame a black man writing in French or English because he happens to stumble in a language that is not his own. Rather, I will be suspicious of him if I come to the conclusion that he is falsifying or misrepresenting the image of Africa. This is a duty, all the more so because Africa was, and still is, in spite of the great efforts being made today, an unknown, a despised and an underestimated world. Is it not therefore the responsibility of a black writer, taking into account what he owes to his people and to his race, to deal first and foremost with all facets of the African civilisation?

Lilyan Kesteloot goes to the heart of the matter in the following passage. Writing in support of Léro and his friends who accused certain West Indian writers of neglecting the lives of the blacks and of hiding their real problems, she says:

> *Qu'entendent-ils par une littérature 'authentique', sinon une littérature ou l'Homme Noir exprimerait son tempérament et ses besoins propres, et par là même révélerait tout l'Univers particulier de sa race.*[1]

[What do they mean by a genuine literature if not a literature where the Black Man expresses his temperament and his needs, thereby revealing the particular Universe belonging to his race.]

Other authors share the same view. Mrs Kesteloot writes elsewhere in her book that among many young writers that she interviewed in

1959, only two attached great importance to literary beauty. Others, she said, were inclined to use their pens simply as a means of passing on their ideas and were satisfied with their styles so long as these could not be described as 'bad' (p. 294). I imagine that a similar survey today would probably produce the same result. This is why, when I agreed to discuss Camara Laye's *L'Enfant Noir* and Ferdinand Oyono's *Le Vieux Nègre et la Médaille*, I made up my mind to explore the ideas expressed in the books rather than to point out their merits as creative writings.

Camara Laye, from the Republic of Guinea, and Ferdinand Oyono, from the Federal Republic of the Camerouns, both wrote these novels while studying in France. *L'Enfant Noir*, published in 1953, is a narrative inclined towards autobiography, written in the traditional personal style, of the childhood and schooldays of a blacksmith's son in Guinea. *Le Vieux Nègre et la Médaille*, which came out in 1956, tells the story of Méka who is manhandled, beaten, flogged and detained in prison on the very day he is honoured with a medal by the French administration in his native land for what the authorities call his exemplary behaviour. The reason: he takes too freely of the wines offered by his hosts and unfortunately enters the white sector of his own town, Doum. And on this particular occasion alcohol is helped by storm, rain, darkness and fatigue to lead him astray.

At present, as far as I know, both authors are living outside their home countries. Camara Laye is in Senegal, in what could be termed an exile; Ferdinand Oyono is in Paris, where he is his country's ambassador. With this in mind, let us take each novel separately, to see how they represent much more than the mere story of an African child and the mere misfortune, like many others, of a colonial collaborator.

Immediately the reader opens *L'Enfant Noir*, he has his first meeting with the little black snake—*le petit serpent noir;* a meeting that he will find interesting or bizarre according to his disposition. The carefree child who has fun playing with snakes that enter his family compound learns that among these, there is one that is not like the others because it is the 'genius of his race', that is to say, the protecting spirit of the family.[2] Soon his father explains the situation to the boy, saying that the reptile first appeared to him in a dream to arrange a rendezvous, that he was really frightened the first time he actually saw it and that this probably made the animal turn away from him. He goes on to say that he saw the very same snake again in a dream and that a kind of confidence was established between two of them (p. 21). This mysterious serpent is always coiled under a sheepskin spread in his father's work-shop when the goldsmith has to work with gold and is thought to be responsible for the man's success and celebrity.

The first reaction of the average man from the western world when confronted with all this is that the story deals with superstitions; as if superstition is a phenomenon met only in the so-called backward corners of the globe. I still remember one of my students who wrote the word 'superstition' on every page of the two early divisions of the novel. We can call it superstition if you like. The author has no qualms about dishing out other superstitions belonging to his people. The initial cuttings in the rice fields just before harvest in the little village of Tindican remove from these fields their inviolability (p. 63). The harvesters do not whistle during the mid-day resting period because they fear that this will cause some misfortune there and then (p. 75). The mother of the central character and her twin brothers have peculiar powers of witchcraft (p. 85). The crocodiles in the River Niger—a river called 'Djoliba' by the villagers—are a danger for every-body except the members of the central family because these animals are regarded as their totems (p. 90). When the young boy is about to travel to Conakry, his mother procures for him some water which is believed to have 'many powers particularly that which develops the brain' (p. 183). His father gives him a small ram horn containing talismans. And to crown it all, they kill an ox as a tribute to the father and they call upon the ancestors to guide and help them all (p. 181).

One should, however, be careful about reacting like my students. An African proverb puts it this way: 'For every finger you point at your neighbour, three other fingers are pointing back at you.' Every society builds up its own beliefs, its own myths and its own legends. Christian societies still uphold the story handed down by the Jews of old that a fallen angel took the form of a serpent to tempt our first parents, Adam and Eve. If this is true, I don't see what prevents a harmless African spirit, the equivalent of the scriptural angel, from taking the form of a black snake to help a mortal of his choice. The western man in the street instinctively 'touches wood' when he wishes to prevent a bad omen or preserve a happy situation. This is not so very different from the feeling of a Malinke who believes that whistling at a certain time could provoke evil forces in his rice field. And again, the Christian medals reading, for example, 'St Benedict, in case of poison' or 'St Christopher, in case of accident', give no more credit to that religion than the 'jujus' do to African fetishism. As for prodigies, they are not lacking in the modern world. The Virgin Mary is believed to have appeared to three Portuguese children and to have delivered through them a significant message for mankind. At Lourdes, thousands of sick people every year crowd over the road leading to a small river that supposedly has acquired healing powers since Our Lady appeared to Bernadette. And in a church situated in Ste-Anne de Beaupré in the Province of Quebec, crutches, wheelchairs, sticks and corsets left by their former owners remain as evidence of 'miracles' that occurred through the influence of supernatural forces. One understands then why Camara Laye said: *'Ces choses incroyables, je les ai vues, je les revois comme je les voyais. N'y a-t-il pas partout des choses qu'on n'explique pas?'* (p. 84). [These unbelievable things, I saw with my own eyes, and I still see them as I saw them before. Are there not everywhere things that one cannot explain?]

Should it not then be more appropriate to consider the mystical in both black societies and in western societies simply as religion? In this case, we have to bring the expression back to its primitive meaning which is 'the relations between man and his Maker': a Yahveh, as with the Jews; a God, as with the Christians; an Allah, as with the Muslims; a Chukwu, as with the Igbos; an Olorun, as with the Yorubas; a Nyame, a Mawu, an Amma, and a Faro as with the Ashantis, the Ewes, the Dogons and the Bambaras.

If we look at it more closely, we would find some similarities between the ox that the father of *l'enfant noir* sacrifices to the ancestors and the sacrifice that a Christian priest offers daily for the living and the dead. The former does not need to deal directly with his God. That Being is so good towards His creatures that they don't feel obliged to pray to Him constantly. They judge it sufficient to settle their differences with His emissaries, that is to say, the ancestors, who are the saints according to tradition, and the spirits who are very much like the angels and the devils. The Christian priest has before him a God who so loved His creatures that He sent His only begotten son to suffer and die on the cross in order to save them from the sins of their original ancestors. The Christian priest has therefore to think of Him more than of His emissaries.

The fetish priest needs the body and the blood of a victim so that his sacrifice may be consummated. As a practical African man surrounded by all that nature can offer, he uses rams, goats, oxen and cocks in his ceremonies. The Christian priest, reminded and reminding always of Christ's sacrifice, offers communicants redemption for their sins through His symbolic body and blood, bread, and wine. Saying as he offers them, 'This is My body which was given for you' and 'this is My blood which was shed for you', he has affinities with the African cutting the throat of his victim and pronouncing words that are secret and necessary.

The father and the mother of *l'enfant noir* are special, privileged persons who have a deeper religious involvement than many others around them, in the same way as priests and religious people in the western world appear to receive light and special grace from above which make them different from ordinary people. Just as the average Christian tries humbly to take his model from Christ and to follow Him in his daily life while leaving to certain exceptional individuals the ecstatic attachment to God and the other world, so too most of the inhabitants of Kouroussa and Tindican (and by extension, the average black man) do not have such intense religious lives as the parents of *l'enfant noir*. The father does not disagree with the other villagers, nor with the few that are as privileged as himself, on the question of religious principles, or dogma (as western mysticism would have it). For him, as well as for others, religion is something to be practised in our lives, both in our devotion to the invisible powers and in our relations with our fellow men, rather than something to be approached with reason. And, as we know, the human mind, in spite of its potentialities, is imperfect and subjective. As for the privileged seer in the Christian religion, he disagrees with many others around him as well as with their religious leaders on the grounds that they are attracted by certain details, rather than by others, on the road to salvation. And he nourishes the hope of converting them one day to his way of thinking without considering at the same time the possibility of adopting their beliefs.

One conclusion can be made from what I have just explained. We have to approach religion in the black societies with the same spirit or tolerance as that of Europe in the sixteenth century. That Europe, after being torn apart by long religious wars, came to peace with the principle of '*Cujus regio ejus religio*', that is to say, 'to each region, its religion'. There is nothing more 'legitimate' about those Africans who have embraced Christianity—a mere accident or by-product of westernisation—than there is about those who still keep to the religion of their forefathers.

There is another aspect of African life that Camara Laye insists upon in his novel. And that is communal life with all that it supposes: a sense of brotherhood in the family, strong ties of friendship in the group, solidarity, widespread hospitality, mutual help, exchange of goods as gifts, and popular rejoicings. The arrival of *l'enfant noir* at Tindican brings out all the women from their huts in answer to the call of the grandmother who announces the coming of the little one (p. 49). And the child talks in these terms of the total solidarity existing among the harvesters:

Ils chantaient, nos hommes, ils moissonnaient; ils chantaient en choeur, ils moissonnaient ensemble; leurs voix s'accordaient, leurs gestes s'accordaient; ils étaient ensemble! . . . unis dans un même travail, unis par un même chant. La même âme les reliait, chacun et tous goûtaient le plaisir; l'identique plaisir d'accomplir une tâche commune.

[They were singing, our men, they were harvesting; they were singing like a choir, they were harvesting together; their voices were in harmony, their actions were in harmony; they were together! . . . united under the same work, and by the same music. Their hearts were one, each and everyone had the pleasure, the identical pleasure of accomplishing a common task.]

Elsewhere in the book, the candidates for circumcision, assembled in the meeting place of Kouroussa, receive gifts from the public. The gifts are made by friends of the families of young 'tam-tam' dancers (p. 13). [Tam-tam is the French expression for dancing drums.] The father of the child, after picking the fruits from his single orange tree, distributes baskets of them among the members of his compound, his immediate neighbours and his customers (p. 149). On the eve of the departure of the child for Conakry, there is a big feast attended by both Muslim and native priests, important personalities, friends and everyone who has taken the trouble to come (p. 180). On the day of his departure, he goes from compound to compound to say goodbye to the old people in the village (p. 183). Finally, the novel deals extensively with the great friendship which binds together Kouyaté, Check and *l'enfant noir*.

I know that some people will say: 'No sir. I lived many years in Africa. I visited many countries. I never saw that social warmth which you and Camara Laye talk about.' To the Africanist in question, I would simply say that he spent those years without really getting into Africa, that he unfortunately never learnt to know what true Africa is all about. If he had sincerely asked the help of history, he would have known that social warmth existed just as Camara Laye describes it,

before the coming of the white man, and that in this respect, our forefathers were in fact more civilised than their civilisers. If our friend had
stooped low enough to mix with the owners of the land, he would have
recognised that that warmth, although considerably diminished today,
still extends to any well-intentioned foreigner. If our expert had as much
goodwill for the black world as he has for his own, he would accept the
fact that there is nothing to prevent independent Africa from recovering
the good ways of life which she lost in the course of history. Moreover,
if our traveller were sufficiently honest with himself and with his race,
he should not need to be told that the white man has invented everything except humanity. Finally, he should admit that the present
world needs to listen to Africa, especially in the search to find a way of
reconciling self-interest with the reciprocal help necessary among men.
Bernard Dadié, in his novel, *Climbié*, sums up this view of Africa:

> *La vie pour nous est un voyage qu'il faut faire avec des compagnons joyeux.
> Et c'est pourquoi nos tam-tams chantent la joie de cultiver en groupe, de
> moissonner ensemble, de construire de même nos maisons. La vie, c'est une
> belle chanson qu'on doit chanter ensemble, en battant toujours des mains.
> C'est la chaude communauté des petits et des grands, des faibles et des
> forts, des jeunes et des vieillards, s'aidant les uns les autres et se serrant
> tous les coudes, contre les forces coalisées.*[3]

> [Life for us is a journey that we have to make with happy com-
> panions. And that's why our drums sing the joys of farming in
> group, of harvesting together, of building our houses in the same
> way. Life is also a beautiful song that we must sing in unison with
> the clapping of hands. It's the warm community made up of the
> big and the small, the strong and the weak, the young and the old,
> helping one another and rubbing shoulders together in their fight
> against the forces in coalition.]

It could be argued that I am reading too much into *L'Enfant Noir*.
As a matter of fact, Camara Laye doesn't deal with 'problems' in his
novel. He exposes the beauties of the authentic Africa and leaves it to
the reader to read between the lines; leaves him free to feel the unjust,
arbitrary, and even absurd nature of the things that humiliate, menace
or destroy that Africa. Many authors choose this way to show their
confidence in their readers. That is why reading a novel is like making
a discovery. We can also ask if Camara Laye is simply acting according
to his temperament. The answer could equally be 'yes'. We cannot be

all contesters, we haven't all got the ability of speaking out against unpleasant things around us. It would be unfair to blame a cat for not being a leopard or a horse for not being an elephant. But the criticism of Sékou Touré's government in *Dramouss*, Camara Laye's third novel, has reduced credibility in that conventional attitude towards the author. Is this a question of cowardice or of strategy? Possibly the author is afraid of displeasing the white man and has purposely planned not to shock readers from the western world. Mongo Béti, a Camerounian novelist whose works are widely translated into English, accuses the Guinean of obstinately closing his eyes to the most crucial realities, the very ones that are carefully kept away from the public.[4]

One thing is certain: the reader of *L'Enfant Noir* does not learn all that he would like to know about colonial Africa. To such unsatisfied appetites, Ferdinand Oyono offers *Le Vieux Nègre et la Médaille*.

Like Camara Laye, the Camerounian paints a picture of Africa in its authenticity. In the book he tries to make us aware of African civilisation in order to make us appreciate its beauty and its value. He gives us details of 'superstitions', of houses, of that special sun that is always there shining solidly on the inhabitants of the black continent. He describes these inhabitants wearing wrappers and towels, and proudly eating their meals of cassava, couscous, lizards and vipers. He describes African brotherhood in communities, in villages, in towns, in clans and on an even wider scale. When the white men honour Méka there are gatherings and discussions. People come from nearby villages to cheer Méka and to rejoice with him. Some have food with them, others imported wines. Eating, drinking and singing become the order of the day. The drums sound out the happiness in every heart.

But if Oyono talks about these things in his novel, it is mainly to introduce us to something else. He is concerned with showing us an Africa which was formerly a good place to live in but which has been destroyed as a result of colonialism. From the first chapter we clearly see the damage caused by the colonial regime. We know that it is an unbearable regime because it is menacing, oppressive and unjust. We learn that the Old Man, Méka, is summoned by the *commandant du cercle*, the regional administrator serving the French government. This summons puts the whole population in a state of anxiety. Everyone has something to say about it and opinions to express which illustrate the position of the blacks oppressed by a foreign power. Méka, the one who is summoned, asks his wife to bring him something to eat because you don't go before a white man with an empty stomach.[5] The villagers, unable to guess the reason for the summons, believe that they are going to have a martyr (p. 19).

Other examples of exploitation abound. The local people are forbidden to drink the 'Arki' (a kind of African wine), so that they are pushed towards drinks and red wine from Europe (p. 24). Kelara, in her panic for her absent husband, would be ready to listen to the reassuring words from the catechist, if the white men were not involved in the whole thing (p. 25). When Méka learns about the medal that the Great Chief of the Whites is coming to pin on him on the 14th of July, he is delighted, but does not want too much fuss about the event. As he murmurs to his wife, you never can be sure when you are dealing with a white man (p. 29). Nti, one of the elders in the village, has lived twenty years in this native section of Doum in order to be able to work as a labourer in the adjacent European quarter known as the city (p. 30). The members of colonial administration are assisted in their exploitation of the blacks by white traders (p. 34).

In the same way, Oyono demonstrates that there is collusion between the Christian churches and colonial administration. Méka confides to his wife: '*Seulement si je ne rentre pas, va le dire au prêtre pour qu'il arrange cela; il me doit bien ça*' ['Only if I don't come back, go and tell the priest, so that he may arrange things; he owes me at least that'] (p. 13). Anything can be 'arranged' between the missionary and the administrator. The priest from his pulpit preaches that Arki blackens the teeth and the souls of the parishioners. Evina, a retired cook for the missionaries, has lost his last tooth in the service of white men (p. 30). All the white men are the same. This collusion is obvious when the colonial officer explains the reasons for the award of the medal. He says to the old man:

Tu as beaucoup fait pour faciliter l'oeuvre de la France dans ce pays. Tu as donné tes terres aux missionnaires et tu avais donné tes deux fils à la guerre où ils ont trouvé une mort glorieuse . . . (p. 33)

[You have done much to facilitate the work of France in this country. You gave your land to the missionaries and you have given your two sons in the war where they died a glorious death.]

And all through the book, details surrounding that famous medal will surface to reinforce the twin truths explained in the beginning. The white man has power. He has no respect for the culture, the customs and the philosophy of the blacks. All he does is mere window-dressing, a mere show that doesn't go beyond appearances. A chief is both honoured and treated as a hideous black criminal on the same day by the people who single him out for his medal. In so doing, they force their ally to turn his back on them and revert to the African way of life. Oyono wants to make the whites understand that if they keep refusing the good things of life to black people, the latter will in their turn refuse to co-operate, will refuse to be exploited and will refuse to be assimilated. Méka says at the end of the book that henceforth he considers himself only as an old man. Oyono suggests that the younger generation will continue the fight from where the older ones stopped and may achieve what their fathers failed to achieve. If we are working today towards the understanding between races, the sharing of knowledge between peoples, the fusion of wisdom from all civilisations, this is because we have heard the message from men like Ferdinand Oyono.

I would like to emphasise at this point that Ferdinand Oyono doesn't show any more sympathy for Méka than for the white oppressors. The reason is that Méka is not working solely for lasting peace and understanding between Africa and Europe. He represents in a way the traditional good nigger, like 'Uncle Tom'. However, he learns his lesson in time and changes, while the character in Harriet Stowe's book endures everything until he is lynched. One can argue that Méka is not to blame, that in the colonial context he could only do what he did. However, this should not make us lose sight of the fact that he is collaborating with the occupants of his native land, that he is somehow an opportunist who banks on profiting from an administration that is crushing his people. One wonders if he agreed to be baptised and if he gave his land because he was really convinced about the principles of Christianity or because he had calculated the advantages that his action would give him over the other villagers. On this basis, he is no better than Ignatius Obebe, the African catechist who is like a one-eyed man in a country of the blind and who is a puppet in the hands of the missionary. He sees that there is prostitution in the African quarter but ignores it in the European quarter; he condemns Arki, the native wine, but has nothing to say against gin or whisky. Nor is Méka any better than the prison warders who surpass their white masters in brutality; who, though Africans, do not recognise an elder in the society; and who make Méka almost smell his blood. This is why Oyono condemns the old man and reserves for him a tragic role in the novel.

The Méka in Oyono's book is not dead; he is still moving about even in independent Africa. In saying this, I think of individuals who pursue their private interests and forget the wrongs being done to their people or to their race. I think of politicians who become mercenaries of imperialism and of exploitation in their own society. I think of some of our leaders who are afraid to take major decisions because of their ties with Paris, with London, with Moscow and with Washington.

Suffering Africa, as presented by Oyono appears to overshadow authentic Africa in *Le Vieux Nègre et la Médaille*. The anger of the Camerounian writer is excessive. His white characters are '*les incirconcis*'—the uncircumcised—and he refuses every other nickname for the Superintendent of Prisons except '*Gosier d'Oiseau*'—bird's throat. But the damage done by the colonialists is real, damage that Oyono makes us feel with all the intricacies of his humour. The loss is there to see in *L'Enfant Noir* for the African delights described there are like things that were and are no more. Camara Laye's novel opens the way to a better appreciation of Ferdinand Oyono.

Is there common ground between these two ways of explaining Africa? The answer is affirmative, for Camara Laye in his way, and Ferdinand Oyono in his own, are both working towards a better Africa. By this I mean an Africa where problems will be minimised and a world where the sons and daughters of Africa, including the blacks of the American continent, will say that all is well as far as they are concerned. Camara Laye is a writer because there are problems. Ferdinand Oyono is a writer because there are problems. The same is true for all those who have made it a duty to speak in the name of Africa. This is what I term African dynamics, a force that sustains all black writings. When that better Africa is recreated we may then have the leisure to try our hands at the new novel which is the most recent manifestation of art for art's sake.

Notes

1 Lilyan Kesteloot, *Les écrivains noirs de langue française: naissance d'une littérature*, Brussels, Université libre de Bruxelles, 1963, p. 320.
2 Camara Laye, *L'Enfant Noir*, Paris, Plon, 1953, p. 16.
3 Bernard Dadié, *Climbié*, Paris, Seghers, 1956, p. 167. The translation that follows is my own.
4 Mongo Béti, 'Trois Ecrivains Noirs', *Présence Africaine*, No. 16, 1954, p. 420.
5 Ferdinand Oyono, *Le Vieux Nègre et la Médaille*, Paris, Julliard, 1968, p. 13.

Isaac Yetiv

Alienation in the Modern Novel of French North Africa before Independence

To speak of alienation is to follow a beaten path through an unknown land. This term has often been used and abused, and even if one disregards the two literal definitions, the legal and the medical, confusion continues to reign among the term's many figurative senses. There is, however, one idea common to all its different meanings: to become, or cause to become, 'alien' or estranged.

Rousseau long ago deplored the alienation of man from nature and exalted the 'noble savage', the natural man. And did not Romanticism, of which he was the precursor, preach a return to a nature which had been forgotten for almost two centuries? In the same fashion, we can view the Communism of Marx as an attempt to 'dis-alienate' man, recently subjugated by a society dedicated to production, as a way of liberating him, according to the author of *Das Kapital*, from that 'human condition in which his own act [the production of consumer goods] becomes a foreign force which overwhelms him and works against him instead of being governed by him'. Today, more than a century after Marx, this 'human condition' has become, in our society of the credit card and the computer, a condition of existence for our generation. Modern man, through his uncontrolled desire and insatiable greed for the acquisition of material goods, has become the slave of his own creations and, consequently, a stranger to himself—like Peer Gynt, that tragi-comic character of Ibsen's theatre who, in his pursuit of material gain, winds up forfeiting instead his fundamental self, the very essence of his human image.

Man today seems alienated from his own thoughts. To prove to himself that he exists, he no longer falls back on the *'cogito ergo sum'* of Descartes. For the Cartesian formula, he has substituted one that is more modern, 'I consume, therefore I am', and often even its converse, 'I am, therefore I consume'. Our contemporary, Erich Fromm, carries his investigation of alienation further, finding it even in the practice of idolatry. According to him, it is not the great number of gods which makes Jehovah jealous, but rather the fact that the idolater worships his own creation and becomes its obedient, soulless and dehumanised slave. Fromm also considers as alienated any man who abandons his will and judgment to a political leader or even to the state.

To these forms of 'alienation', economic or social in their origin, one may add the 'metaphysical' alienation made fashionable by the philosophies of Existentialism and of the Absurd which, despite their somewhat artificial veneer of 'liberty' and 'revolt', are nevertheless full of anxiety and pessimism. The gratuitousness of existence and the contingent nature of human life which is powerless in the face of the most terrible scourges, the negation of a Supreme Power acting as point of reference and source of resignation, instil even more deeply in man the feeling of estrangement from his world, the sense of that unfathomable abyss between what he is and what he would like to be which is the essence of the 'human condition'. Kafka's fragmented man, who does not even have a name, only an initial, is crushed beneath the merciless and implacable wheels of technobureaucracy and totalitarianism; and the all-powerful Roman tyrant of Camus' play discovers, after the death of his sister-mistress, the great cause of the Absurd in existence— that 'men die and are not happy'. K. and Caligula are not of their worlds: the former becomes alienated unwillingly, the latter deliberately.

I have briefly outlined the different 'case-types' of alienation in order to define more clearly the subject of my paper: the alienation of the French North African intellectual as it appears in his written literature and especially in the novel. We should mention at the very start that since the majority of works under consideration here are of an autobiographical nature, it is not always easy to distinguish the author from his hero.

Although the alienation of the French North African writer has its more remote sources in economic and political history, it was directly caused by the head-on collsion of two different, indeed totally opposed, civilisations: the archaic and politically weak civilisation of the colonised natives, and the prestigious, conquering, and arrogant civilisation of the French coloniser. Subjected to this double pressure, the 'suddenly civilised' North African intellectual had to make a choice; the two cultures could not co-exist; to blend them was impossible; it was necessary to do away with the old and substitute the new. There was not therefore a juxtaposition but rather an imposition of the foreign culture over the native culture which was to be banished from all memory and whose very existence was contested by the coloniser. The North African intellectual was condemned to be the spectator of his own painful metamorphosis and to observe with bitterness as his 'I' became more and more 'another'. The gap between himself and his own people who were not affected by the intense acculturation he experienced became deeper each day and more and more difficult to bridge. He became a stranger to his tribe, to his religion, to his traditions, and to himself.

The alienation of the French North African writer is thus by no means a metaphysical one. The suffering he experienced was due to the splitting of the two parts of his being, to his cultural schizophrenia, and had nothing to do with the anguish expressed by the contemporary writers of the Absurd and the 'human condition'. It was not Man transcending time and space which was the object of his thoughts but a specific and well-defined man living in the *'hic et nunc'* and clearly 'situated' in a political and social context: the native, colonised, acculturated North African of the forties and the fifties.

We usually interchange the terms 'Alienation' and 'Identity Crisis'. In fact, Alienation presupposes Identity, just as Death presupposes Life. It is in the final analysis the loss of identity, be it individual or ethnic, and the effort to recapture this lost identity which constitutes the 'Identity Crisis'. Like life itself, identity is a dynamic phenomenon often threatened by certain psychological, socio-political or cultural viruses or by certain 'congenital malformations' due to 'birth defects'. Like a sick person, the individual suffering from an identity crisis fights ferociously, guided and sustained by the same 'instinct of preservation'. If he wins, he recovers his health and identity and leaves the battle immunised and enriched. If he loses, he disappears: the sick man dies and the 'marginal' man or, as he has often been called, 'the cultural hybrid' or 'the historical bastard', completely loses his identity. He has not been able to reconcile the two parts of his mutilated self which have vied so furiously for his allegiance. He will belong to neither. He will recapture his inner peace in the calm immobility engendered by disillusionment, just as a dead man finds his eternal rest. Alienation is thus the static condition which terminates the identity crisis; it is the *dénouement* of the hybrid's tragedy.

After having studied the theme of alienation in the North African novel, I took a close look at the literatures of other hybrid cultures and was surprised by a resemblance which led me to formulate the following outline, one which, in spite of its general nature, seems to me to encompass a representatively large number of members of an equally large number of minorities; it applies equally to the black literature of the United States, Jewish-American literature and the literature of French Canadians, to cite only a few examples. I propose, then, an outline which moves from acculturation to alienation, and I will try, in the course of my explanation, to illustrate its principal stages through examples taken from North African literature before 1956, which is the date of the independence of Tunisia and Morocco and which I have made the cut-off year of my study:

1 the intellectual native makes an enthusiastic discovery of the new culture;
2 he makes a great effort to identify, assimilate, integrate;
3 this effort is often accompanied by a violent scorn for his own culture, family, religion and traditions, even for himself;
4 it is rare that the 'other' will take these affectations seriously and welcome him with open arms; most often, there is total rejection;
5 disillusionment results, followed by a strong self-affirmation and a spontaneous desire to find once again his origins and himself; this is the present situation of blacks in the United States whose slogan, already out of date I believe, is: 'Black is Beautiful!';
6 if things stop there, hope still remains for the culturally colonised individual; but most often, this return to one's origins proves impossible; 'he has rejected the East and the West has rejected him', as Memmi writes. This is alienation.

Let us now try to see how this outline applies to the French North African novel.

Sources of the Malaise: Colonisation and Acculturation

If we take a close look at the indigenous North African literary production, we are continually aware of a force often disguised, but very important and indeed omnipresent: French colonisation, or let us say rather, colonialism. This dynamic force, which has generated changes in attitudes and social and political upheavals, is the common denominator and the backdrop of this entire literature.

One is often inclined to associate with colonialism the idea of the political domination of the colonised people and their economic exploitation. This is true for any colonialism. But the French colonial system has never been satisfied with this alone: its aspiration has always been to promote the 'dissemination of French culture' and its 'civilising mission' in the world. Political observers have often remarked that 'when the English colonise they build businesses, that the Portuguese build churches and the French build schools'. It is precisely this construction of schools which was at the source of the malaise of the North African intellectual. This new type of man, fashioned in the classrooms of the French colonial high schools and colleges or in universities in France itself, is a by-product of colonisation. He is at one and the same time its beneficiary and its victim, the living proof of France's 'civilising mission' and the sad result of its 'cultural oppression'. Having abandoned the Koutab, his traditional religious school, for the French school where instruction is dispensed in French, his native language, Arabic, is forgotten, and this linguistic metamorphosis is the source of all his problems. Once he has been 'thrown to the wolves', to quote Kateb Yacine's well-known comment referring to the start of his career in the French schools, the young North African starts out on his 'learning adventure', an adventure, writes Albert Memmi, which was 'the source of all the suffering, of all the impossible situations which arose in my life'. For the culturally colonised individual is led to believe from the teaching of his masters, the exclusive purveyors of civilisation, that his country was a 'bush fit for jackals', that his people have no history, no culture, no geography even, since he is required to memorise the names of the French departments and their capitals, those of the mountains, waterways, wines and cheeses, and to repeat with all the culturally colonised members of the French colonial empire the famous *'Nos ancêtres les Gaulois'*. ['Our ancestors the Gauls']

For this group of writers, French schools symbolised a break, a brutal separation from their native milieu, an uprooting. All of them have, to a greater or lesser degree, given expression to the anguish of their first crisis. For example, Kateb Yacine: 'Thus I lost at one and the same moment both my mother and her language, the only inalienable treasures and yet, alienated.' Hence, the sorrow of exile, a very frequent theme in this literature, a lament sung by all the Amrouches. The exclamation of Malek Haddad, 'The French language is my exile', is well known, as is his charge against colonialism, which was the cause of his 'language defect'. Long before him and even more painfully, Jean Amrouche wrote in his *Chants de l'Exil* [Songs of Exile]:

Eboulez-vous, montagnes
Qui des miens m'avez séparé.

....

Mère, Ô mère bien-aimée,
Ah! L'exil est un calvaire.[1]

[Smash down, mountains
Which have separated me from my own.

....

Mother, oh beloved mother,
Ah! Exile is a Calvary.]

And his sister, Marie-Louise Taos, in *Jacinthe noire*[2] [Black Hyacinth], the undisputed forerunner of the novel of alienation, also bewails her own exile as she tells us the story of a young Berber woman stranded in Tunis, strange and a stranger to all. To complete the circle of the Amrouches, we might listen finally to the confession of the mother Fadhma Aït Mansour in her *Histoire de ma vie*[3] [Story of My Life], published only five years ago: 'I have remained, always and forever, the eternal exile, who has at no time and in no place felt at home.'

We can very well ask ourselves why, in spite of his suffering, the North African intellectual has so fervently followed this *via dolorosa* of assimilation to French culture and western civilisation which has often led him to a servile imitation of his masters and to its inevitable consequence, an unlimited scorn for the moral and spiritual values of his tribe and family, traditions and customs, often carried to the point of a desperate self-hatred. The answer can only be found in the 'totalitarian' character of French cultural domination which aims not simply at educating and instructing but at 'Frenchifying' the colonised elite. This elite has been 'impregnated' (in the etymological sense of the term) by a French culture whose mark is indelible. In the autobiographical novels of alienation, the author-protagonist recounts his learning adventure and presents it as a veritable rebirth. He discovers the marvellous secrets of the new culture with which he struggles to identify in a rush of enthusiasm that takes him out of himself and thereby creates, through that sort of Bergsonian 'intellectual sympathy', a perfect unity of subject and object. We could cite numerous examples but will limit our discussion to writers who have expressed this feeling directly in their literary production—and no one has done this better than Mammeri and Memmi.

It is in his second novel, *Le Sommeil du Juste*[4] [The Sleep of the Just] that Mammeri, embodied in the protagonist Arezki des Aït-Wandlous, tells of his own 'learning adventure'. In this epistolary novel, the letters go in one direction only, from the young Arezki to his French mentor, Monsieur Poiré, his much-admired teacher from the Ecole Normale. During his two years of residence at the Ecole Normale, Arezki does not once return to Ighzer, the Berber village where he was born. He seems to have already broken the bonds which tied him to his tribe and to his father—whose anger he used to arouse by proclaiming out loud to one and all that there was no God. For, writes Arezki, 'my new knowledge weighed upon me. I burned with the desire to communicate it to others. To do this, I had to begin by sweeping away all obstacles' (p. 135). He buries himself in his books, weeping in anguish over the difficulties of the French language which is not his native tongue. This is, nevertheless, the happiest period of his life. He is jubilant, full to overflowing 'with love, admiration, enthusiasm' for Monsieur Poiré and his humanist teaching. And when the war breaks out, he joyfully enlists to defend the endangered motherland, France. Before entering the army, he writes to Monsieur Poiré: 'It is to you, my dear master, that I shall forever owe my coming to life. Because before you I did not exist' (p. 119). This is an example of the phenomenon of rebirth through learning discussed earlier. There is also in this statement a remarkable echo of the colonialist idea, promulgated by the military, the politicians and the colonisers, to the effect that everything began in 1830 and that there was nothing before the colonial conquest; was it not, for instance, General Giraud who spoke of the 'Algerian void' which preceded the arrival of the French? What interests us here is not the opinion of the coloniser, which is expected, but its spontaneous and naive acceptance by a young member of the culturally dominated native population. And Arezki goes on: 'You broke in the doors of my prison and I was born to the world, a world which, without you, would have passed me by' (p. 120). If we accept Erich Fromm's definition of alienation mentioned earlier, we can easily see that by his total and unqualified identification with a foreign culture and with the teachings of his master, Arezki has already given up claim to his own 'self' and thus finds himself alienated. 'I go to this war with the same fervour I experienced when I drank in your words like a man dying of thirst. . .' he writes to his teacher as he sets off to defend the Tricolour and the ideas of the French Revolution: liberty, equality, fraternity.

Three years before *Le Sommeil du Juste*, Memmi published his first novel, *La Statue de Sel*[5] [Pillar of Salt]. Admitted, by means of a scholarship, to the Lycée Carnot in Tunis, the young Alexandre Mordekhaï Benillouche, an inhabitant of the poorer part of the city's Jewish ghetto, exults for joy. He is transported by 'a sort of immense movement toward the future, by an almost muscular drive' toward the conquest of the world. After the same linguistic difficulties resulting from his late start in studying French, he begins to win prizes at school. He literally weeps with joy at being the first to discover 'the most Racinian line in Racine' in a passage from *Andromaque;* he weeps true tears of suffering and pride as he reads Rousseau and identifies with his humble origins. He admires Vigny for his pride, his stoicism, his melancholy. He is wild about the Enlightenment, in raptures over Robespierre and Saint-Just. He discovers a new world every day and trembles at the idea that he might never have known it, had not chance opened the doors of the West to him. 'Sometimes,' he writes, 'I think with great fear of the darkness in which I might have lived, of the innumerable aspects of the universe which might have remained outside my ken. And I would never even have suspected it! Like a fish from the ocean's deep which is ignorant of the very existence of light.' (p. 77)

The Crisis

However, this jubilation and euphoria of learning exact at the same time a painful toll from the young intellectual. The philtre of knowledge produces disastrous effects on the personality of the culturally dominated individual. The price to be paid is enormous: the loss of identity. He has ceased to be himself; every day, parts of his being, which is in a constant state of renewal, 'break away in pieces', as Benillouche observes. From this strange metamorphosis emerges a new being who, in spite of his conscious or unconscious efforts to bury the past, no longer knows 'which way to turn'. At this moment begins a formidable quest for identity, a long and painful march on the perilous road of discovery of the self, of a name, of belonging. 'Who am I?' cries Jean Amrouche, 'who lives in me and through me? . . . A man can bear hunger and thirst. . . . But we, we must find our very name'[6]—a name without which he feels himself to be a 'bastard, deprived of his heritage' whose identity, 'put into question by the supercilious, almost god-like attitude of the coloniser', is never established, thus condemning him to a perpetual inner struggle.

In *Le Sommeil du Juste*, the young Arezki, after his first flights of enthusiasm, begins to feel the pains of his otherness: 'for a long time, I remained a stranger to everyone', he writes to Poiré, 'I had to tear myself away, each day, from a part of what I had been; I never imagined it would be so hard' (p. 132).

It is, however, the hero of *La Statue de Sel* who carries the identity crisis to its paroxysm, for he is pulled in three directions: his culture is French but he is a colonised native; he is colonised but still a Jew; a Tunisian Jew but with an Italian father and a Berber mother. We can thus easily understand the pathetic note of his desperate cry:

> I could be directly descended from a Berber tribe, the Berbers still would not acknowledge me since I am Jewish, not Muslim, a city-dweller, not a montagnard; I could have the exact same name as the painter [an Italian painter also called Benillouche], the Italians would not accept me because I am African, not European. Always and forever, I will remain Alexandre Mordekhaï Benillouche, a native in a colonised land, a Jew in an anti-Semitic universe, an African in a world in which Europe reigns supreme (p. 89).

Torn as he may be, however, between the two opposing forces which pull upon him (or the three forces in the case of Benillouche), the protagonist in the French North African novels of alienation seems, when the moment of decision is at hand, to choose West over East, French culture over his native culture, the world of the coloniser rather than that of the colonised. While admitting the ambiguity of his feelings and his suffering, Jean Amrouche also recognises the positive results of his transformation, which he attributes to 'historical chance'. In reply to a question one day, he affirms, not without a certain pride: 'I am a French writer.' This affirmation takes different forms for different writers but the message is the same. For Mammeri-Arezki, it is sanctified by action, that of serving in the French army; for Memmi-Benillouche, it takes the shape of an absolute and irrevocable decision:

> I would not be Alexandre Mordekhaï Benillouche; I would go beyond myself and move toward others. I was neither Jew nor Easterner nor poor; I did not belong to my family nor to its religion, I was new and transparent: I was still to be made, I will be a teacher of philosophy (p. 193).

As we see, the choice of the West brings with it the repudiation of the clan's sacred values. For, at this stage in the acculturation-alienation process, the North African intellectual seems to feel almost instinctively that the two worlds cannot co-exist in him, that he must first 'sweep away all obstacles' and cut away the innermost part of what constitutes his 'I' in order to better receive and implant what is 'other'. Arezki hears 'the voice of his heart' crying out to his father: 'dead to the world, but it is you who are dead. . . . If you only knew how I laugh at your fossilised wisdom, your world, your poor little world' (p. 135). Benillouche goes even further in overturning the idols of his people: 'I exposed and detested the tribe,' he says . . . 'I learned to scorn Uncle Aroun . . . to laugh at Uncle Filikche . . . to hate Aunt Foufa . . .' (p. 62). He hates all those dirty, hypocritical 'hirelings of religion', rabbis, grave-diggers, undertakers; he becomes indignant at the beliefs, superstitions and occult practices of his ignorant Berber mother who had become for him 'a stranger . . . buried in the womb of the primitive continents'; and he asks himself in despair: 'what dark bonds chain me to this phantom?' (p. 142).

This hatred of the past and all that it represents is seen in its most violent form in Driss Chraïbi's Le Passé Simple.[7] This novel differs from the others we have discussed in its sarcastically bitter tone, its harsh and incisive style, its violent and often obscene language. Nevertheless, it gives vent to that already familiar and painful cry of the cultural hybrid, the marginal man caught between two cultures, searching for an identity beyond his grasp. The hero, Driss Ferdi, experiences 'a rage at injustice'. He detests his father, a hypocritical tyrant; Islam, outdated and loathsome; his brothers, stupid animals who do not revolt; his mother, who killed herself after a life of vexation and resignation. The present exasperates him, but he hates his past even more. 'I don't like this city,' he says, speaking of Fez, 'it is my past and I don't like my past' (p. 69).

At the cost of a painful effort, the North African intellectual has torn himself away from his native milieu in order to cross into a foreign world. He discovers very quickly the enormity of his mistake; the outstretched hand has been violently repulsed; his hosts want nothing to do with him; their tremendously coveted circles are exclusive, impenetrable, rigorously closed to outsiders, even Frenchified and 'civilised' ones. It is during the war that Arezki makes this terrible discovery and finally understands 'that Man [of Poiré's teaching] did not exist; what existed was the Imann and the others'. The IMANN! It is only then that he grasps the true meaning of these significant initials (Indigène Musulman Algérien Non Naturalisé: Non-Naturalised Muslim Algerian Native) and feels that he too is enveloped in the same scorn that surrounds his faceless people. He becomes indignant over the discrimination against the Imann who spill their blood in a war which is not even theirs: 'according to the regulations . . . the Europeans were to be obeyed above all others', and 'the ranks being equal, the native officer owed obedience to the European one'. Worn out, beaten, in a fit of anger and under the influence of alcohol, he has a superb bookburning of all his French texts, all these 'phials' of poison, as if to exorcise the last remnants of his second personality which has betrayed him during 'twenty-three years of lies'.

The same war also opens the eyes of Mordekhaï Benillouche. Although the conditions are different, the lesson is the same: he is not welcome, he is not European, he is colonised and inferior, he is a Jew under the German occupation. Europe and western civilisation appear at his door in Nazi uniform: 'It was,' says the author-narrator, 'the painful, the astounding betrayal of a civilisation in which I had placed all my hopes, to which I had given all my admiration' (p. 229). Benillouche knows humiliation, the evils and dangers of German forced-labour camps; his best European friends reject and avoid him, and after his liberation, there is the final blow: he wants to enlist in the ranks of De Gaulle but is refused 'because of his name'. After this final rejection, he admits to his defeat and understands at last 'the error of wanting to be what essentially I was not'.

The 'Dénouement'

It is not by chance that the three great novels of alienation, *La Statue de Sel* (Memmi, 1953), *Le Passé Simple* (Chraïbi, 1954), and *Le Sommeil du Juste* (Mammeri, 1956), end with the departure of the hero, his escape after failure and disillusionment. Mordekhaï, the Tunisian Jew, leaves Tunisia for Argentina; Driss Ferdi, the Moroccan Arab, leaves Morocco for France; Arezki des Aït-Wandlous, the Algerian Berber, does not, it is true, leave Algeria, but he puts up no resistance to being thrown in gaol for a crime he did not commit, which is simply another form of abdication, of escape. From the moment they came into contact with the West, these three heroes have gone round unceasingly in a vicious circle; this continual rotation has given them a sensation of dizziness accompanied by a feeling both of anguish and well-being. But once the chains which bound them to the axis broke, they were hurled far away by centrifugal force.

Shaken by the West's rejection of them and by their own disillusionment, Arezki and Benillouche had for a time made an attempt 'to return to the fold' and to reaffirm their primary identity: Arezki had returned to his father's village with 'good intentions'; Benillouche had prayed to his God and chanted the Hebrew national anthem with his coreligionists enslaved in the forced-labour camps. But these were, for both of them, inauthentic and ephemeral acts. The only 'logical' choice for them is flight; Benillouche burns his diary, symbol of the past, and provides himself with a 'blank book' inscribed 'Argentina'. Arezki accepts his sentence with bitterness but also with resignation. Departure and prison put an end to their inner struggles; their 'alienation' is total; they have attained that static condition of which we spoke in our introduction.

Driss Ferdi, the most violent of all during the 'crisis', does not admit defeat; he finds extenuating circumstances for his failure: he is 'small and paltry in the face of the feudal lords' and his departure for France is for him an excuse to 'raid the treasure-house of ideas, social reforms, unions', before returning home to continue the fight. But we know very well that this will not happen, that Ferdi, like Arezki and Benillouche, has lost his battle for identity, that he has remained neither an Arab nor a Frenchman but rather, in his own words: 'An Arab dressed in French!'

We have followed the process of alienation by studying the protagonists of works which, although autobiographical, contain nevertheless an element of fiction, sometimes as embellishment, often for drama; the lyrico-epic nature of Chraïbi's *Le Passé Simple* was for a long time misunderstood. His scandalised compatriots—who wanted to find 'reality' directly transposed onto the 'fictional' plane—raised a public outcry against him and he had to protect himself with confessions and promises. It is therefore important, as we conclude, to follow the personal destiny of the writer himself. Of all the authors cited, and among all those of the 'generation of 1950', only Mammeri remained in Algeria after independence. Memmi, Chraïbi, and many others have settled in France and, having reconverted their themes, seem to have found a place among French writers. They, too, took their leave like the heroes of their fiction. Perhaps they feel enriched by their double culture; perhaps they still suffer from the after-effects of their 'crisis'; no one knows. What is certain is that they constitute, in their lives and works, a document, the prototype of a class of men that reaches beyond the limits of North Africa and is found today on every continent and in every latitude—men of two languages and two cultures who find their own deepest selves in this so very painful yet poetic avowal of Jean Amrouche: 'I am Algerian; I believe I am totally French. France is the spirit of my soul, but Algeria is the soul of my spirit.'[8]

Notes

1 Jean Amrouche, *Chants barbères de Kabylie*, Tunis, Monomotapa, 1939.

2 Marie-Louise Taos, *Jacinthe noire*, Paris, Charlot, 1947.

3 Fadhma Aït Mansour, *Histoire de ma vie*, Paris, Maspero, 1958.

4 Maulūd Ma'marī [Mouloud Mammeri], *Le Sommeil du Juste*, Paris, Plon, 1956.

5 Albert Memmi, *La Statue de Sel*, Paris, Gallimard, 1966; première édition: Paris, Buchet-Chastel, 1953.

6 Noted by J. Déjeux: 'Littérature maghrébine d'expression française', *Présence Francophone*, No. 4, Sherbrooke, Canada, p. 69.

7 Driss Chraïbi, *Le Passé Simple*, Paris, Denoël, 1954.

8 Jean Amrouche, 'Quelques raisons de la révolte algérienne', *Etudes méditerranéennes*, pp. 97–8.

Daniel P. Kunene

Towards an Aesthetic of Sesotho Prose

Sesotho is a Bantu language spoken in Lesotho and its environs. Lesotho is situated in Southern Africa, and is completely surrounded by the Republic of South Africa. The total number of Sesotho speakers, both in Lesotho and elsewhere (in parts of the Republic of South Africa) is approximately 2,000,000 or more.

The first missionaries to come to Lesotho, Arbousset, Casalis and Gosselin, representing the Paris Evangelical Missionary Society, arrived in 1833. Before this there was no system of writing in Lesotho, and all verbal art was dramatic and participatory.

It is important to remember that the missionaries came to Christian-ise, and that whatever other activity they engaged in was conceived as an aid to, and as part and parcel of, the process of Christianisation. The promotion of mother-tongue literacy was one such activity. The fact that education for blacks developed into something bigger and worthy of pursuit for its own sake was purely an accident of history. In the words of Dr James Stewart, himself a missionary in South Africa at the turn of the century, 'If missionary education communicated no other power than ability to read the Bible, it would still justify itself.'

Thus, as will be seen later, in the process of learning to read and write, the black man acquired a new set of values, and inherited the missionary zeal to pass them on to his fellow blacks and, through writing, to his readers. Traditionally, the story-teller had been a moralist, and most of his stories were, to varying degrees, didactic. The writer conceived his task in the same way—he would both entertain and teach.

Motivations, or the Writer's Function as he sees it

First of all, like his oral narrator/performer counterpart, the writer assumes the role, in relation to his characters, of a wise, all-knowing father and guardian. He approves and commends, he disapproves and chides, he teases and mocks with lighthearted playfulness, displaying a paternalistic amusement at, and tolerance for, the human foibles of his characters—a Gulliver among the Lilliputians. In another sense, he is comparable with God's own messenger among men of diminutive moral stature.

The writer, as against the oral narrator/performer, also has the magic power of communicating through a new medium whose acquisition has given him an enhanced status as a man of knowledge, something possessed only by the lucky few.

Secondly, the writer sets out to tell a story which he hopes will, among other things, be entertaining. He is, therefore, a narrator and entertainer, and in this role he creates people and situations which he objectifies for his reading audience. He has the disadvantage, however, in comparison with the oral narrator, that he does not create in the presence of a participating, critical audience which could inspire him to great heights of artistic excellence or, in some cases, bring his creative performance to an abrupt and premature end. He pursues his creative activity individually and in privacy, springs it upon his reading audience who also receive and evaluate it individually and in privacy, and he can only hope that they will both concur and be entertained. Which means that his critics speak after the fact, not during the process of creation.

Thirdly, the writer takes upon himself the role of commentator. Both directly and indirectly he interprets, evaluates and pronounces judgement upon the actions, attitudes and expressed intentions of his characters. He is both the entertainer and the entertained, cuing his audience and hoping that they will endorse his evaluations and judgements. His function, in this respect, could be compared with that of the Greek chorus.

When considered in his first and third roles—as the big father of all his characters and as a critical commentator upon their actions—the writer must be seen as someone who has attitudes towards those characters. The attitudes themselves arise out of a moral code which the writer vehemently upholds and jealously protects. His characters either observe and reinforce this code, or wilfully disregard it and threaten it with destruction. As an involved person with a vested interest in the behaviour of his objectified creatures, therefore, the writer either likes and praises them, or dislikes and vilifies them, as the case may be. Similarly, the oral narrator, in dramatising the actions and words of an actor in an oral tale, implies an attitude towards that character. The eating of the hyena, for instance, would be dramatised by mimicking ravenous eating with all the ugly noises; the size of the lion and his authority and dignity by raising the shoulders and simultaneously bending the head forward to look severely at members of the audience while giving authority to the voice by reaching down to its lowest register; the antics of the trickster by being simultaneously amusing and repugnant, exactly as the trickster sometimes is. He likes them, dislikes them, is amused by them—exact parallels to the writer's attitudes. That means that both the oral narrator and the writer display what I call an Affection/Disaffection relationship with their characters. There are, of course, other manifestations of the writer's involvement.

In sum, then, we come up with a writer who is inescapably didactic, who creates situations which will prove his moral point. He tends to see the world in extremes, in sharp contrasts of black and white, evil and good, ugly and beautiful; and his characters are either doomed or saved. There is no compromise, no merging of extremes—it is either day or night, never twilight or dawn, and the stories of his people are classical fables featuring stereotypes.

In his *Moeti oa Bochabela* (The eastbound traveller) Thomas Mofolo, the well-known Mosotho writer, describes right at the beginning what he considers as the dark age among the Basotho, the period before the coming of the missionaries. Into the powerful image of darkness that he builds, he introduces the contrasting image of light, but it is only a tiny spark which vainly attempts to resist the darkness, but must finally escape to avoid total engulfment by its more powerful rival. To represent these images, Mofolo creates a nation of corrupt men and women who lie and cheat and fornicate and kill, and suffer from a general condition of moral turpitude. The character who illustrates the corruption of the Basotho is a man named Phakoane. He is the personification of evil. Next door to Phakoane lives the protagonist, the young man Fekisi, who is the personification of virtue. In lack of verisimilitude, these characters are, of course, no different from all characters of allegory. But we must see in this, also, the moralist's ubiquitous technique: the twice-told tale with the 'good' character and the 'bad' character involved in turn, the 'good' one making all the right moves and prospering in the end, and the 'bad' one blundering at every turn, and getting punished.

Mofolo believes that the term 'human being'—*motho*—should be reserved only for men of unimpeachable character. The rest are 'beasts'.

Mofolo does not raise the question of corrigibility. Nor indeed that of corruptibility. We get cardboard figures in a rigid, static situation where the 'good' are good forever, and the 'bad' are bad forever. Phakoane and Fekisi are pigeonholed, *inter alia*, by the following descriptions: 'Phakoane was a human being when he had not taken any drink, but when he was drunk, he was a wild beast.' Fekisi, on the other hand, was 'a human being in the full meaning of the word "human being", a human being as the Creator had planned that human beings should be, a true image of Him who made all things, both the visible and the invisible, the very human being described when it was said: All creatures shall fear him, shall be obedient to him and shall honour him, because he has a glory of his own which other creatures do not possess.'

Chaka tells the story of a persecuted young lad, later a courageous but unappreciated young man, a budding warrior thrown to the mercies of his bloodthirsty enemies by his own father (the enemies including his half-brothers and his mother's co-wives), sung by the women but hunted down by the men. At the beginning of the saga, and for some time after, Chaka is a 'human being', and his detractors are 'beasts'. However, when he comes into his own, a social misfit, a sadist and a bloodthirsty Dracula, he is disqualified from 'human beingness', and the label 'beast' is stuck on him. The beginning of this decline is hinted at as Chaka is, by degrees, seduced by the Diviner or Smeller-out, Isanusi. But the process is considered to be complete and irrevocable when Chaka agrees (nay, even begs) to kill his beloved Noliwa on Isanusi's promise that this will bring him greater power and renown: 'Firstly, the last little spark of humanity still remaining in him was extinguished, completely extinguished in the terrible darkness of his heart. . . . Secondly, his being died, died forever, and there entered [into him] the nature truly of a beast.'

Similarly, in *Pitseng*, the people of darkness (equivalent to beasts) are the legions of young men and young women who pervert love into a thing of no consequence, contracting relationships with many partners at the same time, relationships which they ended casually and abruptly, failing to consult with their parents before committing themselves to marriage. These are the 'beasts'. The 'human beings' of the story are Alfred Phakoe and Aria Sebaka who never engage in these frivolities until they discover true love together.

Now we can say that Mofolo loves 'human beings' and hates 'beasts'. We must, however, not lose sight of the fact that, as a writer, he had the power to create and define his own human beings and his own beasts according to his moral code. The moral code Mofolo recognised was that arising from western Christian ethics, a code which, at that time, however, was not shared by the majority of his fellow-Basotho. In this role, Mofolo is an extension of the white missionary, and he is therefore a crusader, a self-styled Moses inspired with the zeal to lead his people out of the bondage of the darkness of *Sothohood* (Bosotho) into the light of *Europeanhood*.

The tensile situation that results from this, that is, where the author no longer subscribes to the same values as his audience (i.e. his readers), calls for a redefinition of didacticism, or, perhaps, an extension of its significance. The oral narrator/performer of premissionary days (in which we include the contemporary remains of this tradition) believes in the same customs, traditions and cultural values as his audience. The didactic tale that he tells illustrates the threat to society of social deviants who would commit rape, incest, murder, fratricide, who would lie, steal and cheat. The narrator passes judgment on them, and his audience concurs and cries 'Vengeance!' It is a reaffirmation of the mores of the social group. It reseals the cracks in the social structure, it heals the wound inflicted on society by a renegade. It either rehabilitates the renegade or ostracises or even destroys him physically.

The audience concurs without any need for cuing from the author; so do the numerous anonymous characters whose omnipresence is felt everywhere in the story, who are always on the side of justice and truth, and always stand ready to help the innocent victim of the social deviant. They stand ready to join those directly involved in passing judgment on the villain, in celebrating a successful and happy conclusion of the story, or in acts of commiseration if all is not well in the end.

This is integrative didacticism, and it belongs to the Africa of premissionary pre-colonial times. It is a feature of oral didactic tales.

The story of Masilo and Masilonyane includes fratricide and theft as its most powerful themes. It is a story of success for the younger brother Masilonyane and failure for his elder brother in finding wealth in a search that takes them away from home. Luck comes to Masilonyane in the guise of an old woman he discovers under an overturned clay pot in the ruins of a village they see along the way. She insists that he should carry her during the rest of their journey. Twice he uses a ruse to get her off his back, and he runs away and hides. On the second occasion, as she comes to where he is hiding, he sets his dogs on her, instructing them not to eat one of her big toes, which was extraordinarily big. He chops it open, and several herds of cattle come out including a beautiful cow whose colour is indescribable. Masilo is envious, and begs him to give him some of his cattle, particularly the beautiful cow. Masilonyane would willingly give him some of the cattle, but not that cow. They go to a fountain to drink. Masilonyane holds the large slab of stone covering the fountain, while Masilo drinks. Then Masilo holds the stone for Masilonyane, but deliberately lets go of it and kills him. He then drives the cattle home. But a little bird keeps appearing and twittering a little song that reveals the murder. It is Masilonyane's heart that has been transformed into this little bird. Masilo in turn kills the bird, grinds it to powder, burns it, but it keeps rising again and singing the same song. Eventually it reaches home just as Masilo is receiving compliments for 'his' beautiful herds and especially for the beautiful cow, and is denying all knowledge of his brother's whereabouts. The truth is revealed and, in the ensuing confrontation, the people indicate that they believe the bird (alias Masilonyane), and when it changes into Masilonyane, Masilo runs away into exile.

Fratricide and theft and lies are negative forces that threaten the solidarity of the society. The crack is sealed when the culprit is punished and the equilibrium restored. It is to be noted that the whole community is involved in the final dispensations and determinations, and that they are on the side of right and justice and of the observance of the society's mores.

A similar story among the Bene-Mukuni tells how a man who kills his pregnant wife, alleging that she has eaten some of his figs, is denounced by the foetus that comes out of the mother and comes running after him dragging its umbilical cord and singing:

> Father wait for me.
> Father wait for me,
> The Little Wombless!
> How swollen are those eyes!
> Wait till the Little Wombless comes.

The Little Wombless One is indestructible and comes to contradict the man's lying about his wife. When he is completely exposed and there is no point in further argument, 'His brothers-in-law tie him. And then . . . all the assegais are poised together in one direction, every one saying: "Now today you are the man who killed our sister . . ."'

'Then they just threw the body there to the west.'[1]

Then comes the literate narrator—the writer who, as previously stated, has willy-nilly embraced the new, aggressive and radically different values which come in the wake of missionary enterprise and colonial subjugation. He has received the skill of writing as part and parcel of the new mores and standards and traditions. He has had to accept everything as a package deal—all or nothing. This way, he has simultaneously inherited the task of the missionary/'civiliser'.

Meanwhile the missionary has recognised that his first and most important task is to create a sense of sin among the people he wishes to convert, and that that will make conversion more plausible. He has had to begin by destroying the structure that he found in order to make room for his own model. The African has thus been placed in a position where he has succeeded in being a sinner without even trying—all he has had to do has been to continue to believe in his own traditions and values.

The writer who comes out of this training is, then, an extension of the missionary--a black ancestor worshipper preaching white Christian values. Like the missionary, he has first to destroy in order to make room for the new ideals, for the brave new world he has discovered. It is a process of destruction, deculturation, disintegration. We thus have to label his didacticism as disintegrative didacticism. In that the disintegration or destruction is undertaken as a means to predisposing the black man to accept the new values, we see that it is not an end in itself, and that some form of reintegration follows close behind. Reintegration is seen as synonymous with the anthropologist's acculturation, while disintegration is equivalent to deculturation. But unlike what it replaces, the disintegrative/reintegrative process is never totally successful either qualitatively in terms of the depth of its penetration, or quantitatively in terms of the number of those who are significantly moved by it.

For example, in Mofolo's *Moeti oa Bochabela*, Fekisi, the puritanical young man who considers everything around him to be evil, fails to change the ways and traditions of the Basotho to accord with the new concepts of 'good' and 'evil' which Mofolo is advocating. Instead, Fekisi has to withdraw from this society and go elsewhere. The Basotho remain stubbornly Basotho in their ways. In fact, we must conclude that the very vehemence with which many writers advocate the acceptance of the Christian religion and western concepts of morality is a barometer of the limited success attained by the whites in their 'westernisation' of the blacks during the early years of contact.

In *Chaka,* Mofolo accepts without apology or explanation the efficacy of the Zulu diviner Isanusi's medicines and potions. Finally, in *Pitseng,* Mofolo personally condemns the new attitude to courtship and marriage that he observes among the modern youth of Lesotho which he says came in with the whites and has destroyed the youth of Lesotho.

Manifestations, or the Writer's Discharge of his Duties as he sees them

For us as critical readers, the first imperative is to accept the validity of the writer's role as a deeply involved individual. This, after all, links him naturally with his predecessor or predecessor/contemporary, the oral narrator/performer. Having done so, however, we have to keep alive in our minds that the writer, in our particular situation, is initially disintegrative—he is a deculturating agent.

The writer's involvement may take the form of *direct, explicit comment.* He interrupts his narrative in order to comment on a situation or a character's behaviour. He either talks to the audience to explain further what has just happened in the story, as when Mofolo concludes a chapter in *Chaka* by saying:

> In this chapter we find that it is indeed true that the fruit of sin is bitter to an amazing degree, because we do not see what transgression Chaka has committed in this matter, yet, even though that is so, his father gives the command that he be killed.

Or he contemplates and muses, as in *Moeti oa Bochabela*:

> Such is drunkenness, it associates one with evil things; its fruit is bitter. When one's mind clears, one is ashamed when one is told, and sees for oneself, the things that one did.

Or he debates a point as in *Pitseng* where Mofolo tells us:

> The days of today, it is said, are days of light, of wisdom, and of progress, and the days of long ago, of the *difaqane,* it is said, were days of darkness, of foolishness, of lack of knowledge. But in a matter such as this one of marriage, we find that to many people those days were of wisdom, and not of darkness and foolishness, and that it is these days of today which are of darkness and foolishness, and not of wisdom and light.

All these evaluations are communicated to the reader with the expectation that he will endorse them—or the hope, at any rate.

One of the problems here is that, in order to do this—that is, to make a direct, explicit comment—the writer has to put his characters in a state of suspended animation, to reactivate them when he has finished saying his piece. A perfect analogue to this is the sudden stoppage of the movement of a film while the commentator explains some detail in the still photo confronting the audience. This objection is sustained by the consideration that the author could convey the same sentiments by building them into the plot, making them emerge as the story moves forward.

A second objection is that explanatory comments, those which reiterate what is already obvious to the reader as against those introducing new elements, are irritating to the reader who rightly feels that he is not trusted to reach the same conclusions without the writer's intervention, nor given the option to conclude differently.

Thirdly, the suspension of the narrative creates a dangerous vacuum which sucks in the closest thing to it, namely whatever the writer may choose to put into it. For one thing, the writer easily turns preacher, particularly since he *is* crusading for a new religion. This is all the more likely since writers like Mofolo and his contemporaries, and for some time after, went through Bible classes and were trained as preachers in addition to being school teachers.

We see that direct comments do not add to the beauty of the narration; on the contrary they detract from it. Indeed, they are not a part of the narration at all. They are thus a negative element, and can be irksome. On the other hand, the author may sustain the narrative, employing various styles to comment. This is *implicit comment*, and it is carried effortlessly, unobtrusively, along with the flow of the narrative, enhancing its elegance.

There are many stylistic techniques which the author employs to insinuate his affection or disaffection for a character into the story. First of all then, affection.

The author may show his affection for a character by a manipulation of the syntax. He inverts the usual relationship that moves from subject to predicate into the less usual movement of predicate to subject. This is *inversion* or *anastrophe*. A brief linguistic orientation is necessary here before we illustrate from the literature. In Sesotho, a verb predicate is structurally related to its noun subject by what is called a subject concord which has a phonological relationship to the noun prefix:

> **Ba***tho* **ba** *makala*
> The people (**they**) were surprised
> **Le***tsatsi* **la** *tjhaba*
> The sun (**it**) rose

In a subject-to-predicate sequence as above, the subject concord and the verb stem (*ba* and *makala*, *la* and *tjhaba* respectively) collaborate to produce, jointly, a verbal predicate—the subject concord relates the predicate to a specific class or gender of nouns sharing the same prefix, the verb stem carries the action.

Inversion of the above two sentences results in the following:

> **Ba** *makala* **ba***tho*
> They were surprised, the people
> **La** *tjhaba* **le***tsatsi*
> It rose, the sun

In these examples, the subject concord has assumed an additional function, that of noun substitute. It also functions in this way when the noun is omitted. This means that the necessity to use the noun is substantially reduced or even totally eliminated. Mention of the noun in these circumstances then becomes a rhetorical device used for poetic effect, as in the following illustrations:

> *A di hana Fekisi*
> He rejected them, Fekisi
> cf. *Fekisi a di hana*
> *Ya qala kgomo e tshwinyana*
> It started, the feminine-white-starred bovine
> cf. *Kgomo e tshwinyana ya qala*
>
> *E ne e se motho yaa ratang ntwa, Fekisi*
> He was not a person who liked fighting, Fekisi
> cf. *Fekisi e ne e se motho yaa ratang ntwa*

It is important to note that, in addition to the inversion, the prosody is slightly but significantly modified. The word just preceding the delayed subject carries a longer length in its penultimate syllable, a phenomenon which would occur if such word were final in the sentence. This means that the process of changing the subject and the predicate around is *inversion plus*, rather than simply inversion. The bestowal of final occurrence prosodic features on the word just before the delayed subject must be seen as reinforcing the argument that, once removed from its usual position, i.e. before the predicate, the noun subject becomes an appendage, syntactically speaking, which is only loosely linked to what precedes it. But there, precisely, lies its rhetorical power.

The noun subject is sometimes omitted, being deducible from the subject concord. In ordinary discourse, such omission serves to avoid the cumbersome repetition of a noun which is already 'understood'. In a *rhetorical omission of the noun*, however, there is no need to assume that the omitted noun is 'understood'. The rhetorical effect depends precisely on the challenge to the reader to supply the correct noun.

Mofolo uses this to great advantage in *Moeti oa Bochabela*, especially in his reference to the sun. In a paragraph where he likens the sun to a royal messenger (with God as King), he rhetorically omits the noun *letsatsi* (sun) from seven key positions of *letsatsi* (subject) plus verb (predicate). So we get *la tjhaba* (it rose) three times and *la hlaha* (it appeared) four times.

The rhetorically omitted noun need not be in subjectival relationship; it could also be an object, or be related to a qualifying word or phrase. In all these situations, an appropriate concord (for example object concord, relative concord, etc.) is used to reveal the class gender and hint at the identity of the omitted noun.

The writer sometimes shows his admiration of a character through the *filial relationship* technique, whereby the character is related to his or her parentage, specifically to his or her father. He is called *son of . . .*, and she *daughter of. . . .* There are two important motivations for this. First, the relationship establishes the character as someone who belongs within a definite line of descent, not a nobody whose antecedents are not known. This harks back to the genealogical references so common in heroic poetry. The common practice whereby a Mosotho will greet another, or express gratitude or appreciation by simply declaiming the clan name of the one he is addressing, emphasises the importance, to a Mosotho, of being recognised as having origins through reference to the ancestral father and/or the ancestral home.

Secondly, and very important, the use of the filial relationship technique does not depend, for its validity, on the illustriousness of the father. Rather, it emphasises the illustriousness of the person praised, suggesting that he or she rubs off fame onto anything with which he or she is related, however remotely. In the sentence

> *Ho bile jwalo ho shwa ha Noliwa,* **moradi wa Jobe**
> So it was, the death of Noliwa, **daughter of Jobe**

from *Chaka*, we know, of course, that Jobe was a famous king. But his fame only adds to the amount of praise that, in Mofolo's eyes, Noliwa has already earned for herself through her 'human beingness' and her sheer beauty.

But in the numerous references to Alfred Phakoe as *mora wa Phakoe* (the son of Phakoe) and Aria Sebaka as *moradi wa Sebaka* (the daughter of Sebaka), or even to Chaka as *mora wa Senzangakhona* (the son of Senzangakhona), neither Mr Phakoe nor Mr Sebaka nor indeed Mr Senzangakhona is particularly famous. In fact the reader does not even know Phakoe and Sebaka since they are merely referred to in passing in *Pitseng*, the book in which their children are central characters. It is rather Alfred and Aria and Chaka who are illustrious.

Phrases of *associative relationship* are also sometimes used. These relate the character to his clan or to a wider socio-cultural group and to his place of origin. This also is reminiscent of heroic poetry. Thus Mofolo refers to Chaka as

> *Tau ya hlaka la ha Zulu*
> Lion of Zulu descent

and as

> *Tlou e kgolo*
> Great elephant

As with filial relationship, one important aspect of the above descriptions is their reaffirmation of the belongingness of the person praised.

There are other, similar, relationships which are, however, not as frequently employed in prose as they are in heroic poetry. Noliwa, in the sentence relating her to Jobe, is also referred to as

> *kgaitsedi ya Dingiswayo*
> sister of Dingiswayo

and

> *mosadi wa Chaka*
> wife of Chaka

In many, perhaps most, cases of inversion, the subject, if a person whose father is known, is expressed through a phrase of filial relationship rather than through the given name of the character. For example:

> *a sa kena ntweng mora wa Senzangakhona* . . .
> he just entering the battle, the son of Senzangakhona.

Warm feelings towards a character or an animal or other actor in the story are sometimes conveyed through a *special use of the adjective*. Here the normal function of the adjective—to distinguish an individual from a class of things which have a basic sameness—is suspended. In describing the graceful movements of the beautiful, well-fed, well-groomed, lively horse mounted by an immaculate suitor who comes to propose love to Aria Sebaka, Mofolo says

> *ya hakala* **pitsi e sootho**
> it excelled, **the dark brown horse**

Mofolo is using the adjective as an indication of his admiration of the horse. But what is important is that he is not admiring the horse because of its dark brownness—he is admiring the dark brownness because of the horse. Thus the horse could have been any other colour, and that colour would have been equally admirable because the thing in which it inheres is admirable. In this context, such directly opposed descriptions as black and white, short and tall, large and small, are all potential instruments for the expression, by one and the same writer, of the admiration of him who, or that which, is admired.

We must conclude, therefore, that in this context there is nothing in these adjectives *per se* that evokes feelings of admiration. They borrow glory rather than impart it, so that, as with filial relationship, the admired object rubs off its fame onto something else, that is, an otherwise irrelevant inherent quality; that is, it bestows fame on the adjective. Here are further examples:

> *A hana hona teng* **Fekisi e mosootho**
> He outclassed them even there, **the dark brown Fekisi**

> *Ya tjho ya hlomolana* **kgomo e pudutswana**
> Doing thus, it created tearful admiration, **the feminine-grey bovine**

> *Ya tla e tiile ho yena* **kgomo e tshehla**
> It came to him at full gallop, **the yellow bovine** (i.e. the lion)

> *. . . e tsositse mohlahla, e tonne mahlo, e tiisitse mohatla,*
> **namane e tshehla**
> . . . its mane raised, its eyes staring, its tail taut, **the yellow calf** (i.e. the lion)

> *a e nyafa ka* **le lephatshwa**
> he stabbed it deep with **the black and white one**
> (refers to spear; this was the colour of Chaka's spear)

As seen from the examples given so far, these techniques are sometimes combined. Usually, inversion is combined either with filial relationship or with given name plus special use of adjective. Illustrations of these can be found easily among the examples already provided.

These expressions of admiration by the author should help us understand why some prose works contain occasional paragraphs of poetry. In the following description, in *Chaka*, of the lion that is about to attack the men looking for it in tall grass, the six-line poem praising the lion constitutes the delayed subject of the inverted syntax in exactly the same way as *the yellow bovine* and *the yellow calf* do above:

> *Ya re feela ham-m-m, ya be e se e le ka hare*
> *Tshehla ya boMothebele, kokomoha,*
> *Tshehla, thokwa-lekakuba,*
> *Ekare o sa je tsa batho,*
> *O itjella dirobala-naheng!*
> *Motjhana a se na babo-moholo,*
> *O a n'a bolaya a be a ratha!*

> It just went ham-m-m, and was immediately among them,
> Tawny One, brother of Mothebele, rise up,
> Tawny One, fawn-coloured king of the wilds,
> Why, you eat not what belongs to men,
> But eat, for your part, the sleepers-in-the-veld!
> A nephew bereft of uncles
> Kills and lays claim to all the booty!

In other words, we have here the same stylistic technique as employed about half a page down from the above quotation:

> *Yare ha e kgaruma, ya tjho e se e tlotse*
> *namane e tshehla*
> *sebata sa meru*

> And when it roared, it did so already having jumped
> the yellow calf
> beast of the forests

The only difference is that in the last illustration Mofolo writes the second and third lines (as arranged by me above) so that they run-on with the narrative that precedes them, and of which, indeed, they are a part.

The praises of the hyena which is laid low by Chaka's spear constitutes a substantival statement in apposition to the absolute pronoun *yona* (it) occurring as the possessor in a possessive qualificative phrase. Here is the sentence:

> *E ne e tshajwa thamahane, batho ba thothomela ha ba utlwa tsa yona*
> *Thamahane, phiri, sephaka-thamaha,*
> *Rangwan'a tau le letlonkana,*
> *Ngwana wa merara ee matswedintsweke.*
> *Thamahane, ngwana wa dika-tsholo-la-ka-phirimana*
> *Ana motsheare o tshaba'ng ho le dika?*
> *Ke tshaba molato nthong tsa batho.*

It was feared, the hyena and the people trembled when they heard of its deed
> Brown hyena, wolf with a brown-coloured fore-arm,
> Little father of the lion and the spotted hyena,
> Child with zig-zag tattoo, mark of brave warriors,
> Brown hyena, child who is a warrior who hunts by night,
> What makes you fear to hunt by day?
> I fear accusations of stealing men's stock.

The admired person or animal or object is sometimes praised by means of a eulogy as in heroic poetry. Thus Fekisi, the main character of *Pitseng*, is called

> *ngwana wa setsoha-le-pelo-ya-maobane*
> child who is getter-up-with-the-heart-of-yesterday,

that is, one who is constantly good-intentioned toward other people.

And now, just a brief mention of *disaffection* and how the writer conveys it. Here the writer mainly relies on well-chosen emotive words. For example, in *Pitseng*, Mofolo tells how some diviners sit outside during a thunderstorm in an attempt to ward off the lightning. The author regards them as trying to control the might of God, and this makes him view them with contempt. The lightning strikes one of them and the rest run inside, but before they reach safety, it kills a second one. To describe their flight, Mofolo chooses the ideophone *naka-naka*, which denotes running and simultaneously connotes the futility of a tiny creature trying to run away from a might or force that is all-pervasive, and from which there can be no escape, like an ant trying to run away from a tidal wave. The sentence is

> *Ba re ba sa re naka-naka, la bata e mong hape*
> Even as they ran futilely, it struck yet another one.

Mofolo never fails to show contempt for those who unjustly provoke a fight, especially when they are given a good, well-deserved beating by an upholder of right and justice, or simply by the one whom they despised. This he does with great effect where Fekisi, during the early part of his journey, beats off several men who are about to murder another one. He does it more elaborately, and with a lot more venom, when Chaka fights for his life against his half-brothers and their supporters after his father gives the order that he be killed. Mofolo's descriptions of the miserable deaths of Chaka's assailants are very lively. One feels, however, that the dramatic effect would be greatly enhanced by oral presentation with all the vocal effects, the gestures and grimaces of the narrator. The following comments and translations of some of the words and phrases used, however, will capture some of the sentiments Mofolo is expressing here:

The word *motho* or the phrase *motho wa bona* roughly denotes an insignificant, little known person; a nonentity. It is used often in the description referred to above.

bokwana is a diminutive of *boko* (brains). The effect of the diminutive is to show contempt; perhaps 'petty brains' might be fitting. The brains referred to are those of someone whose head Chaka has just smashed with his stick.

a shwa a bohla jwaleka motho yaa nweleng jwala haholo: he died belching like someone who had drunk too much beer. Death, usually regarded with awe and solemnity is associated with the repulsive act of belching—or perhaps retching—of someone who has taken too much drink.

motho a shwa hampe yeo: what an ugly death that man died!

leihlo a le dukula la wela fatshe e le pataolo e kang ya nku: as for the eye, he dug it out and it fell to the ground, a big, round thing like that of a sheep (i.e. Chaka dug out his opponent's eye).

a shwa a dikeditse meno fatshe: he died with his teeth dug deep into the ground.

Mfokazana madi a kopotseha ka hanong, ka dinkong, ka ditsebeng, a phalla jwaleka a nku ee kgaotsweng molala: As for Mfokazana, blood flowed freely through his mouth, his nostrils, his ears, it flowed like that of a sheep whose neck had been severed.

The associations are animalistic, the victims are mostly considered as being of no importance, of no known origin.

Towards the end, when Mofolo has begun to express the same uncomplimentary sentiments for Chaka, he evinces unmistakable annoyance and contempt as he caricatures Chaka as a trickster in his exaggerated and hypocritical wailings in connection with the death of his mother whom he himself has killed. He makes Chaka cry aloud:

Joo, joo, mme o shwele wee! Joo, joo, malapeng a mang mosi oa thunya, heso ha o thunye!

Joo, joo, my mother is dead, oh-h! *Joo, joo,* from other homes the smoke goes up, from my home it does not go up!

The effect of this is to provoke derisive laughter on the part of the reader. But again the dramatic effect would be much enhanced by theatrical presentation.

Conclusion

There are other ways, apart from affection/disaffection, in which the author conveys his involvement in the story. For example, he may show pity for a character in trouble, or he may be part of the audience and watch from the sidelines reflecting his emotional reactions with appropriate interjections. Beyond this, one might further pursue the topic of this paper by describing stylistic techniques which are outside the sphere of author involvement, but nevertheless natively Sesotho.

From the above discussion, however, the conclusion is inevitable that the author is a very deeply involved person, one who not only creates, but also reacts; one who loves some of his characters and likewise hates others, and reflects these feelings in basically the same way as the heroic poet praising the warrior on the home side and pouring scorn on the enemy. And he seeks the concurrence of his audience.

Perhaps future Basotho writers will develop in some direction away from these relationships, which is not to say that such a break is necessarily desirable. For the present, however, we have to recognise that a significant number of the stylistic techniques the contemporary writers employ arise out of, and reinforce, this role. We have to accept the validity of this role, and let our critical statements begin at the point where we consider *how* the writer fulfils it.

Notes

1 J. Torrend, *Specimens of Bantu Folklore from Northern Rhodesia*, New York, Negro Universities Press, 1969, p. 17. (First published by Kegan Paul, Trench, Trubner and Co., Ltd, 1921).

Rowland Smith

The Johannesburg *Genre*

Recently there has been a welcome surge of interest in the writing of black South Africans. Not only are some of the most prominent contemporary figures writing about South Africa people classified as 'non-white' in that country's unique Wonderland of racial terminology, but also historians and social scientists are beginning to study the reactions of that vast 'non-white' majority to events that had previously been viewed solely from a white perspective. Part of the arrogance of white domination in South Africa has always been the assumption that South African affairs (particularly cultural affairs) *are* the affairs which affect whites and those in which whites are involved. Even as recently as twenty years ago, 'South African literature'—if it were considered at all—would have been generally considered to be that body of literature written by white South Africans, whether they wrote in English or Afrikaans.

Writers such as Peter Abrahams, Ezekiel Mphahlele, Alex La Guma, Lewis Nkosi, Arthur Nortje, and Dennis Brutus have put an end to that myth over the last twenty years. In a sense their assertion of the 'non-white' voice has been so successful that there are signs of a contemporary attitude that *this* writing is the only real or legitimate South African literature. The reasons for this view are easy enough to find in both the long history of neglect which black South African intellectuals have suffered and in the continued, monstrous oppression of the South African black population.

In this essay I shall concentrate entirely on the writing of white, English-speaking South Africans. This is not to 'take sides' with the white writers against the 'real' voice of South Africa, nor to neglect, in arrogance, the writing of black South Africans. It is only in the sub-sub-culture (Nadine Gordimer's phrase) of English-speaking white South Africa that the theme I wish to discuss could be appropriate. It is intimately connected to the whiteness of the authors I deal with, and, in most cases, the guilt associated with their white status. The dwindling influence of English-speaking whites in South Africa itself and the growing confidence of the international public in the voice of the dispossessed 'non-white' population may already have relegated to history the pattern of response which is my concern in this essay

An obviously recurring theme in the literature of English-speaking white South Africa is that of estrangement. Many writers have stressed their sense of shock at the harsh, unrelenting reality of their day-to-day world in contrast with the more varied, polished and flexible world of European myth and literature on which they have been spiritually nourished. Guy Butler's poem, 'Myths', gives a beautifully direct statement of this theme:

> Alone one noon on a sheet of igneous rock
> I smashed a five-foot cobra's head to pulp;
> Then, lifting its cool still-squirming gold
> In my sweating ten separate fingers, suddenly
> Tall aloes were also standing there,
> Lichens were mat-red patches on glinting boulders,
> Clouds erupted white on the mountains' edge,
> All, all insisting on being seen.
> Familiar, and terribly strange, I felt the sun
> Gauntlet my arms and cloak my growing shoulders.
>
> Never quite the same again
> Poplar, oak or pine, no, none
> Of the multifarious shapes and scents that breed
> About the homestead, below the dam, along the canal,
> Or any place where a European,
> Making the most of a fistful of water, splits
> The brown and grey with wedges of daring green—
> Known as invaders now, alien,
> Like the sounds on my tongue, the pink on my skin;
> And, like my heroes, Jason, David, Robin Hood,
> Leaving tentative footprints on the sand between
> The aloe and the rock, uncertain if this
> Were part of their proper destiny.[1]

The violent, glare-ridden, un-European environment evoked with such startling clarity in these opening stanzas, is itself the focus of interest for many of the earlier white writers. Their need to capture on the page the emptiness of their vast, bleak, pioneering world gives the peculiarly intense stamp to scenes such as the opening of *The Story of an African Farm* or the ghastly treks through Pauline Smith's godforsaken Little Karroo. Implicit in these descriptions of life in 'frontier' communities is a sense of their rawness and roughness. But it is not until the pioneering days are clearly over that English-speaking, white writers incorporate that same harshness and bleakness of environment into a picture of provincial or colonial manners.

Even when the real frontier has ceased to exist, the frontier manner lives on. And the satirists of the 1920s, such as Roy Campbell and William Plomer, repeatedly allude to the outlandish quality of life in either Banana- or Lembuland. By the 1920s the attitude of the white ruling class—even in the back of beyond—is portrayed as increasingly complacent. Its smugness about the 'progressive' and privileged status which it enjoys in contrast to that of the indigenous blacks is as much a target for the sarcasm of Plomer and Campbell as is the roughness of the environment and culture.

In *Turbott Wolfe* the barbarous racism of the white farmers and officials is at the centre of Plomer's disgust. But the other-worldly quality of nightmare life in Lembuland is heightened by descriptions of the absurdly inappropriate mores of even sympathetic characters like the Fotheringhays. Mr Fotheringhay is the English Church priest at Aucampstroom. His Rectory is heated by fire (*à l'anglaise*) even on the hottest days. His 'dressing room' is a ramshackle storeroom filled with junk and a rickety washstand. From the Fotheringhays' window Turbott Wolfe watches 'two little unwashed white girls, four or five years old, mocking at a drunken native in the street'[2] while his hosts reminisce about their Victorian English past. And on his last night in the district, Wolfe dines with the Fotheringhays who insist on walking after dinner 'in the garden'—most conspicuous for its spidery, ramshackle earth-closet smelling strongly of sheep-wash, its seedy cabbages, and one pallid, wasted rose.

There is a problem in preserving one's concept of oneself in such inauspicious surroundings. And the primitive facilities, together with the boorishness of the settlers, force the Fotheringhays back on their English past for emotional succour. The effect is twofold: not only are their reveries totally disconnected from the day-to-day reality of their lives (Turbott Wolfe wonders if Africa has ever really registered in Mrs Fotheringhay's mind), but also those reveries themselves as well as their 'different' house (with its 'dressing room', 'garden', and fire) distinguish the Fotheringhays from the greyness of their surroundings. As a result, their quirks are in a way prized possessions, desperately needed to indicate their difference—their separation—from the ordinary life of Lembuland. The difficulty in being ordinary in Lembuland, in being able to accept and submerge oneself in one's surroundings, is a minor suggestion in *Turbott Wolfe*. But it becomes a recurrent theme in the literature written by white South Africans in the 1950s and 1960s. By that time the frontier has ceased to exist even metaphorically. But the provincial self-importance of the English-speaking white world—against which the post-war writers react so consistently—grows from alienation similar to that of the Fotheringhays.

Roy Campbell's repeated outbursts against the claustrophobia of Natal in the 1920s are far more personal than Plomer's. And as a result they continually suggest the impenetrable complacency of an increasingly secure and yet still primitive white world. Campbell's hostility towards his native culture was an effect of his feeling rejected by it. As a result, there is a personal virulence in his attacks on the myopic self-sufficiency of colonial tastes:

> As for the 'boundless spaces'—wild and free
> They stretched around as far as eye could see,
> Which, though not very far, was yet enough
> To show a tree, four houses and a bluff.
> Geographers, who say the world's a sphere,
> Are either ignorant, or mazed with beer,
> Or liars—or have never read two pages
> Of any of our novelists or sages
> Who tell us plainly that the world's more wide
> On the colonial than the other side,
> That states and kingdoms are less vast and grand
> Than ranches, farms and mealie-planted land.[3]

When faced with the armour-plated smugness of the white Natal culture, Campbell himself reacted by adopting the persona of the rejected, lonely genius, scorned by the group and yet superior to it. Even in resorting to this persona Campbell was epitomising the problem of self-esteem for an English-speaking white South African. His role as an isolated, exceptional figure was, ironically enough, adopted as a defence against the bland self-importance of his compatriots. The backwardness of their milieu and their social privileges seemed to be interdependent. And it was with the stupefying effects of that particular combination that he was obsessed. Campbell's feeling of rejection was complex and was to pursue him through other societies and groups. His subsequent career was in many ways a continual search for a group or society which he could call his and in which he could happily submerge himself. But his role of outsider became institutionalised, even when he was proclaiming loyalty to esoteric coteries in France, Iberia and the British army.

Since the war, the most prominent English-speaking white South African writers have not set out openly to attack or chastise their own cultural milieu. However bitter their views have been and however dark the picture they have drawn, they have not taken a *Voorslag* to the public hide. Their depictions of South African life have been subtle, analytical and varied. There has been no successful polemic such as Roy Campbell's and little sustained satire. And yet writers such as Dan Jacobson, Nadine Gordimer and Jillian Becker show a remarkable similarity when discussing (from quite dissimilar viewpoints) the ensnared and isolated position of many characters in their created white world.

In a sense the situation had become more acutely provincial. In spite of the industrialisation of the land, and its apparent modernity, it was still an undeveloped country in many respects. The life of black peasants deteriorated as the flashy white cities grew. And with the growth of the opulent suburbs there coincided a growth of the hopeless black slums and heartless mining compounds. The affluent English-speaking whites inhabit an apparently sophisticated world, and yet they are surrounded by both the teeming black slums and the harsh countryside of dust and khaki-weed and farms worked by convict or squatter labour. Not only are their inherited British customs inappropriate to this world, but also their ordered, affluent, games-playing, middle-class milieu—which on the surface seems most British—depends for its existence and protection on a particularly un-British, brutal monolithic regime intimately connected with what is most primitive in the land.

A beautiful picture of this schizophrenic situation is provided in Nadine Gordimer's novel, *The Lying Days*. The central character is brought up on a mine just outside Johannesburg. Her father is mine secretary, and the family life is regimented around the infinitely genteel world of the mine officials, who, with their tennis club and social round, seem to epitomise the decorum of earlier British imperial classes. Yet the girl has to travel each day to university by train, using the mine siding with its tin office, bleak platform, debris, khaki-weed, stinking grass burnt brown with urine, and hordes of black miners—properly segregated, of course.

The trapped quality of life in this unreal, self-important white world is a topic on which Jillian Becker, Nadine Gordimer and Dan Jacobson all dwell. And the paradox in the picture they paint is that a sense of alienation grows out of the superiority which the English-speaking middle class professes either because of its borrowed customs or because it dissociates itself from its sordid surroundings; one of the most liberating effects of escape into the metropolitan world is the ability to be ordinary or anonymous.[4]

In *The Keep* by Jillian Becker, the neurotic, wealthy Freda Leyton reflects in this way on her imprisoned existence as a particularly sensitive creature in crass Johannesburg:

> She had to face it, face it, her life was a stupid and empty thing. The occasional party; clothes-buying; birthdays and anniversaries—the dull, private and only festivals; the annual holiday; and now and then, twice in fact in the last ten years, the venture into the civilization of Europe, which for all the glamour of its nouns crystallized into a cluster of hotels, theatres, opera-houses, and galleries through which she strolled wondering what was the proper attitude to adopt, what the right emotions to feel, what the right thoughts to think. Europe could never repeat that first surprise it had given her with its rich evidence of ultimate dust and perfect levelling. . . . So she did not lose faith in Europe; and although so far no one had lived up to her expectations of cosmopolites, she delivered every letter of introduction. And then the scenery in Europe was well arranged, easy to admire. Not only was it small and well-worked, but it was amply described in so many books. It had every stamp of approval and it was friendly.
>
> But here she was in this raw country, among these people, in this house. Trapped.[5]

Freda is, of course, an ass with no talents and hardly any feelings. But even as she is being mocked here, her plight is presented as real. She has both an instinctive feeling of superiority and an utter bewilderment about any feature of the world around her. Not only is Europe the only place with 'real' values; it is also the only place where the model on which to base her responses is occasionally accessible. Yet even though literature and tradition apparently give her more guidance in regulating or preparing her European responses, the most fascinating aspect of Europe is its 'rich evidence of ultimate dust and perfect levelling'. On her first visit she fell in love with ruins. And for someone as dead as Freda Leyton this is not surprising. But beneath her affinity for monuments to the dead lies a dim response to the 'rich' evidence of 'levelling'—the freedom from the death-like decorum and ritual in her status-ridden, identity-conscious provincial pond.

A similar undertone ripples through a passage in Nadine Gordimer's *The Lying Days*. The central character, as a child, leaves the Saturday afternoon torpor of the mine property (her parents are at the tennis courts) and wanders across the veld to the string of mine concession stores patronised by the black miners. The shops are dirty, dingy, filled with cheap junk and the paraphernalia of an indigenous medicine store. Around her is the dust and weed and urine-burnt grass that she is later to encounter again at the railway siding. The rawness of the place is something quite excluded from her own belawned, behedged environment. Yet as the child observes the comprehensive, inclusive, teeming life of the scene her sense of new-found release and excitement is related to her colonial predicament:

To me, brought up into the life of a South African mine, stories of children living the ordinary domestic adventures of the upper-middle-class English family—which was the only one that existed for children's books published in England in the thirties—were weird and exotic enough. Nannies in uniform, governesses and ponies, nurseries and playrooms and snow fights—all these commonplaces of European childhood were as unknown and therefore as immediately enviable as the life of princesses in legendary castles to the English children for whom the books were written. I had never read a book in which I myself was recognizable; . . . So it did not need the bounds of credulity to be stretched to princes who changed into frogs or houses that could be eaten like gingerbread to transport me to an unattainable world of the imagination. The sedate walk of two genteel infant Tories through an English park was other world enough for me.

Yet now as I stood in this unfamiliar part of my own world knowing and flatly accepting it as the real world because it was ugly and did not exist in books (if this was the beginning of disillusion, it was also the beginning of Colonialism: the identification of the unattainable distant with the beautiful, the substitution of 'overseas' for 'fairyland') I felt for the first time something of the tingling fascination of the gingerbread house before Hansel and Gretel, anonymous, nobody's children, in the woods.[6]

What the child senses are the magic possibilities of shaking off the limitations of her identity as the mine secretary's daughter and entering the exotic, sordid, amorphous reality of the world outside the official gentility of her home. But the fascinating part of the description is its suggestion that to be 'anonymous, nobody's children' is to be able to approach the wider world without apology.

In this passage the colonialism in the girl's mind is shown to result in her equating the real world with her own drab, day-to-day surroundings, and the unattainable world elsewhere with the beautiful. A more profound disorientation can result from the inversion of the same phenomenon. To some white South African writers the spiritual plight resulting from an English-speaking upbringing is shown to be that the real world is an unattainable realm approached through books or legends or fashions from Europe, and that one's daily environment is a half-real, makeshift substitute.

In Nadine Gordimer's second novel, *A World of Strangers*, the hero is an Englishman sent out to South Africa to manage the South African branch of the family publishing house. He lives a split existence, dividing his leisure between a group of moneyed white socialites who congregate at the mansion of a mining magnate and a group of vital blacks who live on the fringes of the underworld in the lower depths of the black townships and slums. He is incapable of making any connections between these two worlds although his closest friend is a flashy black man and his mistress is a flashy, horse-riding white girl. A meeting between the two is out of the question. And again the effect is obviously a feeling of unreality, of a living schizophrenia. Toby, the hero, describes himself floating in the magnate's swimming pool and instantly succumbing to its mood of opulence: 'an Orpheus, I passed from one world to another—but neither was real to me. For in each, what sign was there that the other existed?'[7]

Toby is an Englishman, so that although he lives in the unreality of this Johannesburg world, he has no doubts about his own roots or background. But the problem is compounded for those white South Africans who belong to the place. A Johannesburg bookseller scornfully discusses the locals over lunch in a new and therefore crowded coffee bar: ' "It's pathetic," he said. "They've got so little to hold them together, they'll rush to any new rallying point you offer them like dogs tearing after a bitch. Specially if they can pretend they're somewhere else; Italy, for example" ' (p. 68). The problem is the inversion of little Helen's reaction after blundering onto the strip of concession stores in *The Lying Days*. After describing the bookseller's comments, Toby remarks: 'That was the first time I encountered what I was soon to recognize as a familiar attitude among South Africans; an unexpressed desire to dissociate themselves from their milieu, a wish to make it clear that they were not taken in, even by themselves' (p. 68).

There are obvious strains inherent in living with an identity which depends on dissociating oneself from one's surroundings, particularly when it is the dissociation itself which makes one special, knowing, an insider. Just as the condescending bookseller is a bitter, lonely character, so too the whites who 'know better' are lonely, apologetic characters. In *A World of Strangers*, Anna Louw, the white lawyer who works for black legal aid and ends up a treason trialist, explains the apologetic instinct to Toby:

> I used to think it was because everything in town life here relates to another world—the plays are the plays of Europe, the cabaret jokes are those of London or New York. . . . You know what I mean? Johannesburg seems to have no *genre* of its own. . . . But now I think there's something else. Loneliness; of a special kind. Our loneliness. The lack of a common human identity. The loneliness of a powerful minority (p. 80).

To be able to merge with one's surroundings; to accept one's environment; to be content to be ordinary or anonymously part of it—all these are presupposed in the concept of 'a common human identity'. And it is these same features which appeal most directly to writers describing the release which the metropolitan world offers to the lonely minority described by Anna Louw.

Dan Jacobson dwells most directly on the problems of adjusting to the cosmopolitan after growing up as a privileged provincial. In an article entitled 'Settling in England' he describes his boyhood in Kimberley, and the typical English values (at one remove) which he imbibed.

> The character of Kimberley has almost altogether changed since those days, for a number of reasons, which can be summarized by saying that all that was un-English then has become dominant

now, and that what was 'English' has become even more faded and tenuous than, looking back, I realize it already was. But I have mentioned the 'Englishness' of the city as it appeared to me in my boyhood because this may help the reader to understand how it was that in a hot tin-roofed mining town on the edge of the Karroo, I felt myself to be involved very deeply, and very early, with an idea of England. . . .

. . . it was the books I read which ultimately had authority over me, and these books were practically all English. The headmaster could only confirm what the books had already told me—namely, that everything I saw in Kimberley which was not recognizably 'English' did not properly exist. The veld, the sun, the heat, the black people of the town, even the Afrikaans-speaking whites, my own position as the son of an immigrant Jewish family—these were all unwritten about, without confirmation, without background, without credentials. There was something unreliable, not to say fishy, about them all. We did not live as people should live; we did not live where people should live. It was wrong that summer should have come in December and winter in July; it was wrong that I never saw snow, wrong that our servants were black men and women who could not speak English instead of apple-cheeked wenches and impertinent Cockneys. . . .[8]

As the title of the essay indicates, it deals with Jacobson's decision to settle in that richly described country. It is the 'immense benefit of the privacy of the life in England' which he points to. And in choosing 'privacy' as one of the great advantages of living at the centre of things, he is merely exhibiting a facet of the theme I have been tracing. Privacy, ordinariness, anonymity are all associated with the ability to accept and merge into one's surroundings. In 'Settling in England' Jacobson writes: 'What I chiefly feel toward England is gratitude: gratitude for its peace, its order, *even its indifference* [my italics]' (p. 27).

Like their author, many of the characters in Dan Jacobson's novels travel overseas, and in some cases settle there. In *Evidence of Love* the plot hinges on the love that develops between a 'coloured' man and a white girl, both from Lyndhurst (Jacobson's fictional Kimberley). In that hierarchical, segregated town the two meet briefly as employer's daughter and the humiliated, insubordinate son of a jobbing 'coloured' handyman. In London, however, they meet as equals (she does not at first recognise him and takes him to be white) in the nondescript, seedy surroundings of a language school. The plot deals mainly with Kenneth's guilt-ridden decision to return with his white wife as an illegally married second-class citizen to his country and his people. They reject him, and both he and Isabel are sentenced to terms of imprisonment for immoral cohabitation. The main interest in the story is certainly not on the adaptations they have to make to life in England. But the freedom and privacy which that country offers them in contrast to their own is always implied. During his guilty courtship of the woman to whom he at first cannot confess his real identity, one of the most satisfying features of the London in which Kenneth is falling in love is that here their love is not the headlined horror it would be in Lyndhurst. Its ordinariness is what is so special:

> The uniqueness and the privacy of the love they were beginning to know, was Kenneth's pride, and so, too, was the commonness of what they were doing, their submission to a fate that was shared by every couple they passed in the street.[9]

In *Evidence of Love* it is obvious that Kenneth and Isabel will have to return to England after serving their terms. Kenneth has formally expiated his guilt of abandoning his family and kind in the desperate respectability of their modest corrugated iron homes in Lyndhurst's 'Coloured Camp'. His break with South Africa will have to be final, irrevocable. In Jacobson's later novel, *The Beginners*, the problem of leaving South Africa is returned to. But it is discussed with more complexity than is the crisis which faces Kenneth Makeer; and it involves questions of identity and fulfilment raised by several of its characters.

The Beginners describes the dissatisfaction felt by the second generation of a prosperous South African family of ex-Lithuanian Jews. The emptiness of life in post-war Johannesburg is particularly oppressive to the son, Joel, who has been in the army overseas. The novel traces his coming to terms with his sense of emptiness through a sojourn in Israel and final settling in London. But the sense of uneasiness and malaise among his Johannesburg acquaintances and student friends is beautifully woven through the book. Just as their feeling of confinement and vacancy is a continual presence in the earlier sections of the novel, so too there is a marvellously evocative *leitmotif* of the contrast between the frightened, empty, guarded, tomb-like night streets in the white suburbs and the noisy, crowded, vital and dangerous streets in the black areas.

The political reasons for Joel's turning away from South Africa are clear enough. And it is to Palestine and the new Israel that he first turns:

> Then, within the same month as the declaration of independence of the State of Israel, the Afrikaner Nationalists came into power in South Africa. Joel's reaction to the news of the Nationalist victory was a selfish one; it was almost one of relief. Now he knew he had been right to want to sever himself from this country; the country, in coming into the hands of the Afrikaner Nationalists, had severed itself from him. Everything that was least welcoming in it, everything that was most provincial, most bigoted, backward, barren, cramped, divisive and suspicious, had been given power.[10]

On this level the statement of Joel's motives is precise and organic to the mood of suffocating passivity which has been created around descriptions of his Johannesburg life. But on another level, Joel's urge to leave is much more complicated. Although he cannot join the middle-class assembly line to wealth, power or professional status in Johannesburg, he is perturbed by the apparent triviality of his rootless existence. The girl he ultimately marries in London does bring him tranquillity. But long before that he has a casual relationship with her in Johannesburg. Even there she exudes peace of a kind which he cannot yet comprehend (although she too is to suffer—through a disastrous first marriage—before her fulfilling union with Joel in London). During their South African period, it is her acceptance of the trivial and the ordinary which sets her apart from Joel. When he asks her what she is committed to, she replies that she is committed to whatever happens to her. 'And when it's trivial?' he asks. She replies, 'I'd hate more to miss anything because I was afraid it might be trivial. How can you tell? How do you know what a lot of trivialities put on top of each other might amount to?' (p. 122). The liberating effect of submitting to an ordinary life in the anonymity of London is strongly suggested at the end of the book. But during this early conversation Pamela has the last thematic word:

> I don't suppose you've ever thought that some people do what they do—whatever it is—for the sake of what they're doing, and do it as well as they can because that's exactly the way to make it worthwhile. You're just afraid of being ordinary, that's the trouble with you—and because you're afraid, you're less than ordinary, you're nothing at all. (p. 124)

She has accurately diagnosed Joel's problem, and it is fitting that she should offer him relief from it in an environment where he is not afraid to be ordinary. His history professor at the university in Johannesburg suggests to Joel the possibility of transcending the problem of self through scholarship, which is both personal and public—a part of the world at large. Through Professor Viljoen, Joel sees an image of a life 'filled with a personal involvement so total as to be dispassionate and disinterested; so unregarding of self as to be fully expressive of everything within him' (p. 135). But neither scholarship nor life on a kibbutz can give Joel peace of mind. Metropolitan London is different, however, and in it he marries and comes to terms with his guilt about South Africa, his collective Jewish past and his personality. Before they know they are in love with each other, Pamela and Joel walk on Primrose Hill. And the emotional shelter in the anonymity and indifference of the place is made quite clear. Joel says he does not want to return to South Africa:

> 'Because of the politics and everything else. Because I like it better here than there.' He added, adopting exaggeratedly the posture of a defeated politician, his hand on his heart, 'Because I've retired altogether from public life.'
> 'And you think this is the place to do it in?'
> 'Don't you think so?'
> She did not answer; she just said emphatically, 'I don't want to leave.' She moved away at once, having spoken; as if, Joel thought, the exposure of their position on the skyline challenged them to justify their choice. How could it be done in the face of that vast indifference, the city sprawled immeasurably beneath them. Yet the indifference was surely one of the reasons for their choice.
> (pp. 428–9)

There is more to this obsession with ordinariness than a mere commonplace about provincials breaking away from their past. Joel and many other characters in *The Beginners* are revolted by the provincialism of Johannesburg, but their sense of guilt and impotence in an ostensibly comfortable middle-class life is peculiarly South African. So too the complete rejection by Joel and others in the novel of professional, material or social success and importance in South Africa is typical of the alienation common in the work of the South African writers I have been discussing. In *The Beginners* the setting is less obviously outlandish than Plomer's Lembuland and less absurdly complacent than Campbell's Bananaland. But complacent and outlandish it still is, with a new prosperity and a new, institutionalised violence. The novel shows booming commercial and material success to be puffing into power and status both the seedy and the bland people from whom Joel and others like him feel most estranged in torpid, half-real Johannesburg society.

The theme I have been discussing is so insistent a feature in the work of the writers discussed that it is almost mannered.[11] All of those writers knew life in a South Africa more closely involved with Britain and British ways than it is today. The Sharpeville emergency in 1960 and the change to a Republic are convenient symbols of the complete turning away from British ways which the Nationalist government began in 1948. Dan Jacobson and Nadine Gordimer write about events in post-Sharpeville South Africa, and record them with great accuracy and insight. Nadine Gordimer in particular continues to explore new themes in both *The Late Bourgeois World* and *The Conservationist*. The former sums up the impasse of white English-speaking culture in the sixties after the spectacular failure of 'liberal' sabotage, and the latter opens a new elegiac discussion on continuing white possession in the seventies. But the sensibilities of both authors were formed in a more humane environment in which the example of the metropolitan model was more accessible. Bizarre though life still is in white South Africa, it is less obviously copied than it was. Anna Louw's complaint in *A World of Strangers* that Johannesburg has no *genre* of its own is probably less true. This is certainly not a compliment; in addition to indigenous films and magazines, the Johannesburg *genre* now includes Radio South Africa, the absence (at the time of going to press) of television, and the banning or heavy cutting of almost all vogue films. In a way this increases the outlandishness of milieu with which a writer has to deal. But the appeal of metropolitan anonymity is also less strong because it, too, is farther away.

The current interest in the writing of black South Africans coincides with the success of a new kind of South African thriller by Peter Driscoll and J. McClure. These thrillers show no trace of the obsession I have been discussing. They use the stage props of the police state as an exotic background for its own sake. *The Wilby Conspiracy* opens with the escape of a political prisoner from Robben Island and follows his fortunes from that point in the manner of a skilful, glossy screen script. No sense of estrangement is possible in this *genre*. One of the more interesting works to appear recently by a black South African writer is D. M. Zwelonke's *Robben Island*, which uses the brutal facts of life on that notorious prison in a searing indictment of its monstrous in-humanity. Again, no sense of estrangement is possible in such a com-mitted work, written by one of the regime's victims. All the writing of black South Africans has this sense of commitment which distinguishes it so completely from the works I have been discussing. Even accounts of life in the black areas of an officially white country inevitably involve an element of protest and outrage. Not only does this facet of black life distinguish literary accounts of it, but also that life itself is less derivative than the life of the English-speaking white world. Township life cannot be a distant copy of another metropolitan model. It is as unique as the pass laws.[12]

One wonders whether the next generation of English-speaking white writers will describe a world of estrangement in the same way as did their predecessors. Perhaps with the withering of Commonwealth ties and the waning of English culture in South Africa the sense of estrange-ment will diminish for English-speaking white writers. And Dan Jacobson's description in *Evidence of Love* will cease to apply: 'England is like a mirror in which they see their deepest selves reflected, the selves they have sought for and never found, and have known only by the sense of incompleteness that haunted all their previous days' (p. 131).

Notes

1   Jack Cope and Uys Krige, editors, *The Penguin Book of South African Verse*, Harmondsworth, Penguin Books, 1968, pp. 103–4.

2   William Plomer, *Turbott Wolfe*, 1925, rept. London, Hogarth Press, 1965, p. 113.

3   Roy Campbell, *Collected Poems*, Volume One, London, Bodley Head, 1949, p. 24.

4   Even Turbott Wolfe imagines that an inconspicuous London life will offer him some relief after his defeat in Lembuland. Wolfe tells his storeman, Caleb, that he has to leave his trading station and aban-don Africa: 'I have just enough money to go and live quietly in Eng-land. I shall live in London. I shall dress neatly and inconspicuously, but with distinction' (p. 200).

5   Jillian Becker, *The Keep*, 1967, rept. Harmondsworth, Penguin Books, 1971, p. 66.

6   Nadine Gordimer, *The Lying Days*, New York, Simon and Schuster, 1953, p. 10.

7 Nadine Gordimer, *A World of Strangers*, 1958, rept. Harmondsworth, Penguin Books, 1962, p. 197.

8 Dan Jacobson, 'Settling in England', *Commentary*, 29, 1960, pp. 23–24.

9 Dan Jacobson, *Evidence of Love*, Boston and Toronto, Little, Brown and Company, 1960, p. 186.

10 Dan Jacobson, *The Beginners*, 1966, rept. Harmondsworth, Penguin Books, 1968, p. 237.

11 Athol Fugard's plays do not fall within the pattern that I have been describing. Not only do they deal exclusively with the wretched on both sides of the colour bar, but they also establish their own bizarre norms of personal interdependence in the mode of Pinter and Albee. Fugard's work is *sui generis*, and its dramatic effectiveness often seems to transcend its South African context in spite of the welter of political material which it contains.

12 Ezekiel Mphahlele's novel, *The Wanderers*, offers a pointed contrast to those I have been discussing. It deals with the decision of its Black hero to leave South Africa and settle elsewhere. He moves to West Africa where he revels in his new-found freedom and dignity, but where he misses the closeness of his old South African slum community. In particular, he worries about the difficulty he has in becoming a part of the West African community which has strong traditions of its own. He takes a short trip to London and meets the 'pathetic colony' of exiles and refugees from South Africa:

> Timi did not bring back any fond memories of London at all. That South African English accent the whites spoke, which constantly assailed him as he moved among the exiles irritated him as it had never done in his home country. When he was through with seeing people and was compelled to move among things like museums and parks and art galleries, he decided to leave. He could not tolerate the sight of things as an institution for long; he was always wanting to be surrounded by people; often he wanted this desperately. He could not survive in a condition of anonymity. He wanted just as many people as could feel his presence and give him a sense of community. (Ezekiel Mphahlele, *The Wanderers*, New York, Macmillan, 1971, p. 234.)

Nadine Gordimer

Writers in South Africa:
The New Black Poets

> Poetry does indeed have a very special place in this country. It arouses people and shapes their minds. No wonder the birth of our new intelligentsia is accompanied by a craving for poetry never seen before. . . . It brings people back to life.

This was written of the contemporary Soviet Union by Nadezhda Mandelstam, widow of the poet Osip Mandelstam, in her autobiography, *Hope Against Hope*. But perhaps the same might be said of the new poetry being written in South Africa by black South Africans. Three individual collections have been published within recent months. I know of at least two more that are forthcoming. An anthology representative of the work of eleven poets is in the press at the time of writing. Poems signed with as yet unknown names crop up in the little magazines; there are readings at universities and in private houses, since the law doesn't allow blacks to read to whites or mixed audiences in public places. For the first time, black writers' works are beginning to be bought by ordinary black people in the segregated townships, instead of only by liberal or literary whites and the educated black elite.

In the 1950s and early 1960s prose writing by black South Africans was some of the best on the continent. Nearly all those seminal black writers went into exile in the sixties, and their works are banned. The lopping-off of a young indigenous tradition—as distinct from the central tradition of the European language the black writer uses—has had a stunting effect on prose writing. No fiction of any real quality has been written since then by a black writer still living in South Africa. It seems that a certain connection has been axed between black fiction writers and their material. Aspirant writers are intimidated not only by censorship as such but also by the fear that anything at all controversial, set out by a black in the generally explicit medium of prose, makes the writer suspect, since the correlation of articulacy and political insurrection, so far as blacks are concerned, is firmly lodged in the minds of the Ministers of the Interior, Justice and Police. Polymorphous fear cramps the hand. Would-be writers are so affected that they have ignored gigantic contemporary issues that have set their own lives awash. Such stories as there are, for example, repulp the clichés of the apartheid situation—the illicit drinking den, the black-white love affair—that have been so thoroughly blunted by overuse in literature good and bad that they can be trusted to stir the censors and the police as little as they can be trusted to fire the people's imagination. Meanwhile, apartheid has bulldozed on over black lives since the 1960s, and brought experiences such as forced mass resettlement that makes the shebeen and the bedroom marginal by comparison.

Out of this paralytic silence, suspended between fear of expression and the need to give expression to an ever greater pressure of grim experience, has come the black writer's subconscious search for a form less vulnerable than those that led a previous generation into bannings and exile. In other countries, writers similarly placed have found a way to survive and speak through the use of different kinds of prose forms. Perhaps, if black writing had not been so thoroughly beheaded and truncated in the sixties, there would have been creative minds nimble enough to keep it alive through something like the *skaz*—a Russian genre, dating from Czarist times, which concentrates a narrative of wide-ranging significance in a compressed work that derives from an oral tradition of story-telling, and takes full advantage of the private and double meanings contained in colloquial idiom. Both the oral tradition and the politically-charged idiom exist in black South Africa.

Or the solution might have been found in the adoption of the Aesopean genre—as in a fable, you write within one set of categories, knowing your readers will realise that you are referring to another, an area where explicit comment is taboo. Camus used this device in *La Peste*, and again, Stalin's generation of writers learned to be dab hands at it.

The cryptic mode is a long-established one; it has been resorted to in times and countries where religious persecution or political oppression drives creativity back into itself, and forces it to become its own hiding-place, from which, ingenious as an oracle, a voice that cannot be identified speaks the truth in riddles and parables not easily defined as subversive. In South Africa there are 97 definitions of what is officially 'undesirable' in literature: subversive, obscene, or otherwise 'offensive'. They are not always invoked, but are there when needed to suppress a particular book or silence an individual writer. Seeking to escape them, among other even more sinister marks of official attention, black writers have had to look for survival away from the explicit if not to the cryptic then to the implicit; and in their case, they have turned instinctively to poetry. Professor Harry Levin defines a poem as 'a verbal artifact' whose 'arrangement of signs and sounds is likewise a network of associations and responses, communicating implicit information'. In demotic non-literary terms, a poem can be both hiding-place and loud-hailer. That was what black writers within South Africa were seeking.

There will be many people whose toes will curl at this crude prag-matic conception of how poetry comes to be written. One cannot simply 'turn' to poetry. It is simply not there, available to anybody with a few hours of home study to spare, like a correspondence course in accountancy or learning to play the recorder. As a prose writer, I don't need reminding of the levels of literature, where poets sit on Kili-manjaro. That snowy crown is not within reach of everyone who wants to write; even those who can start a grassfire across the prose plain will find themselves short of oxygen up at that height.

Poetry *as a last resort* is indeed a strange concept; and a kind of inversion of the enormous problems of skill and gifts implied in electing to write poetry at all. Many who are doing so in South Africa today are not poets at all, merely people of some talent attempting to use certain conventions and unconventions associated with poetry in order to express their feelings in a way that may hope to get a hearing. One of them, James Matthews, has said:

> To label my utterings poetry
> and myself a poet
> would be as self-deluding
> as the planners of parallel development.
> I record the anguish of the persecuted
> whose words are whimpers of woe
> wrung from them by bestial laws.
> They stand one chained band
> silently asking one of the other
> will it never be the fire next time?

From the Icelandic saga to Symbolism, from a Chaucer creating English as a democratic literary medium to a Gunter Grass recreating areas of the German language debased by Nazi usage, writers in their place at the centre of their particular historical situation have been forced by this kind of empiricism and pragmatism to 'turn to' one form of expression rather than another.

There are two questions to ask of the black writers who have 'turned to' poetry in South Africa. In the five years since this spate of poetry began, these questions have been shown to be so bound together that I don't know which to put first. So, without prejudice at this point: Question—through the implicit medium of poetry, are black writers succeeding in establishing or re-establishing a black protest literature within South Africa? Question—are they writing good poetry?

These questions, as I have said, seem to have demonstrated an indivisibility that I hesitate to claim as a universal axiom. Where protest speaks from a good poem, even one good line, both questions are answered in a single affirmative. When Mandlenkosi Langa, in his 'Mother's Ode to a Still-born Child', writes:

> 'It is not my fault
> that you did not live
> to be a brother sister
> or lover of some black child
> that you did not experience pain
> pleasure voluptuousness and salt in the wound
> that your head did not stop a police truncheon
> that you are not a permanent resident of a prison island'

his irony says more than any tract describing in spent emotives the life-expectations of the black ghetto under white oppression in the police state. When, writing again of a new-born child already dead—symbol of the constant death-in-life that runs through this black poetry—Oswald Mbuyiseni Mtshali in 'An Abandoned Bundle' makes the image of dogs 'draped in red bandanas of blood' scavenging the body of a baby dumped on a location rubbish heap, he says more about black infant mortality than any newspaper exposé, and by the extension that the total vision of his poem provides, more about the cheapness of life where race is the measure of worth.

The themes chosen by the new black poets are committed in the main to the individual struggle for physical and spiritual survival under oppression. 'I' is the pronoun that prevails, rather than 'we', but the 'I' is the Whitmanesque unit of multimillions rather than the exclusive first person singular. There is little evidence of group feeling, except perhaps in one or two of the young writers who are within SASO (South African Students' Organisation), the black student organisation whose politico-cultural manifesto is a combination of Negritude with Black Power on the American pattern.

The themes, like those of the poets who preceded the present generation (they were few in number and were forced into exile), are urban—although it is doubtful whether one can speak of the tradition or influence of a Kunene or a Brutus, here. Few of the young aspirants writing to-day have read even the early work of exiled writers: it was banned while they were still at school. The striking development of Dennis Brutus's later and recent work, for example, is unknown except to a handful of people who may have spotted a copy of Cosmo Pieterse's *Seven South African Poets* or *Thoughts Abroad* that has somehow slipped into a bookshop, although the statutory ban on Dennis Brutus would mean that the book itself is automatically banned.

It is axiomatic that the urban theme contains the classic crises: tribal and traditional values against Western values, peasant modes of life against the modes of an industrial proletariat, above all, the quotidian humiliations of a black's world made to a white's specifications. But in the work we are considering I believe there also can be traced distinct stages or stations of development in creating a black ethos strong enough to be the challenger rather than the challenged in these crises.

The starting-point is essentially post-Sharpeville—post-defeat of mass black political movements: the position that of young people cut off from political education and any objective formulation of their resentments against apartheid. The stations are three: distortion of values by submission to whites; rejection of distortion; black/white polarity—opposition on new ground.

In terms of the personal, immediate and implicit within which the poems move, the first station—distortion by submission—is often demonstrated by apartheid through the eyes of a child. Mike Dues writes in his poem 'This Side of Town':

> Rested near swinging
> sliding playground
> with eager-eyed black faces
> 'can we play on the swing'
> a cowing no
> in town the voice pleads
> 'I want to pee'
> a hackneyed no
> leads to the edge of town.

And James Matthews in 'Two Little Black Boys':

> Two little black boys
> standing in front of a public lavatory
> one not bigger than a grasshopper
> the other a head of hair taller
> you can't go in there
> the tall one said, pointing to the board
> it's white people only.

It is not insignificant that incidents such as this are written about again
and again. Through the recurrence of apparent trivialities in a child's
life, certain objects—a swing, a public lavatory—can be seen becoming
reified with the value of a sacred totem of white supremacy from whose
ground the black child learns he is excluded without knowing why. But
the question will come. James Matthews' poem ends:

> Puzzled, the grasshopper replied
> don't white people shit like me?

And Mike Dues, more ominously:

> Later the face stronger
> and voice bigger
> will ask why.

A child's three questions in one of Oswald Mtshali's poems 'Boy on a
Swing' —'Mother!/Where did I come from?/When will I wear long
trousers?/Why was my father jailed?'—illustrate by their unconscious
grouping how victimisation undergoes transformation into one of the
immutable mysteries of a natural order. The experience of these black
children takes on a dreadful logic as preparation for their sort of future
in Stanley Mogoba's poem 'Two Buckets' in which two buckets side by
side, one a lavatory, the other filled with drinking water, define prison
as a destination. Thrown into a cell at night, a man stumbles over the
buckets:

> In this startled manner
> I made my entry
> Into a dark world
> Where thousands of men
> Pine and are forgotten.

It is the world of the pass laws, and the pass document is not a
booklet of simple identification but a hateful possession that must be
cherished because one cannot live without it—another inversion of

values demanded by the white man. In 'City Johannesburg', Mongane Wally Serote addresses the white city:

> This way I salute you;
> My hand pulses to my back trouser pocket
> Or into my inner jacket pocket
> For my pass, my life
> . . . My hand like a starved snake rears my pockets
> . . . Jo'burg City, I salute you;
> When I run out, or roar in a bus to you,
> I leave behind me my love—
> My comic houses and people, my donga and my
>   ever-whirling dust
>
> My death
> That's as related to me as a wink to the eye.

The city as an environment of distortion as well as dispossession creates the image in Njabulo Ndebele's poem:

> I hid my love in the sewerage
> Of a city; and when it was decayed,
> I returned:
> I returned to the old lands.

Oswald Mtshali's country bird is shedding his identity along with his feathers when he takes a job as a city cleaner and says in 'The Moulting Country Bird':

> I wish
> I was not a bird
> red and tender of body
> with the mark of the tribe
> branded on me as fledgling
> hatched in the Zulu grass hut.
>
> Pierced in the lobe of the ear
> by the burning spike of the elderman;
> he drew my blood like a butcher bird
> that impales the grasshopper on the thorn.
>
> As a full fledged starling
> hopping in the city street,
> scratching the building corridor,

I want to moult
from the dung-smeared down
tattered like a fieldworker's shirt.
tighter than the skin of a snake
that sleeps as the plough turns the sod.

Boots caked with mud,
wooded stoppers flapping from earlobes
and a beaded little gourd dangling on a hirsute chest,
all to stoke the incinerator.

I want to be adorned
by a silken suit so scintillating in sheen,
it pales even the peacock's plumage,
and catches the enchanted eye
of a harlot hiding in an alley:
'Come! my moulten bird,
I will not charge you a price!'

Njabulo Ndebele, one of the youngest of the new writers, is surely speaking of the same man when he writes, in 'I hid my love in the sewerage':

O who am I? Who am I?
I am the hoof that once
Grazed in silence upon the grass
But now rings like a bell on tarred streets.

Ultimate submission is the acceptance of white materialist values as a goal while at the same time they are by definition unattainable. Again Mtshali has understood this incomparably. In much-imitated poems his city black wears shoes made in America, has a wife who uses lightening cream, a mistress, a car, but:

He knows
he must carry a pass.
He don't care for politics
He don't go to church
He knows Sobukwe
he knows Mandela
They're in Robben Island
'So what? That's not my business!'
('The Detribalized')

This city black does the 'Chauffeur Shuffle', 'a carving of blackwood/ in a peaked cap/ clutching the wheel of the white man's car in white-gloved hands'; he is 'Always a Suspect', dressed like a gentleman in white shirt and suit but trudging 'the city pavements/side by side with "madam"/who shifts her handbag from my side to the other/and looks at me with eyes that say /"Ha! Ha! I know who you are;/beneath those fine clothes ticks the heart of a thief." '

The Sartrian and Fanonist theory of realising oneself in terms of the Other, of becoming someone else's projection rather than oneself (the orphan Genet a thief because that is the image in which society recognises his existence) reaches its apogee in the term 'non-white'. That is the official identity of any South African who is black, brown, coffee-coloured or yellow. Mtshali's non-white describes himself:

> If I tell the truth
> I'm detestable.
> If I tell lies
> I'm abominable.
> If I tell nothing
> I'm unpredictable
> If I smile to please
> I'm nothing but an obsequious sambo.
>   ('Always a Suspect')

And he accepts his non-white non-value by seeing, in turn, fulfilment as the vantage point from which the white man makes this valuation:

> I want my heaven now,
> here on earth in Houghton and Parktown;
> a mansion
> two cars or more
> and smiling servants.
> Isn't that heaven? ('This Kid Is No Goat')

The ironic note of the last phrase—no trumpet call, but ringing in the ears just the same—serves to mark the transition to the second station in the development of the black ethos as reflected in these poets. Mike Dues uses irony both as approach and technique in a terse poem, 'You Never Know', that is at once also an anecdote and a wry joke. We are eavesdropping on a telephone call to a sports event booking service:

'Hello. Duncan Taylor here.
I want nine tickets for Saturday.'
'Nine you said. Hold on I'll check the booking.
I can give you eight in one row. One in front or back.'
'Thank you. I'll collect at the gate. How much?'
'Well, nine at R1.25. That is R11.25, Sir.'
'Why the difference? A friend paid seventy-five cents last night.'
'Oh! But that's non-white.'
'That's what we want.'
'I'm sorry, you sounded white.'

Soon the ironic note grows louder. Mandlenkosi Langa sets the scene in a 'Non-Whites' pension office with a white official behind the counter:

I lead her in
A sepia figure 100 years old.
Blue ice chips gaze
And a red slash gapes:
'What does she want?'
I translate: 'Pension, sir.'
'Useless kaffir crone,
Lazy as the black devil.
She'll get fuck-all.'
I translate.
'My man toiled
And rendered himself impotent
With hard labour.
He paid tax like you.
I am old enough to get pension.
I was born before the great wars
And I saw my father slit your likes' throats!'
I don't translate, but
She loses her pension anyhow. ('The Pension Jiveass')

The rejection of distortion of self, the rejection of reification, take many attitudes and forms. What has to be dismantled is three hundred years of spiritual enslavement; the poet is supremely aware that though the bricks and mortar of pass offices and prisons can be battered down, the bastille of Otherness must have its combination locks picked from within. And this is not easy. In creative terms, there is a casting about

for the right means. The reference of the metaphors of sexual love is
extended to become a celebration of blackness as a kind of personal
salvation, as in Njabulo Ndebele's love poems:

> I am sweeping the firmament with the mop
> of your kinky hair;
> . . . I shall gather you
> into my arms, my love
> and oil myself,
> Yea, anoint myself with the
> Night of your skin,
> That the dust of the soil may stick on me;
> That the birds of the sky may stick on me;
> . . . let me play hide-and-seek
> With an image of you in the
> Dark, plum-dark forests of
> your kinky hair,
> And I shall not want. ('Five Letters to M.M.M.)'

(Echoes here of Léon Damas' *Rendez-moi mes poupées noires*.) Another
means has been a use of the blues idiom of the Langston Hughes-
Bessie Smith era, resuscitated in 'cat' vocabulary by Black Power
writers in America.

Pascal Gwala uses it, writing from Durban:

> Been watching this jive
> For too long.
> That's struggle.
> West Street ain't the place
> To hang around any more
> . . . At night you see another dream
> White and Monstrous
> Dropping from earth's heaven,
> Whitewashing your own Black Dream.
> That's struggle.
> Struggle is when
> You have to lower your eyes
> And steer time
> With your bent voice.
> When you drag along—
> Mechanically.

Your shoulder refusing;
Refusing like a young bull
Not wanting to dive
Into the dipping tank
Struggle is keying your tune
To harmonize with your inside.
. . . Heard a child giggle at obscene jokes
Heard a mother weep over a dead son;
Heard a foreman say 'boy' to a labouring oupa
Heard a bellowing, drunken voice in an alley.
. . . You heard struggle.
Knowing words don't kill
But a gun does.
That's struggle.
For no more jive
Evening's eight
Ain't never late.
Black is struggle. ('Gumba Gumba Gumba')

Mongane Wally Serote uses the jazz beat but with vocabulary and imagery less derivative or obviously localised—generalised definitions of blackness, or anything else, are not for him. He puts a craftsmanlike agony to making-by-naming (Gerald Moore's and Ulli Beier's definition of the particular quality of African poetry) in a vocabulary and grammar genuinely shaped by black urban life in South Africa. There is a piercing subjectivity in his work, in which 'black as struggle' becomes at times an actual struggle with the limits of language itself. He can discipline himself to the device of plain statement:

White people are white people
They are burning the world.
Black people are black people
They are the fuel.
White people are white people
They must learn to listen.
Black people are black people
They must learn to talk. ('Ofay-Watcher, Throbs-Phase')

He can see the elements of an almost untainted black identity in the old people and children who are recurring lyrical motifs in his work. But when he seeks to recreate that identity by learning how it was destroyed, deeply wounded and marked himself, he wanders among the

signs of signs, the abstractions of abstraction. The persona of his poems
is often named 'Ofay-Watcher'—one who watches Whitey, a definition
that has overtones of the negative Non-White clinging to it like grave-
clothes around the resurrected. Ofay-Watcher says:

> I want to look at what happened;
> That done,
> As silent as the roots of plants pierce the soil
> I look at what happened,
> Whether above the houses there is always either smoke or dust,
> As there are always flies above a dead dog.
> I want to look at what happened.
> That done,
> As silent as plants show colour: green,
> I look at what happened,
> When houses make me ask: do people live there?
> As there is something wrong when I ask—is that man alive?
> I want to look at what happened,
> That done
> As silent as the life of a plant that makes you see it
> I look at what happened
> When knives creep in and out of people
> As day and night into time.
> I want to look at what happened,
> That done,
> As silent as plants bloom and the eye tells you: something
>   has happened.
> I look at what happened
> When jails are becoming necessary homes for people
> Like death comes out of disease,
> I want to look at what happened. ('Ofay-Watcher Looks Back')

Not only to look, but to express his findings in the long expletive of
'What's In This Black "Shit" ', gagging on its own bile of force-fed
humiliation:

> It is not the steaming little rot
> In the toilet bucket,
> It is the upheaval of the bowels
> Bleeding and coming out through the mouth
> And swallowed back,

Rolling in the mouth
Feeling its taste and wondering what's next like it.

Finally he turns the term 'black shit' on those who joined it:

I'm learning to pronounce this 'shit' well,
Since the other day
At the pass office
When I went to get employment,
The officer there endorsed me to Middleburg
So I said, hard and with all my might, 'Shit!'
I felt a little better;
But what's good is, I said it in his face.
A thing my father wouldn't dare do.
That's what's in this black 'Shit'.

The Word becomes Weapon. At times, for this writer, there is no calligraphy capable of containing the force of resentment and he destroys his very medium by exploding the bounds of coherence:

WORDS.
Trying to get out.
Words. Words. Words.
By Whitey
I know I'm trapped.
Helpless
Hopeless
You've trapped me Whitey! Meem wann ge aot Fuc
Pschwee ep booboodubooboodu blllll
Black books
Flesh blood words shitrrr Haai,
Amen. ('Black Bells')

You taught me language; and my profit on't| Is I know how to curse.
Not from the political platform or the prisoner's dock, but howling from the subconscious, hate is conjured up in Serote's work. Yet he himself is not free to hate; he is tormented by its necessity for the black in South Africa:

To talk for myself
I hate to hate
But how often has it been
I could not hate enough. ('That's Not My Wish')

Preoccupation with the metaphysics of hate belongs to the station of rejection of the distorted black self-image: James Matthews refers to the book he has published with Gladys Thomas as a collection of 'declarations' and the unspoken overall declaration is that of those who have learned how to hate enough, and to survive. His is the manifesto of the black ethos as challenger, confronting the white ethos on black ground. In a kind of black nursery jingle by Gladys Thomas, entitled 'Fall To-morrow', it speaks to blacks:

> Don't sow a seed
> Don't paint a wall
> To-morrow it will have to fall

and to whites:

> Be at home in our desert for all
> You that remade us
> Your mould will break
> And to-morrow you are going to fall.

The book is called *'Cry Rage!'* and the theme is often expressed in terms of actual and specific events. James Matthews is not diffident about taking a hold wherever he can on those enormous experiences of the long night of the black body-and-soul that prose writers have ignored. His obsession with the subject of resettlement is no more than an accurate reflection of the realities of daily life for the tens of thousands of blacks who have been moved by government decree to find shelter and livelihood in the bare veld of places dubbed Limehill, Dimbaza, Sada, Ilinge—often poetic names whose meanings seem to show malicious contempt for the people dumped there:

> Valley of plenty is what it is called;
> where little children display their nakedness
> and stumble around on listless limbs
> . . . where mothers plough their dead fruit into the soil
> their crone breasts dry of milk
> . . . where menfolk castrated by degradation
> seek their manhood in a jug
> of wine as brackish as their bile. ('Valley of plenty')

Njabulo Ndebele invokes the intimate sorrows of forced removal less obviously and perhaps more tellingly. Limehills, Dimbazas—these valleys of plenty seldom have adequate water supplies and the new 'inhabitants' often have to walk a long way to fetch water:

> There is my wife. There she is
> She is old under those four gallons of water,
> It was said taps in the streets
> Would be our new rivers.
> But my wife fetches the water
> (Down Second Avenue)
> We drink and we eat.
> I watch my wife: she is old. ('Portrait of Love')

And Oswald Mtshali also takes as subjects some dark current events. He uses the Aesopean mode to write devastatingly of a ghastly recent disaster anyone living in South Africa would be able to identify instantly, although its horrors are transliterated, so to speak, into Roman times. A year or two ago a prison van broke down on the road between Johannesburg and Pretoria; the policemen in charge went off to seek help, leaving the prisoners locked inside. It was a hot day; the van was packed; they died of suffocation while the traffic passed unconcerned and unaware:

> They rode upon
> the death chariot
> to their Golgotha—
> three vagrants
> whose papers to be in Caesar's empire
> were not in order.
>
> The sun
> shrivelled their bodies
> in the mobile tomb
> as airtight as canned fish.
>
> We're hot!
> We're thirsty!
> We're hungry!
>
> The centurion
> touched their tongues
> with the tip
> of a lance
> dipped in apathy:

'Don't cry to me
but to Caesar who
crucifies you.'

A woman came
to wipe their faces.
She carried a dishcloth
full of bread and tea.

We're dying!

The centurion
washed his hands. ('Ride Upon The Death Chariot')

James Matthews writes of the Imam Abdullah Haron, one of the number of people who have died while in detention without trial. He writes of 'dialogue' as 'the cold fire where the oppressed will find no warmth'. Perhaps most significantly, he reflects the current black rejection of any claim whatever by whites, from radicals to liberals, to identify with the black struggle.

They speak so sorrowfully about the
children dying of hunger in Biafra
but sleep unconcerned about the rib-thin
children of Dimbaza. ('They Speak so Sorrowfully')

And again, in a poem called 'Liberal Student Crap!':

The basis of democracy rests upon
Fraternity, Equality and not LSD
I should know fellows
Progressive policy the salvation of us all
You just don't understand
There's no-one as liberal as me
Some of my best friends are
Kaffirs, Coolies and Coons
Forgive me, I mean other ethnic groups
How could it be otherwise?
I'm Jewish; I know discrimination
From the ghetto to Belsen
So, don't get me all wrong
'Cause I know just how you feel
Come and see me sometime
My folks are out of town.

Whatever the justice of this view of young white people militant against apartheid—and increasing numbers of them are banned and restricted along with blacks—on the question of white proxy for black protest he has a final unanswerable word:

> can the white man speak for me?
> can he feel my pain when his laws
> tear wife and child from my side
> and I am forced to work a thousand miles away?
>
> does he know my anguish
> as I walk his streets at night
> my hand fearfully clasping my pass?
>
> is he with me in the loneliness
> of my bed in the bachelor barracks
> with my longing driving me to mount my brother?
>
> will he soothe my despair
> as I am driven insane
> by scraps of paper permitting me to live?
> ('Can The White Man Speak For Me?')

He does not spare certain blacks, either, nor fear to measure the fashionable against the actual lineaments of the black situation. He addresses one of the black American singers who from time to time come to South Africa and perform for segregated audiences:

> Say, Percy dad
> you ran out of bread that you got to
> come to sunny South Africa to sing soul
> or did you hope to find your soul
> in the land of your forefathers?
> . . . Say, Percy dad
> will you tell nina simone back home
> that you, a soul singer, did a segregated act
> or will you sit back flashing silver dollar smiles
> as they cart the loot from your Judas role to the bank.
> ('Say, Percy Dad')

And he accuses:

> my sister has become a schemer and
> a scene-stealer

. . . songs of the village
traded in for tin pan alley
black is beautiful has become as artificial as the wig she wears.
('My sister has become a schemer')

Matthews uses indiscriminately the clichés of politics, tracts, and popular journalism and these deaden and debase his work. But occasionally the contrast between political catchwords and brutal sexual imagery carries a crude immediacy:

democracy
has been turned
into a whore
her body ravished
by those who pervert her
in the bordello
bandied from crotch to hand
her breasts smeared
with their seed . . . ('Democracy has been turned into a whore')

And in the context of fanatical laws framed in the language of reason, within which he is writing, even clichés take on new meaning: they mock the hollowness of high-sounding terms such as 'separate development' or clinical ones such as 'surplus people'—the behaviouristic vocabulary that gives a scientific gloss to mass removals of human beings.

James Matthews is a paradigm of the black writer in search of a form of expression that will meet the needs of his situation by escaping strictures imposed on free expression by that situation. He is older than other writers I have discussed; more than a decade ago he was writing short stories of exceptional quality. There were signs that he would become a fine prose writer. Whatever the immediate reasons were for the long silence that followed, the fact remains that there was little or no chance that the themes from the cataclysmic life around him he would have wished to explore would not have ended up as banned prose fiction. He stopped writing. He seems to have accepted that for him to have dealt honestly in prose with what he saw and experienced as a coloured man slowly accepting the black heritage of his mixed blood as his real identity, might be written but could not be read. He is the man who wrote the words I quoted at the beginning of this survey: 'To label my utterings poetry/and myself a poet/would be self-deluding . . .'

He is indeed not a poet, although his old creative gifts, uneasy in a medium to which they are not suited, now and then transform his 'declarations' into something more than that. And so he is also an example of yet another distortion, this time within a black literature that expresses rejection of distortion and the assertion of new values for blacks: the black writer's gifts can be, and often are squeezed into interstitial convolutions that do not allow him to develop in the direction in which development is possible for him as an artist.

At its best, 'turning to poetry' has released the fine talents of an Mtshali and a Serote, a Dues and a young Ndebele. At its least, it has provided a public address system for the declarations of muzzled prose writers like Matthews. But if he stands where I have put him, as the symbolic figure of the situation of black writing, the sudden ban on his book '*Cry Rage!*' (during the very time when I was preparing these notes) suggest that black writing in South Africa may once again find itself come full circle, back again at a blank, spiked wall. This is the first book of poems ever to be banned within South Africa. If there were to be a lesson to be learned in a game where it seems you can't win for long, it would seem to be that only good writing with implicit commitment is equal both to the inner demands of the situation and a chance of surviving publication, whatever the chosen literary form.

In terms of a literary judgement, yes, it is never enough to be angry. But unfortunately this does not hold good as an assurance that black poetry of real achievement can continue to be published and read in South Africa. Some of the best writing ever done by South Africans of all colours has not escaped, on grounds of quality, banning in the past. Black Orpheus, where now? How? What next?

G. D. Killam

Notions of Religion, Alienation and Archetype in *Arrow of God*

What I first proposed to attempt in this paper was a comparison between two novels of widely differing backgrounds, Chinua Achebe's *Arrow of God* and Robertson Davies' *Fifth Business*. I had been reading these novels (along with others) with students in a course on Commonwealth Literature and a number of similarities between both the books and their authors struck me. The heroes of both books seek to find and, as far as it is possible, explain religious meaning. Both books deal with the emphasis placed on affluence and the pursuit of material ends which results in a sense of spiritual loss and personal alienation. I think it would be quite easy to show that, for both these writers, the alienation experienced by their heroes and indeed by most of the people in their books, proceeds from the same source—the unprecedented material progress which has been achieved since the Victorian period with the consequent social upheaval and loss of religious faith to which this gave rise. So the legacy of the encounter with Europe is common to both novels and accounts for much of what goes on in them. Other similarities between the two writers are apparent in their attempts to define what it is to be a modern writer of Canadian or Nigerian fiction and to show their readers, in Achebe's words, 'in human terms what happened to them, what they lost'. The parallels are not, of course, perfect, but a comparison, I think, could be sustained and would prove interesting.

But it was a specific statement by Robertson Davies in an interview with Donald Cameron which seemed to me to have as much bearing on *Arrow of God* as on Davies' own writing and suggested a useful way of looking at Achebe's book. Davies says:

> . . . and then I gradually began to look into the works of Jung and found a much more—to me—satisfying attitude toward religion, but it was not an orthodox Christian one. Orthodox Christianity has always had for me the difficulty that it really won't come, in

what is for me a satisfactory way, to grips with the problem of evil. It knows an enormous amount about evil, it discusses evil in fascinating terms, but evil is always the other thing: it is something which is apart from perfection, and man's duty is to strive for perfection. I could not reconcile that with such experience of life as I had, and the Jungian feeling that things tend to run into one another, that what looks good can be pushed to the point where it becomes evil, and that evil very frequently bears what can only be regarded as good fruit—this was the first time I'd ever seen that sort of thing given reasonable consideration, and it made enormous sense to me. I feel now that I am a person of strongly religious temperament, but when I say 'religious' I mean immensely conscious of powers of which I can have only the dimmest apprehension, which operate by means that I cannot fathom, in directions which I would be a fool to call either good or bad. Now that seems hideously funny, but it isn't really; it is, I think, a recognition of one's position in an inexplicable universe, in which it is not wholly impossible for you to ally yourself with, let us say, positive rather than negative forces, but in which anything that you do in that direction must be done with a strong recognition that you may be very, very gravely mistaken.[1]

Early in the novel Achebe has Ezeulu meditate on his status as Chief Priest of Ulu in a passage which foreshadows the course that the whole of the action of the novel is devoted to working out.

Whenever Ezeulu considered the immensity of his powers over the year and the crops and, therefore, over the people he wondered if it was real. It was true he named the day for the feast of the Pumpkin Leaves and for the New Yam feast; but he did not choose the day. He was merely a watchman. His power was no more than the power of a child over a goat that was said to be his. As long as the goat was alive it was his; he would find it food and take care of it. But the day it was slaughtered he would know who the real owner was. No! the Chief Priest of Ulu was more than that, must be more than that. If he should refuse to name the day there would be no festival—no planting and no reaping. But could he refuse? No Chief Priest had ever refused. So it could not be done. He would not dare.[2]

Arrow of God embodies a complex of forces, and dramatises the process whereby a homogeneous society under pressure from these forces is destroyed. The result is that man is alienated from his land, the product of his work (the novel would stand pretty careful scrutiny along Marxist lines), and from his fellow men. Most destructive of all, he is alienated from his religious beliefs which supply the ethical, moral and social bases of his society. In regard to the central position of religion and the profound need it fulfils in society, *Arrow of God* is perhaps a unique modern novel. Many modern works are concerned with the alienation which results from a loss of religious faith and with the substitutes which are sought (never satisfactorily) for this, but none so far as I know describes, as Achebe's novel does, the beginning, middle and ending of a religion and with it a way of life. Indefinable and intangible as the religion of Ulu ultimately is (as with all religions), Ulu, and the system of beliefs and observances attached to him and expounded by his Chief Priest, was created to fulfil a specific purpose. The god was created by agreement to supersede other deities whose powers were not sufficient to provide protection against slave-raids which were endemic at the time of his creation. The religion unified and strengthened the people it served and who served it, sustaining them for several generations even when subjected to a number of specific internal pressures. But it is dramatically and inexorably cast aside when it fails to be functional, when it runs contrary to the consensus of opinion which created it in the first place.

Arrow of God is the most complex and difficult of Achebe's four novels and its complexity and difficulty arise most out of the dramatisation of the place of religion in Ibo society. At the level of realistic narrative *Arrow of God* is a continuation of *Things Fall Apart*—the quality and texture of traditional Ibo life are faithfully portrayed at the realistic and ritualistic level. We have presented a society with a stable system of values, with precedents of long-standing acceptance, supported by an oral tradition expressed often in proverbial fashion. But while he works at the realistic level Achebe also works at the levels of symbols. In *Things Fall Apart* Achebe reveals how, through white encroachment with its alien and more powerful system of government, law and Christian religion, coupled with the introduction of a cash economy, the traditional balance between the temporal and spiritual, the male principle of acquisitiveness of which Okonkwo is the archetype, and the female principle of religion embodied in Ani, the Earth Goddess, is upset. Achebe has written in this connection:

Ibo society has always been materialistic. This may sound strange because Ibo life had at the same time a strong spiritual dimension—

controlled by gods, ancestors, personal spirits or *chi* and magic. The success of the culture and the balance between the two, the material and the spiritual. . . . Today we have kept the materialism and thrown away the spirituality which should keep it in check.[3]

The exploration of the process of disintegration, initiated in *Things Fall Apart*, is carried through the four novels so that by the time of *A Man of the People*, the religious element in Ibo life, symbolised by the masks which represent the continuity and quality of religious experience of the society, is rendered inconsequential. We need only look at the scene in Chief Nanga's compound on Christmas Day (in *A Man of the People*) where the masks are reduced to the status of entertainers, and compare this with the scene showing the destruction of Okonkowo's compound in *Things Fall Apart*, to understand how complete has been the disintegrative process and to understand, in the context of the novel, how unrestrained acquisitiveness has come to prevail.

Arrow of God is poised in time between the other two novels: Christian imperialism has established itself and the alienation process at the societal level is under way. It is shown in a variety of subtle ways, none of which obtrude on the novel's central enquiry. *Arrow of God* catches this sequence poised at the point when the traditional mode of existence is being replaced by a modern form. Marxist interpreters claim that the first organised system of alienation was slavery and that the last will be wage labour. In *Arrow of God* the process is in the middle: wage labour is coming in various forms—in the wages, paltry as they are, paid to workers on the road, and to servants in the homes of Europeans; there is even enforced labour as when Obika and his age set are commandeered to work on the road. The wish to get established in the cash economy is expressed in the desire of John Nwodika to establish himself in the tobacco trade.

But the principal purpose of *Arrow of God* is to explore the 'relationship between a god and his priest', to examine the 'old question of who shall decide what shall be the wish of the gods. . . .' Ezeulu epitomises the values of his society, just as Okonkwo did in the first novel, but from a different point of view, that of the spiritual life of the Ibo. Ezeulu ponders the reality of this life which extends from his innermost being to encompass all the six villages. The extent of this power, unspecified and enigmatic as all such power is, is suggested in the passage cited above on the nature of the power which Ezeulu possesses and his wonder over its reality. The power he possesses and the role he fulfils has the effect of isolating Ezeulu from the community from the outset. Even to Akuebue, his closest and perhaps his only friend, Ezeulu remains a mystery, likened to a 'madman laughing on a solitary path'. Ezeulu claims that loneliness is as familiar to him as are corpses to the earth:

> I have my own way and I shall follow it. I can see things where other men are blind. That is why I am Known and at the same time I am Unknowable. You are my friend and you know whether I am a thief or a murderer or an honest man. But you cannot know the Thing which beats the drum to which Ezeulu dances. (p. 163)

One is able both to distinguish the various qualities and elements of Umuaro life and at the same time to view them as facets or aspects of its chief priest. And this is consolidated within Ezeulu's own compound in the disparate natures of Ezeulu's own sons. Edogo, the somewhat sullen first-born, and Obika, the handsome and aggressive second son, can be taken to represent the meditative and active facets of Ezeulu's personality, or what one might describe as the masculine and feminine sides of his nature. Throughout the novel Obika and Edogo are constantly compared by Ezeulu and by the villagers as well. These facets of personality show themselves in various ways in the novel and operate to explicate and elaborate Ezeulu's personality and function. For example, in a fit of ill-will towards his father, Edogo recalls a saying of his mother about Ezeulu (echoed in many comments by other characters) which reveals the fundamental element in his nature, the one which ultimately cracks his mind:

> . . . Ezeulu's only fault was that he expected everyone—his wives, his kinsmen, his children, his friends and even his enemies—to think and act like himself. Anyone who dared say no to him was an enemy. He forgot the saying of the elders that if a man sought for a companion who acted entirely like himself he would live in solitude. (p 114)

Edogo is the passive facet of Ezeulu's being. Ezeulu acknowledges in the imagery of fire begetting ash, that 'hot' must have 'cold' to establish its own reality and that the two sons are an organic entity born of the same fire. And while Edogo's refusal to fight infuriates Ezeulu, he nevertheless sees that much of his own spiritual quality is revealed in Edogo's desire to commune with the ancestral spirits, in the peace he achieves in the solitude of the spirit house, and in his ability to give himself totally to his art as a carver. The complexity of his nature is revealed, for example, in his reactions to the mask he carves for Agaba. He is troubled by the gentleness in the features which he judges to be out of place in the kind of mask he is creating. He refuses a seat in the *okwolo* in order to be free to move around and see his mask in action. The scene seems another way of suggesting the necessity of achieving a balance between the male and female principles as a dynamic in the society.

> There was something about the nose which did not please him—a certain fineness which belonged not to an Agaba but to a Maiden Spirit. . . . Looking at it now that it had come to life the weakness seemed to disappear. It even seemed to make the rest of the face more fierce. (pp. 250–1)

Obika, on the other hand, is always associated with things masculine and most resembles his father in looks and temperament. Edogo uses the same words to describe Ezeulu as the father uses to describe Obika— neither of them could look away from trouble. That they were so much alike in temperament accounts for the constant contention and argument between them. When, for example, the wicked medicine man, Otakekepeli, appears at the Agaba festival it is Obika, prowling 'like a leopard' who attacks him, causing Ezeulu, 'biting his lips', to observe: 'It would be Obika, he thought, the rash, foolish Obika. Did not all the other young men see Otakekepeli and look away? But his son could never look away.'

Yet even while condemning Obika's temper and impulsiveness, Ezeulu nevertheless finds him preferable to the 'cold ash' of Edogo. When berating Edogo for his lack of action at the Nkwa market, Ezeulu's temper shows itself like that of Obika.

> 'Don't you hear him?' asked Ezeulu of no one. 'My first son, somebody says to your hearing that your father has committed an abomination, and you ask me what you should have done. When I was your age I would have known what to do. I would have come out and broken the man's head instead of hiding in the spirit-house.' (p. 64)

This aggressiveness, shared by Ezeulu and Obika, is one feature of Ibo life which accounts for its continuity. And it is this which is sacrificed to the new order in Obika's death and the mental collapse of Ezeulu. Obika's death and what it will imply have been foreshadowed in his being likened to a sacrificial ram. Offended by Wright's actions, while working for him on the new road, Obika drops his matchet and instinctively charges the white man:

> At the same time Mr Wright's two assistants jumped in quickly and held Obika while he gave him half a dozen more lashes on his bare back. He did not struggle at all; he only shivered like the sacrificial ram which must take in silence the blows of funeral dancers before its throat is cut. (p. 101)

Obika is thus offered in symbolic form on the altar of the Christian God.

Oduche, the least favoured son, represents Ezeulu's understanding of the leprous nature of the white man's handshake. He has been sent to the mission school to be his father's 'eye and ear' there and to learn the white man's ways. But there is more to it than this. Edogo suggests to Akuebue that Ezeulu wishes Oduche out of the way so that Nwafo, the youngest of the four, may succeed his father as priest of Ulu. Edogo further perceives what he fears his father does not; that is, in sending Oduche to the mission-school he, Ezeulu, is guilty of planting dissension among his children, similar in kind to that which informs the whole of society.

Confronted with Edogo's sentiments by Akuebue, Ezeulu reveals he has a deeper purpose. This is the central speech in the novel. It demonstrates the extent to which Ezeulu will go to preserve his religion. It specifies the terrifying risk he is prepared to take to achieve this: he will use Oduche if need be in the way his forefathers used a kinsman to establish and enforce their faith. The speech, moreover, suggests the impenetrable ambiguities which constitute faith and belief. And the imagery connected with Oduche and the Christians is that of sacrifice and similar in kind to that associated with Obika. Seen in this context Ezeulu is the agent of resolving the conflict between two contending faiths as it is worked out in an apocalyptic contest in which he deliberately places his two sons as the principal pawns.

> 'Shall I tell you why I sent my son? Then listen. A disease that has never been seen before cannot be cured with everyday herbs. When we want to make a charm we look for the animal whose blood can match its power; if a chicken cannot do it we look for a goat or a ram; if that is not sufficient we send for a bull. But sometimes even a bull does not suffice, then we must look for a human.

Do you think it is the sound of the death-cry gurgling through blood that we want to hear? No, my friend, we do it because we have reached the very end of things and we know that neither a cock nor a goat nor even a bull will do. And our fathers have told us that it may even happen to an unfortunate generation that they are pushed beyond the end of things, and that their back is broken and hung over a fire. When this happens they may sacrifice their own blood. This is what our sages meant when they said that a man who has nowhere else to put his hand for support puts it on his own knee. That was why our ancestors when they were pushed beyond the end of things by the warriors of Abam sacrificed not a stranger but one of themselves and made the great medicine which they called Ulu.'

Akuebue cracked his fingers and moved his head up and down. 'So it is a sacrifice,' he muttered. . . . (p. 165)

Both Edogo and Akuebue recognise the risk that Ezeulu is prepared to take and the high cost it will demand either way. The dramatic centre of the novel occurs in this scene, though there is no acknowledgement by the priest of the possible consequences of the gamble to himself. Akuebue points out the risk when he says to Ezeulu in reminding the priest that a great man's compound, especially if he is a leader, must embrace 'people of all minds' so that whatever tune is played, someone will always be ready to dance to its beat. At the level of conscious understanding Ezeulu knows this as well as anyone. But he does not give expression to his recognition.

Better than any of his people Ezeulu knows that the world is changing. Since the land dispute with Okperi, the fighting that resulted and the intercession of Winterbottom, Ezeulu has felt that Umuaro is 'challenging its "chi" '. He says that 'the world is spoilt and there is no longer head or tail in anything that is done'. Thus the gamble he is prepared to take and thus Achebe ascribes a sense of the inevitability of fate to the life of Ezeulu, the destruction (or desertion) of Ulu and the ultimate destruction of the traditional life of Umuaro. Speaking to Ezeulu of the demands made on the villagers by Ulu after the priest has been released from jail, Ofaka says that the people are trying to obey two calls at once. And this sums up the conflict in Ezeulu's own mind, and accounts for his long period of deliberation about whether or not he will punish Ulu, who intercedes, to delay the New Yam festival.

The intervention of Ulu, who speaks for the first time to the priest is, if one chose to describe it in Jungian terms, the assertion of the Self, if we define this as the inner guiding factor that is different from the conscious personality. At the surface level Ezeulu has been appeased by the recognition his villagers have given him, the welcome they have offered on his return from prison. Just as his reaction against them on the surface level was not, because it was personal, sufficient justification for punishing them, so his abandonment of the plan makes simple good sense at the level of everyday conduct. But something more fundamental is at stake: the religion of Ulu itself. And Ulu must intercede at this point to make this plain to the priest. The situation is apocalyptic. The god may abscond: but a priest is a priest and in a contest as mighty as this one he must serve his god, whatever the consequences to him personally. So the god makes it plain to Ezeulu that despite the fact that the world is changing 'like a mask dancing' his first responsibility is to lead Umuaro and to confront the danger. It is ironic that it is Oduche's teacher who tells the villagers to harvest their yams 'in the name of the son' and when Oduche is sent from his father's presence in shame for failing to tell his father that this is so, just before Obika's death, the ending and the outcome of the contest is symbolically fore-shadowed. Perhaps at the deepest level of apprehension Ezeulu knows that the changing world held no place for Ulu.

This notion is reinforced when one considers Nwafo, the fourth and youngest of the sons. He has been chosen, in so far as it is possible for Ezeulu to choose, to be his father's successor as chief priest. Nwafo leans intuitively towards the celebration of Ulu and is unobtrusively but almost constantly present in his father's *obi*. It is because of his intuitive attachment to the god that Ezeulu designates him as a possible, even likely, successor. It is Nwafo who most keenly misses his father when Ezeulu is in prison. And it is Nwafo, stifling his instinctive re-action, who inadvertently and ironically precipitates the famine, the tragedy of his father and the collapse of the religion. He watches in the absence of his father for the New Moon:

> . . . as dusk came down Nwafo took his position where his father always sat. He did not wait very long before he saw the young thin moon. It looked very thin and reluctant. Nwafo reached for the *ogene* and made to beat it but fear stopped his hand. (p. 205)

Fear, which is a luxury that Ezeulu does not permit himself, protects Nwafo from the fate which overtakes his father.

We have seen that there are important symbolic associations con-nected with the recurring image of the dancing masks and the sacrificial ram which involve Ezeulu, Obika and Edogo. These associations act as unifying agents in the novel and serve to contrast the opposing natures of the sons with that of their father and to describe each as a facet of the symbolic sacrifice in which each becomes involved. Nwafo, too, becomes involved in an incident connected with the imagery of the ram when village children substitute Ezeulu's name in a song which is used to taunt the Udo rams.

> . . . he [Obielue] put Ezeulu's name in the song children sang whenever they saw an Udo ram, one of those fierce animals that belonged to the shrine of Udo and could come and go as they wished. Children enjoyed teasing them from a good distance. The song, which was accompanied by clapping of hands, implored the ram to remove the ugly lumps in its scrotum. To which the singers answered (on behalf of the ram): How does one remove yam tubers? The request and the response were sung in time with the swinging of the tubers. In place of *ebunu* Obielue sang *Ezeulu*. Nwafo could not stand this and gave his friend a blow in the mouth which brought blood to his front teeth. (p. 264)

The children's song is used to foreshadow the final sacrifice. And as the climax of the conflict is reached everyone in Ezeulu's household feels enclosed in the hostility of the six villages. All the family are made to feel Ezeulu's guilt and isolation. The intensity of the hostility, and the shaping climax, are specified in Ezeulu's recognition that the atmosphere permeating Ulu's shrine is intensified by the sound of the Christian bell:

> As Ezeulu cast his string of cowries the bell of Oduche's people began to ring. For one brief moment Ezeulu was distracted by its sad, measured monotone and he thought how strange it was that it should sound so near—much nearer than it did in his compound. (p. 263)

The end is reached with Obika's death. Running as Ogbazulobodo, despite his fever and yet determined to act in support of his father, his family and his faith, Obika transcends himself, feels as if he were two persons 'one running above the other'. As he runs, Obika's life passes before his eyes and he achieves a sort of ultimate illumination where he is at once blind and full of sight. This illumination is supported by the seeming chaotic flood of images and proverbs which pass through his mind as he runs. The completion of the ritual and his death come at the same moment and with them the end of the religion. Ulu, in allowing the death of Obika, has absconded and this recognition is more than the mind of the priest can take.

> The matchet fell from his hand and he slumped down on both knees beside the body. 'My son,' he cried. 'Ulu, were you there when this happened to me?' He hid his face on Obika's chest. . . . Ezeulu sank to the ground in utter amazement. It was not simply the blow of Obika's death, great though it was. Men had taken greater blows; that was what made a man a man. They say a man is like a funeral ram which must take whatever beating comes to it without opening its mouth; only the silent tremor of pain down its body tells of its suffering. (pp. 284–6)

The god has claimed his harvest and it is the Christian God that reaps it. The public and political opportunities in the worsening situation in Umuaro have not been lost on Goodcountry the missionary who allows the pagans to harvest their wasting crops if they will only serve Christ. Ezeulu has been sacrificed on the altar of something greater than his own will or ability to resist. One wonders at the end, in the bow of which god he has been the arrow? The questions posed by Ezeulu at the outset of the novel and cited above are not answered— they are by their nature incapable of ultimate solution; but possible answers are rendered ambiguously in the rage of questions and doubts which assail Ezeulu's mind before it cracks:

> Why, he asked himself again and again, why had Ulu chosen to deal thus with him, to strike him down and cover him with mud? What was his offence? Had he not divined the god's will and obeyed it? When was it ever heard that a child was scalded by the piece of yam its own mother put in its palm? What man would send his son with a potsherd to bring fire from a neighbour's hut and then unleash rain on him? Who ever sent his son up the palm tree to gather nuts and then took an axe and felled the tree? But today such a thing had happened before the eyes of all. What could it point to but the collapse and ruin of all things? Then a god, finding himself powerless, might take to his heels and in one final, backward glance at his abandoned worshippers cry:

> > If the rat cannot flee fast enough
> > Let him make way for the tortoise! (p. 286)

The book is about the place of religion in society and the nature of religion. Ultimately, then Ezeulu's relationship with, and response to, his deity is no more easily comprehended than that, say, of Moses with Jehovah. The universal quest for understanding is a continuing one. Ezeulu has gambled and lost and he does not understand why this is so. In the end Akuebue's recognition that 'when brothers fight a stranger inherits their father's estate' is proven. He is talking about consequences and not causes. So are the leaders and villagers of Umuaro when they interpret the fate which overtakes Ezeulu in these terms:

> To them the issue was simple. Their god had taken sides with them against his headstrong and ambitious priest and thus upheld the wisdom of their ancestors—that no man however great was greater than his people; that no man ever won judgement against his clan. (p. 287)

Achebe's novel is a particularly good example of the forces of modernism at work in the contemporary novel for the reasons I suggested above: it shows a culture intact at its opening wherein general accord about the policies and proscriptions of life and living are agreed upon. At the end, Ibo society is smashed and an important part, perhaps the finest part, is lost. At the end of this novel another god is found and the alienation process continues by the cultivation of the pursuits which were operative in destroying Ezeulu and causing Ulu to flee. One senses that Ezeulu is happier in his madness (and in this state he is a reminder to those who care to bear witness to him) than if he had been left to understand the destruction of his culture in the name of civilisation, religion and progress.

Two quotations by Jung discussing this process and its consequences seem particularly relevant here in describing the course of events in Ibo life which Achebe's four novels reveal. The first reads:

> Modern man does not understand how much his 'rationalism' (which has destroyed his capacity to respond to numerous symbols and ideas) has put him at the mercy of the psychic 'underworld'. He had freed himself from 'superstition' (or so he believes), but in the process he has lost his spiritual values to a positively dangerous degree. His moral and spiritual tradition has disintegrated, and he is now paying the price for this break-up in world-wide disorientation. [4]

And the second:

Anthropologists have often described what happens to a primitive society when its spiritual values are exposed to the impact of modern civilization. Its people lose the meaning of their lives, their social organization disintegrates, and they themselves morally decay. (p. 84)

But Achebe's purpose seems to be to do more than simply explore the nature of religion and the function of a priest in expounding it. He is on record in a variety of places in stating his conception of the artist's function in society. And the burden of his writing seems to be to direct readers to the recognition that what has been lost might be regained with time and through deliberate action. He says, for example, that

Those who want to resurrect an illustrious ancestor to grace their celebration may sometimes receive a great shock when the illustrious ancestor shows up. But, I think, it is still necessary that he should appear. What I have said must not be understood to mean that I do not accept the present day as a proper subject for the novelist. . . . But what I mean is that owing to the peculiar nature of our situation it would be futile to try and take off before we have repaired our foundations. We must first set the scene which is authentically African; then what follows will be meaningful and deep. This, I think, is what Aimé Césaire meant when he said that the short cut to the future is via the past.[5]

Jung's notion that so-to-say primitive society is more whole because closer to its roots and that the consequences of mechanisation and affluence (or the faith in these and the quest for them) which in turn promotes isolation, alienation and lack of communication is implicit in this comment. Jung further suggests that the price modern man pays for trying to get rid of his gods and demons is high.

. . . in recent times civilized man has acquired a certain amount of will power, which he can apply where he pleases. He has learned to do his work efficiently without having recourse to chanting and drumming to hypnotize him into the state of doing. He can even dispense with a daily paper for divine aid. He can carry out what he proposes to do, and can apparently translate his ideas into action without a hitch, whereas the primitive seems hampered at each step by fears, superstitions, and other unseen obstacles to action. . . .
Yet, in order to sustain his creed, contemporary man pays the

price in a remarkable lack of introspection. He is blind to the fact
that, with all his rationality and efficiency, he is possessed by
'powers' that are beyond his control. His gods and demons have
not disappeared at all; they have merely got new names. They
keep him on the run with restlessness, vague apprehensions,
psychological complications, an insatiable need for pills, alcohol,
tobacco, food—and, above all, a large array of neuroses.[6]

All of these modes of action and reaction specify the isolation of the
individual and his alienation not only from the group but from a
unifying system of belief, whether in the religious or the general societal
mode. The most tragic form of alienation, represented by Ezeulu's
ultimate madness, is loss of the capacity to communicate.

The capacity to communicate has become the most fundamental
attribute of man, of his quality as a human being. Without communication, there can be no organized society because without
communication there is no language and without language there is
no intelligence.[7]

Achebe's novel represents the process of alienation as it happened
in Africa and there are many examples of this sort of fiction. In fact,
of novels set in the contemporary period coming out of Africa it is hard
to name one which is not about the alienation of the individual from
his society. The artist tries to find words to give expression to the sense
of alienation and to communicate in order to stave off madness and
despair. The quest for contact takes as many forms as there are sensibilities in search of the means to achieve it.

Notes

1 Donald Cameron, *Conversations with Canadian Novelists*, (part one),
   Toronto, MacMillan of Canada, 1973, p. 41.
2 Chinua Achebe, *Arrow of God*, London, Heinemann, 1964, pp. 3–4.
3 Chinua Achebe, 'The Role of the Writer in a New Nation', *Nigeria
   Magazine*, 81, June 1964, p. 159.
4 Carl G. Jung, *Man and His Symbols*, New York, Dell, 1972, p. 72.
5 Chinua Achebe, 'The Novelist as Teacher', *New Statesman*, 29
   January 1965, p. 2.
6 Carl G. Jung, *Man and His Symbols*, p. 71.
7 *Ibid.*

Kofi Awoonor

Tradition and Continuity in African Literature

We must make certain assumptions about the principle of continuity which seems to be at the heart of a great deal of our literature. By this I mean that the African writer creates within a cultural tradition, a tradition that defines its own aesthetics and functions. For literature and art in tradition were not limited in their role to a utilitarian system *per se*, but expressed the continued endurance of a certain theological order. More important, the art forms of the traditions had as their primary impulse a concern with a fundamental process of integration and survival, integration as opposed to a dichotomised process of evil and good, beautiful or ugly, and, furthermore, opposed to what I may call an itemistic concern, a fragmentation, and, therefore, to the destructive absolutism of a one-dimensional totality.

The traditional artist is both a technician and a visionary. There is no division between the two roles for him. His technical competence enables him to select and utilise material: words, wood, raffia, or whatever, which in themselves carry a spirituality or an innate essence. It is from here that the transformation into the visionary realm is primarily fed. Forms and motifs already exist in an assimilated time and world construct, and so he serves only as the instrument of transforming these into an artistic whole based on his own imaginative and cognitive world, a world which exists and has meaning only within the larger world. In this process, he releases the ambiguity of the larger communal world in the dynamic impulse of the details of the medium which will bear his stamp. He is not a visionary artist *per se*, like the European artist who projects into space and time structures which simply were not there before. There is no otherness locked in the private psyche of his vision. Individually, of course, there are perplexing moments when forms and motifs achieve a power over him, creating fear and apprehension. But the ultimate shaping spirit of the wider world concept of the community returns him to a resolution, to an integration (which per-

haps was briefly threatened but never really in danger), to a restoration
of calm and quietude which is necessary for the widening of the circle
into waves that ultimately will constitute the only human progress.
In this, the proper reality, therefore, is part of the process of transformation, fundamental to a combined physical and beyond physical
totality, defying fragmentation, defying time, defying space. And man,
therefore, is defined by the tree, by the beast, by the deity, but is never
all-powerful because there is no room for that kind of absolutist horror.
The transformation, the artistic process, entails a primary exchange
of energies through what we might call the magical projection. Shocks,
surprises, dislocations into irregularities, basic splinterings, and all kinds
of mercurial transmogrifications are essential aspects of the inner dynamics of the total process. Anyone who has read Amos Tutuola's books
will understand exactly what I am saying.

Everything is irreducible because everything counts. The process
therefore also encloses a self-generating ecstasy, moments of delirious
madness, the breaking of the formalities of the perceived reality. The
models of this lunacy exist in the artist, the carver, the storyteller, the
poet-cantor, the music maker. The crises of these models are over-
stepped, they are conquered, subdued if need be, for the calm
integration, the making of the units into one total whole, the reas-
semblement of the fragments, and, therefore, the restoration of the real
life.

The danger and the joy are part of the same indivisibility. Raymond
DeChamp-Villon's remark, 'The sole purpose of the arts is neither
description nor imitation but the creation of unknown beings which
are always present but never apparent,' stood on its head and reunder-
lined for the artist of the African tradition (the continuing tradition to
which I believe a lot of us belong) will mean the recognition of the
pattern of transformation as the energetic, lunatic, ecstatic process
that restores the felt and the long recognised beings to their proper
world, and creates the reunification of all things in a primary universal construct.

In an essay in *The American Scholar*, xxxii, 4, 1963, Wole Soyinka,
writing specifically of Amos Tutuola, discovers:

> . . . a largeness that comes from an acceptance of life in all its mani-
> festations; where other writers conceive of man's initiation only
> in terms of photographic rites, Tutuola goes through it as a major
> fact of a concurrent life cycle, as a progression from a physical

insufficiency through the Quest into the very psyche of Nature. The *Palm-Wine Drinkard*, as with Fagunwa's Ogboju Ode and universal myth, is the epic of man's eternal restlessness, symbolized as always in a Search. . . . For Tutuola involves us in a co-operation of the spiritual and the physical, and this is the truth of his people's concept of life. The accessories of day-to-day existence only become drawn into this cosmic embrace; they do not invalidate it.

If we accept the premise that Tutuola is a writer whose art rests and has meaning only within the larger world construct of Yoruba thought and ontology, then we will understand Soyinka's statement here to be in a direct reference to the whole process of art in Africa.

In his novel *The Interpreters*, Kola, Sagoe, Egbo, Bandele, and Sekoni, the protagonists, represent a composite or combined artistic sensibility that seeks to infuse a moral balance into a fast disintegrating world of man's waking hours, and each struggle of this combined artistic impulse is toward that restoration which I referred to. Kola, in his person, carries the urgent energy of the artist as he seeks to create on his great canvas the reassembled folk psyche, peopled by deities and men in a unified community. This search is at the centre of his restlessness. It marks his dissatisfaction with a continuing line of surrogates.

Sagoe, the apostle of voidancy, of the extended joke, almost totters on the brink of cynical destructiveness. Yet he expresses the inner progression, toward that reintegration of the sacred and the profane, the agitated and the serene, the vulgar and the sublime. What struggles in his bosom is a wounded and a fragmented humanity that has suffered and continues to suffer the affront of a total immorality, the immorality that rejected and excluded all other possibilities.

But it is Egbo, the Ogun character, who in his creative urge is the reincarnation of Ogun himself, stands at the centre of the universal conflict, astride the non-dichotomised world. In an essay entitled, 'The Fourth Stage: Through the Mysteries of Ogun to the Origin of Yoruba Tragedy', that appeared in *Morality of Art* edited by D. W. Jefferson, published by Routledge and Kegan Paul, Soyinka attempts to link in the restorative role of art the placid essence of Obatala, the god of creation, and the creative urge and destructive instinct of Ogun. The link here lies in the tenuous, quivering trance of the transitional abyss before which Egbo, like Ogun, hesitates. But the mystic chasm summons him to complete the essence of that dread power, the act of immersion, predicated upon the attainment of the tragic climax, the calm of release which is the Obatala self-awareness, asserted in creative control of the universe. This is aesthetic joy. The struggle is not to be seen, Soyinka shows, in terms of Nietzschean original oneness but entails the restoration to the original womb, the serenity of release born out of suffering, and the contained fragmentation. So of Egbo in *The Interpreters* he wrote, 'The spectre of generations rose now about him and Egbo found he would always shrink, although incessantly drawn to the pattern of the dead. And this waiting near the end of the journey, hesitating on the brink, wincing as he admitted, was it not an exhumation of a better forgotten past?' I submit that this doubt, this hesitation, is at the heart of the movement toward the resolution.

Bandele in *The Interpreters* is Obatala, the authority of Ogboni: just, balanced, enduring, and yet retaining the capacity to undergo a needful, even if limited, suffering and alienation in order that the restoration should be complete. It is not for nothing that his voice is the ultimate voice of the novel. It is he who restores through the serenity of his person all the fragmented energies of his friends and of the world to a state of calm which is a precondition and prelude to the progression and the expansion of the human circle. In the process, therefore, there are the contradictions that exist within the same mythic continuum, expressing both a limited tragic spirit and a limited cosmic essence. The gulf and the bridge of inevitable separation will be bridged and crossed through the ritual sacrifice, in its ultimate and primary role. That is why Soyinka rejects a total tragic vision, the doom of repetition, which the Western tragic concept or outlook from the Greeks right down to our present time, entails. In the same essay he states:

> Yoruba myth is a recurrent exercise in the experience of disintegration, and this is significant to the isolation of Will among a people whose mores, culture and metaphysics are based on seeming resignation and acceptance but are, experienced in depth, a statement of man's penetrating insight into the final resolution of things and the constant evidence of harmony.

And so the suffering and the pain are negated only in the restorative moment and are yet rendered oppositional as this leads to the fragmentation and the truncation that I talked about. There is futility only in the context of fulfilment. The accompanying rites of music, the ritual, the sacrifice, provide the ingredients of the archetypal restoration, part of the transformation based in that numinous territory of transition in which ancestor, living, and the yet unborn unite to express the only cosmic reality. Man, Ogun, the protagonist of the abyss, dares, and in his day-to-day living underscores the elemental restorative scope of his artistic and therefore ritualist role. Poetry, dance, carving, represent in their finished states the serenity which is the enduring aspect of the resolved crisis of our divine person.

Let me quickly cover the relevance of what I am saying by reference to my own prose poem, *This Earth, My Brother*. What most reviewers of this work seem to be professionally unaware of is that I have used, taken, and utilised motifs from Ewe cosmology or ontology: motifs that are existing, extant, active. To any casual reader it should be quite clear that the work does not concern itself with the politics of the Nkrumah era, contrary to what a lot of people have said. In fact, when people compare my book with Ayi Kwei Armah's *The Beautyful Ones Are Not Yet Born* and regard us as the eloquent critics of the excesses of Nkrumah's rule, they are paying me a compliment I do not deserve or wish to share with Mr Armah. I wasn't talking about that. I was concerned with a total ongoing historical process of fragmentation and decay. It's true the hero of my book is a lawyer and, therefore, he's the most removed person from the primary area of that cultural impulse; he's the one who makes the journey; he's the one who assumes the role of the archetypal hero. He is, in fact, the Ogun essence through whom the restoration will be achieved. He epitomises alienation, *ennui, angst*, but these are the preconditions that are attendant upon his search and the restoration and the awareness.

Theoretically the book attempts to create a fragmented world of opposites, and any careful reader will note that as we move towards the end of the book, the fragmentation dissolves and the so-called 'a' sections vanish, and we move into a unified area of both poetry and prose, if you like those terms. Unified, because there is no longer any dichotomy in the person. The images of dunghill, the field of butterflies, the woman of the sea, who is very, very central, are all part of this process of transforming the mundane and the spiritual, uniting the fragments, thus muting the edges of the agonised sensibility that is predicated upon the returning balance towards the end. There is too the return of the primal good nature of the anthropomorphic female essence, the woman of the sea. She eliminates the dichotomised conflicts and the palpable contradictions. She is Earth. She is Africa. But where do all these come from? One critic, Richard Priebe, in a recent article in *Ariel*, has suggested that to understand African literature one must also examine the concept of liminality, (borrowing, I think liberally, from the work of Mary Douglas, particularly the book *Purity and Danger: An Analysis of the Concepts of Pollution and Taboo*, published in 1966) establishing a firm place for the so-called marginal persona. This means that all artists in the African society are people who exist on the periphery of the community; they do not exist in the centre. And in this, correctly I believe, he sees this artist as a priest, as a mediating agent between men and gods, a man who dares the dangerous frontiers of insanity, relative anguish and despair, in order to achieve for man the restoration. Much as I agree with this idea of liminality, *per se*, I also think that liminality connotes a predetermined boundary, a boundary which has been responsible for the dichotomised ethical and visionary concepts. And so when we place man on the periphery, we have removed him, therefore, from the centre of human activity. Accepting the theory in its most broad-based sense, we must guard against the possibility of demarcations. For man the visionary is also man the nonvisionary. Man the ethical being is also the abstract or man the physical being. If we use a circle, therefore, as our construct, the hero of *This Earth, My Brother* stands at a wider periphery, liminal yet central. His burden, also defined by his responsibilities beyond such characters that crowd the whole canvas in their brief and tormented appearances, marks him as the one who states for them the need for the restoration.

Chinua Achebe as a writer, I suggest, stands on the other side of what I am saying, the other side of the same system. His art is derived not only from the ritualistic structure, as specifically basing itself on a continuing survival motif, but also on the basic assumption or presupposition that we know that if this home is threatened, we shall proceed to a new ground and build for ourselves a new place of human habitation. In other words, things actually did not fall apart; the centre held, for it was only Okonkwo who decided to commit suicide; Umuofia refused to commit suicide; Umuofia still stands. And in his *Arrow of God*, Ezeulu, the priest, half-priest, half-man, half-deity, refuses to eat the yam and therefore imposes hardship upon the community. Thus he was the one who had stepped aside. And, as Achebe puts it, when they brought in the harvest, they brought home the harvest in the name of the son, which critics have decided means that the Christian religion had won in the end. But it is not a victory for Christianity. It was victory for Umuaro.

Tradition, therefore, stands at the heart of this literature. In our work we have essayed consciously or unconsciously to step out on the long journey of the restoration that I have spoken about. Our concern is not with that regime or that singular condition. It is, as in the work of the poets, the griots, the carvers of the older traditions, a process of fragmented world, of seeing the world from the African view, of making the African landscape physical and mythical, the point from which to see the world. That is why after all his wanderings, Amamu, the protagonist of *This Earth*, returns to that aboriginal landscape in order to fulfil his destiny. Any critic who does not see him within the context of that construct of Ewe mythology or ontology in which such images of the river, the dunghill, the sea, the desert, the drum, and the passion of love itself, being the eternal, elemental invocations of the ultimate ritual of his own and the communal restoration, had better leave the work alone.

Wole Soyinka

Drama and the African World-View

Contrary to popular assumptions, the serious divergences between a
traditional African approach to drama and the European will not be
found in lines of opposition between creative individualism and communal creativity, nor in the level of noise from the auditorium—this
being the supposed gauge of audience participation—at any given performance. They will be found more accurately in what is a recognisable
western cast of mind, a compartmentalising habit of thought which
periodically selects aspects of human emotion, phenomenal obser-
vations, metaphysical intuitions and even scientific deductions and
turns them into separatist myths (or 'truths'), sustained by a proliferat-
ing superstructure of presentation idioms, analogies and analytical
modes. I have evolved a rather elaborate metaphor to describe it;
appropriately it is not only mechanistic but represents a technology
which marked yet another phase of western man's comprehensive
world-view.

You must picture a steam-engine which shunts itself between some
rather short-spaced suburban stations. At the first station it picks up a
ballast of allegory, puffs into the next emitting a smokescreen on the
eternal landscape of nature truths. At the next it loads up with a
different species of logs which we shall call naturalist timber, puffs into
a half-way stop where it fills up with the synthetic fuel of surrealism,
from which point yet another holistic world-view is glimpsed and
asserted through psychedelic smoke. A new consignment of absurdist
coke lures it into the next station from which it departs giving off no
smoke at all, and no fire, until it derails briefly along constructivist
tracks and is towed back to starting-point by a neo-classic engine.

This, for us, is the occidental creative rhythm, a series of intellectual
spasms which, especially today, appears susceptible even to commercial
manipulation. And the difference which we are seeking to define
between European and African drama as one of man's formal

representations of experience is not simply a difference of style or form, nor is it confined to drama alone. It is representative of the essential differences between two world-views, a difference between one culture whose very artifacts are evidence of a cohesive understanding of irreducible truths and another whose creative impulses are directed by period dialectics. So, to begin with, we must jettison that fashionable distinction which tends to encapsulate western drama as a form of esoteric enterprise spied upon by fee-paying strangers as contrasted with a communal evolution of the dramatic mode of expression, this latter being the African. Of far greater importance is the fact that western dramatic critique does habitually reflect the abandonment of a belief in culture as a definition within man's knowledge of fundamental, unchanging relationships between himself and society and within the larger context of the observable universe.

Let us, by way of a paradigmatic example, take a common theme in traditional mask-drama: a symbolic struggle with chthonic presences, the goal of the conflict being a harmonious resolution for the well-being of the community.[1] Any individual within the 'audience' knows better than to add his voice even to the most seductive passages of an invocatory song or to contribute a refrain to the familiar sequence of a liturgical exchange among the protagonists. The moment for choric participation is well defined but this does not imply that, until such a moment, participation ceases. The so-called audience is itself an integral part of that arena of conflict, it contributes spiritual strength to the protagonist through its choric reality which must first be conjured up and established, defining and investing the arena through the protagonist's incantations. The drama would be non-existent except within and against this symbolic representation of earth and cosmos, except within this communal compact whose choric essence supplies the collective energy for the challenger of chthonic realms. Overt participation when it comes is channelled through a formalised repertoire of gestures and liturgical responses. The 'spontaneous' participant from within the audience does not permit himself to give vent to bare impulse or euphoria which might bring him out as a dissociated entity from within the choric mass. If it does happen, as of course it can, the event is an aberration which may imperil the eudaemonic goals of that representation. The interjector—whose balance of mind is regarded as being temporarily disturbed—is quietly led out and the appropriate (usually unobtrusive) spells are cast to counter the risks of the abnormal event.

I would like to go a little deeper into this ritualistic sense of space since it is so intimately linked with the comprehensive world-view of the society that gave it birth. We shall treat it firstly as a medium in the communicative sense and, like any other medium, it is one that is best defined through the process of interruption. In theatrical terms, this interruption is effected principally by the human apparatus. Sound, light, motion, even smell can be used just as validly to define space, and ritual theatre utilises all these instruments of definition to control and render concrete, to parallel—this is perhaps the best description of the process—to parallel the experiences or intuitions of man in that far more disturbing environment which he defines variously as void, emptiness or infinity. The concern of ritual theatre in this process of spatial definition which precedes—as we shall discover—the actual enactment must therefore be seen as an integral part of man's constant efforts to master the immensity of the cosmos with his miniscule self. The actual events which make up the enactment are themselves, in ritual theatre, a materialisation of this basic adventure of man's metaphysical self.

Theatre, then, is one arena, one of the earliest that we know of, in which man has attempted to come to terms with the spatial pheno-menon of his being. Again, in speaking of space, let us recognise first of all that with the advancement of technology and the evolution—some would prefer to call it a counter-evolution—of the technical sensibility, the spatial vision of theatre has become steadily contracted into purely physical acting areas on a stage as opposed to a symbolic arena for meta-physical contests. The pagan beginnings of Greek theatre retained their symbolic validity to dramaturges for centuries after the event, so that the relative positions of suppliant, tyrant or *deus ex machina*, as well as the offertory or altar, were constantly impressed on their audience and created immediate emotional overtones both in the event of their utilisation and by their very act of being. (I do not, for the purpose of this essay, wish to debate whether the very fixity of these positions did not, contrasted with the fluid approach of African ritual space, detract from the audience's experience of cosmic relations.) Medieval Euro-pean theatre in its turn, corresponding to the religious mythology of its period, created a constant microcosmos by its spatial correspondences of good and evil, angels and demons, paradise, purgatory and hell. The protagonists of earth, heaven and hell enacted their various trials and conflicts in relation to those traditional positions, and the automatic recognition of those hierarchical situations of man created spiritual anxieties and hopes in the breasts of the audience. But observe, the apprehended territory of man has already begun to contract! Cosmic representation has shrunk into a purely moral one, a summation in terms of penalties and rewards. The process continued through successive periods of European partial explorations of what was once a medium of totality, achieving such analytical aberrations as in this sample of compartmentalisation which claims that the right (actor's) wing of the stage is 'stronger' than the left. We will not encounter any proofs of this ludicrous assertion in the beginnings of theatre—Greek or African.

Ritual theatre, let it be recalled, establishes the spatial medium not merely as a physical area for simulated events but as a manageable contraction of the cosmic envelope within which man—no matter how deeply buried such a consciousness has latterly become—fearfully exists. And this attempt to manage the immensity of his spatial awareness makes every manifestation in ritual theatre a paradigm for the cosmic human condition. There are transient parallels, brief visual moments of this experience in modern European theatre. The spectacle of a lone human figure under a spotlight on a darkened stage is, unlike a painting, a breathing, living, pulsating, threateningly fragile example of this paradigm. It is threatening because, unlike a similar parable on canvas, its fragility is experienced both on the level of its symbolism and in terms of sympathetic concern for the well-being of that immediate human medium. Let us say he is a tragic character: at the first sign of a check in the momentum of a tragic declamation, his audience becomes nervous for him, wondering—has he forgotten his line? Has he blacked out? Or in the case of opera—will she make that upper register? Well, ritual theatre has an additional, far more fundamental anxiety. Indeed, it is correct to say that the technical anxiety, even where it exists—after all it does exist, the element of creative form is never absent even in the most so-called primitive consciousness—so, where it does exist, it is never so profoundly engaged as with a modern manifestation. The real unvoiced fear is: will this protagonist survive confrontation with forces that exist within the dangerous area of transformation? Entering that microcosmos involves a loss of individuation, a self-submergence in universal essence. It is an act undertaken on behalf of the community and the welfare of that protagonist is inseparable from that of the total community. [2]

This ritual understanding is essential to a profound participation in the cathartic processes of the great tragedies. To attempt to define it even more clearly I would like to refer once again to painting, that essentially individualistic art. In surmounting the challenge of space and cosmos, a Turner, a Wyeth or a Van Gogh utilises endless permutations of colour, shapes and lines to extract truly harrowing meta-physical statements from natural phenomena. There is, however, no engagement of the communal experience in this particular medium. The transmission is individual. It is no less essential to the sum of human experience but it is—even when viewed by a thousand people simul-taneously—a mere sum of fragmented experiences, individual and vicarious. The singularity of theatre is its simultaneity in the forging of a single human experience—at its most successful. That it often does not succeed is true enough, but it does not invalidate the truth that, at the very roots of the dramatic phenomenon, this affirmation of the com-munal self was the experiential goal. The search, even by modern European dramatists for ritualist roots from which to draw out visions of modern experience, is a clue to the deep-seated need of creative man to recover this archetypal consciousness in the origins of the drama-tic medium.

Ritual theatre, viewed from the spatial perspective, aims then to reflect through physical and symbolic means, the archetypal struggle of the mortal being against exterior forces. A tragic view of the theatre goes even further and suggests that even the so-called realistic or literary drama can be interpreted as a mundane reflection of this essential struggle. Poetic drama, especially, may be regarded as a repository of this essential aspect of theatre—being largely meta-phorical, it expands the immediate meaning and action of the pro-tagonists into a world of nature forces and metaphysical conceptions. Or, to put it the other way round, powerful nature or cosmic in-fluences are internalised within the protagonists and this implosive factor creates the titanic scale of their passions even when the basis of the conflicts seems hardly to warrant it. (Shakespeare's *Lear* is of course the greatest exemplar of this.) Indeed, such a view of theatre sees the stage as a constant battleground for forces beyond the petty infractions of habitual communal norms or patterns of human relationships and expectations, beyond the actual twists and incidents of action and their resolutions. The stage is endowed, for the purpose of that communal presence which alone creates it—and this is the fundamental defining concept, that the stage is brought into being by a communal presence—so, for this purpose, the stage becomes the affective, rational and in-tuitive milieu of the total communal experience: historic, race-forma-ative, cosmogonic. Where such theatre is encountered in its purest form, not as re-created metaphors for the latter tragic stage, we will find no compass points, no horizontal or vertical definitions. There are no reserved spaces for the protagonist for his very act of representational being is defined in turn by no less than the infinite cosmos within which the origin of the community and its contemporaneous experience of being is firmly embedded.

Drama, however, exists on the boards; in the improvised space among stalls in the deserted or teeming market, on the raised platform in a school or community hall, in the secretive recesses of a nature-fringed shrine, among the push-buttons of the modern European stage or their equivalents in Africa—those elegant monstrosities raised to enshrine the spirit of misconceived prestigiousness. It is necessary always to look for the essence of the play among these roofs and spaces, not confine it to the printed text as an autonomous entity. For this reason the deductions of plays which have had the benefit of actual production are more instructive and, for the rest of this paper, I intend to utilise two different but representative plays which have had the benefit of realisation before both European and African audiences. Critical responses are in themselves an index to dramatic attitudes and are, even more relevantly, a reflection of those world-views which separate and profoundly affect the relations of art and life in differing cultures. A common ground to all fortunately makes comparative references possible: the creative man is universally involved in a subtle conspiracy, a tacit understanding that he, the uncommissioned observer, relate the plight of man, his disasters and joys to some vague framework of observable truths and realities. The differences are the various levels of realities, relative comprehensiveness of vision and the assumptions which the creative mind feels traditionally entitled to make or turn into acceptances—from the forcefulness of his art—coerced from the most unwilling audience.

Our first example, *Song of a Goat*, a play by J. P. Clark, has the advantage, for this exercise, of fitting into the neat category of tragedy in the European definition of this genre. It was first performed in Europe at the 1965 Commonwealth Festival of the Arts, London; its reception was not of the best, and for very good reasons. First, the production was weak and amateurish. An inexperienced group playing on a London stage for the first time in their lives found that they could not match the emotions of the play with the technical demands of the stage and auditorium. The staging of the play was not particularly sensitive, in addition to which there were the usual unscripted happenings which seem to plague amateur productions everywhere. A rather lively goat (another practical mistake) tended to punctuate passages of intended solemnity with bleats from one end and something else from the other. The text itself—we may as well get over the critical carps at once—the text, written in verse, betrays a self-conscious straining for poetic effect, leading to inflated phrasing and clotted passages. For a company which was not wholly at home in the English language, the difficulties were insurmountable. In an English audience it created resistance, even hostility.

The drama takes place in a fishing village. The characters are Ijaw, a riverine people on the Niger delta. Two brothers, Zifa and Tonye, Ebiere, the wife of the elder Zifa, and Orukorere, a scatty old aunt of the two brothers, are the central characters. The old lady provides a Cassandra presence throughout the unfolding of the tragedy which is centred on the sexual impotence of Zifa.

At first Zifa sends his wife to consult the Masseur, a doctor-cum-seer who diagnoses the real problem without difficulty, recognising that it is the husband not the wife who is the real patient. He suggests that the younger brother, Tonye, take up the marital duties of the elder, an idea which is violently rejected by Zifa (who later consults him) just as Ebiere indignantly spurned it in her turn. But the inevitable does happen. In one of the most credibly sexual scenes of progressive frustration Ebiere goads the brother into taking her. Zifa suspects, manoeuvres the guilty pair into a revelatory ritual—this ritual is made the climactic moment of the play—and tries to kill Tonye. He escapes, but only to hang himself in the loft. Zifa walks out to sea and the house of Zifa is left to the bats and goats.

I have touched on some of the technical reasons why, unlike some African audiences before whom this play has since been staged, the European audience found itself estranged from its tragic statement. One other reason, however, was voiced by the newspaper critics and this had nothing to do with the fortuitous events of stage presentation but rather chose to limit, in far more general terms, what areas of human unhappiness may contain the tragic potential. It underlined yet another aspect of the essential divergencies of the European cast of mind from the African: that, on the one hand, which sees the cause of human anguish as viable only within strictly temporal capsules and, on the other, whose tragic understanding transcends the causes of individual disjunction and recognises them as reflections of a far greater disharmony in the communal psyche. The objection was this: sexual impotence was a curable condition in modern medicine (or psychiatry). In addition, child adoption provided one remedy, among others, for sterility; therefore sexual impotence or sterility were outside the range of tragic dimensions for a European audience.

There was something familiar in that plaint. I had heard it some years before after a London production of Ibsen's *Ghosts*. Syphilis, asserted a critic or two, was no longer an incurable disease. Ibsen's play had consequently lost any tragic rationale it might have had in the mercury days of venereal science. I could not help recalling this particular critical thesis when I found myself in Sydney a year or two later and encountered an Australian poet who, with his wife cheerfully supplying the details, boasted that he had caught a completely new mutation of the syphilitic virus which had the entire Australian medical profession stumped. Nicknamed the Golden Staphylococcus because of its appearance under the microscope, it had developed powerful resistance to all known antibiotics. Research and consultations with international laboratories would shortly, I was relieved to learn, put an end to the reign of the Golden Staphylococcus, but I could not help wondering aloud if Ibsen's *Ghosts* should not quickly be declared the definitive antipodeal tragedy of the sixties.

Our critic would have found consolation, however, even confirmation of his views, in the quite cheerful attitude towards the acquisition of a new and rather menacing virus. He would fall back on the argument that the social atmosphere created by a demystification of diseases, the removal of the puritanical burden of opprobrium which attached to the 'social' diseases have combined to destroy the genetic doom which gave Ibsen's tragedy its dimension of the inescapable. The same goes for O'Neill and his tuberculosis-infested drama. And so attitudes which consider sexual impotence as insufficient cause for a statement in tragic terms are logical results of sociological changes, a relaxation of traditional attitudes to masculine virility and, the existence of opportunities through which the creative constriction in the victim can be channelled. Indeed, to sum it up in the most contemporary terms, Women's Lib. and the tragedy of sexual impotence, or even infidelity, are mutually exclusive. *The Father* is dead; long live *The Female Eunuch!*

The socio-political question of the viability of a tragic view in itself in a contemporary world is of course one which has preoccupied schools of social vision since the preliminary clashes of the empirical stance against metaphysical religious orthodoxies. This has become crystallised in, I suggest, two main attitudes: one, represented by the Marxist view of man and history, which denounces the insidious enervation of social will by the tragic afflatus. The other is the rearguard action of crumbling defences. It speculates that there has been a decline in tragic understanding (i.e. the referential basis from which man is convincingly projected in confrontation with forces beyond his remedial understanding). From this basis of suspicion and a related awareness that this represents a quite unnecessary loss in creative territory, an almost comprehensive list of major twentieth-century dramatists have felt compelled, at one time or another, to rifle and re-present Greek tragedy as containing statements of relevance even to post-Marxian times.

Among the literary beneficiaries of the first attitude, the principle of revolutionary rejection of the ineffable is, of course, the French neo-fiction movement of the late fifties and early sixties (Robbe-Grillet, etc.) whose manifesto enjoins the fictional realisation (observe the contradiction!) of objective superficies. Rooted in as deep a fallacy as the involuted Surrealist ontology which it appears to oppose, the theory of the new fiction not only creates a gulf between man and his physical environment but declares such a gulf unbridgeable. What we are in fact confronted with in both these seemingly antagonistic views are two faces of the same European tradition: one which assumes and seeks to transcend a gulf between man and the essence of being, thought, feeling, etc., between object and the pure state of being; and the other which, claiming to rectify the anti-social pursuit of an intangible kingdom by this and other schools of world-perception, legislates a gulf between man and the materiality of his environment and proceeds to employ consciously mechanistic devices to widen the unproven, purely hypothetical abyss.

George Steiner observes, in his diagnosis of the decline in tragic grandeur of the European dramatic vision,[3] a relatedness between this decline and that of the 'organic world-view and of its attendant context of mythological symbolic and ritual reference'. The implication of this, a strange one to the African world-view, is that, to expand Steiner's own metaphor, the world in which lightning was a cornice in the cosmic architecture of man collapsed that moment when Benjamin Franklin tapped its power with a kite. The assimilative wisdom of African metaphysics recognises no difference in essence between the mere means of tapping the power of lightning—via ritual sacrifice, through the purgative will of the community unleashing its justice on the criminal, or through the agency of Franklin's revolutionary gadget. What George Steiner effectively summarises is that at one time or the other of some intellectual hypothesis, at some phase or the other of scientific exploration, at each supposition by European man on the possible nature of things, that architectonic unity which is the basis of man's regulating consciousness (of which the most personalised expression is his art) suffers the same fate of redundancy as the assumptions and theories themselves. For cultures which pay more than lip-service to the protean complexity of the universe of which man is himself a reflection, this European habit of world redefining appears both wasteful and truth-defeating.

We must return to the stage manifestation, to the dramatic expression which confronts its audience with such human revelations as breed an awareness of a play of forces which contradict a technologically reme-diable world, this being the most easily isolated challenge of the tragic intrusion. It becomes necessary to examine the nature of the concrete event which, when successfully mirrored, deranges the technological rationale with which the healthy, well-adjusted audience entity is conditioned to ward off penetration of the 'pathetic fallacy'.

And the most significant discovery, or more accurately, recognition is that we encounter in such plays a complete, hermetic universe of forces or being. This is the most fundamental attribute of all true tragedy, no matter where geographically placed. In *Lear* for instance, the world of the court, the world of Old Man Frost in the disordered community of wind and heather is rounded and entire. The relation-ship of seemingly disparate entities such as Court and Nature is estab-lished through character transitions—Lear, Kent, Edgar and Fool out from one and into the other environment and back again, then the progressively vixenish daughters in near physical transformations. Such is the spatial architecture of the play that the specialised world of cronies, villains, principles of inheritance and courtly protocol becomes accessible to and paralleled by whatever world the audience inhabits, with its own laws, norms and values. The universe of a *Hamlet* is wrapped in a similar envelope, so are the haunting habitations of John Synge, Garcia Lorca, even Wedekind at his most uncompromising interiority. Encapsulation of these exclusivist spheres of existence within which all action is unravelled appears to be the first prerequisite of all profound drama, and tragedy most specifically. Its internal cogency makes it impervious to the accident of place and time.

In relating *Song of a Goat* to such drama, I make no exaggerated claims for its actual achievement. It remains, however, excellent pre-mises from which to enter the matrical consciousness of the African world. The play is contained within a microcosmic completeness as already described, with especially strong affinities—again for ease of reference—to the world of Lorca. A play of brooding violence, its central motif, the symbolic design may be described as one of contained, poetic violence. We encounter human beings whose occupation and environment are elemental and visceral. Flood and ebb affect their daily existence, their language, their spectrum of perception. Mists and marsh colour their mood. Within this claustrophobia of threatening metaphors, existence is economic and intense; its expansion into an awareness of immediately exterior forces merely reinforces their circumscribed intensity of being. From this closed relationship a thread of potential violence is gradually drawn, consistently prepared through metaphors within the dialogue of action. Until we are brought at last, bound to the protagonists, to the climactic image which, for the principal sufferer, is also the image of revelation—a sacrificial pot and the ram's head within it, a precariously contained force, barely held, barely restrained. It parallels that core of sexual frustration, that damming up of natural continuity and beneficent release by sterile opposition compounded with individual pride, self-deception, a code of morality which presupposes normal circumstances.

The whole point, however, is that the circumstances are abnormal, even unnatural. The interaction of man and nature so pervasively rendered in the play demands a drastic redress of these abnormal circumstances and it is a demand which cannot be pushed aside by the pride of one man. The poetic containment of violence is very much the environmental reality of *Song of a Goat*. Storms do not occur every day nor are fishermen washed off their canoes on every fishing-trip. But the hovering claims of this natural cycle dominate the natives' daily awareness, giving to rituals of appeasement an integrated essentiality for every event. Thus the death of an individual is not seen as an isolated incident in the life of one man. Nor is individual fertility separable from the regenerative promise of earth and sea. The sickness of one individual is a sign of, or may portend, the sickness of the world around him. Something has occurred to disrupt the natural rhythms and the cosmic balances of what is the total community.

> There, another blow
> Has been dealt the tree of our house, and see
> How the sap pours out to spread our death. I
> Believe it, now I believe it. White ants

Have passed their dung on our roof-top.
Like a tree rotten in the rain, it
Topples. What totem is there left now
For the tribe to hold on to for support.

Passages like this, displaying little of the lapses of language which mar a good portion of the play, convey an unselfconscious conjunction of the circumcentric worlds of man, social community and Nature in the minds of each character, irrespective of role. And one important, even vital element in the composition of the elaborate interiority of such tragic drama is of course its moral order. This must not be understood in any narrow sense of the ethical code which society develops to regulate the conduct of its members. A breakdown in moral order implies, in the African world-view, a rupture in the body of Nature just as the physical malfunctioning of one man. And the literature of this viewpoint is not to be found in the ruminative asides or debates among principals but in the metaphor of existence in the most mundane or in the most exalted circumstances. We find, to revert to J. P. Clark's play, that moral disorder is not simply a matter of sleeping with another man's wife, especially if that man is your brother. This is of course an anti-social act and is recognised as such. It is neither desirable nor is it condoned. Deviations from harmonious conduct such as this are dealt with by set processes which vary from society to society. But this anti-social act can be—depending on circumstances—a far less dangerous threat to communal well-being than, for instance, Zifa's self-delusion and sterile pride.

Where society lives in a close inter-relation with Nature, regulates its existence by nature phenomena within the observable processes of continuity—ebb and tide, waxing and waning of the moon, rain and drought, planting and harvest—the highest moral order is seen as one which guarantees a parallel continuity of the species. We must try to understand this as operating within a framework which can conveniently be termed the metaphysics of the irreducible: knowledge of birth and death as the human cycle, the wind as a moving, felling, cleansing, destroying, winnowing force, the duality of the knife as blood-letter and creative implement, earth and sun as life-sustaining verities, etc., etc. These serve as matrices within which mores, personal relationships, even communal economics are formulated and reviewed. Other 'irreducible' acceptances may evolve from this; for instance, the laws of hospitality or taboo on incest, but they do not possess the same strength and compulsion as the fundamental matrix. They belong to a secondary category and may be reversed by accident or human error.

The profound experience of tragic drama is comprehensive within such irreducible hermeticism. Because of the visceral intertwine of each individual with the fate of the entire community, a rupture in his normal functioning not only endangers this shared reality but threatens existence itself.

The African world-view is not, however, as though by implication, stagnant. This may seem a surprising assertion to those who consider that the kind of society which has emerged so far from the foregoing fits rather disturbingly into Karl Popper's[4] primitive blueprint for the modern totalitarian society. Karl Popper's inadequate knowledge of the societies which he attempts to force into his specially constructed closed circle has of course been adequately exposed by several of his critics. His fundamental assumptions are inaccurate. They bypass the code on which this world-view is based, the continuing evolution of tribal wisdom through an acceptance of the elastic nature of knowledge as its one reality, as signifying no more than reflections of the original coming-in-being of a manifestly complex reality.[5] European scholars have always betrayed a tendency of substituting the myth, the lore, the social techniques of imparting knowledge or of stabilising society for the evidence of orthodox rigidity. Yet the opposite, an attitude of philosophic accommodativeness is constantly demonstrated in the attributes accorded most African deities, attributes which deny the existence of impurities or 'foreign matter' in the god's digestive system. Experiences which, until the event, lie outside the tribe's cognition are absorbed through the god's agency and converted into yet another piece of the social armoury in its struggle for existence or enter the lore of the tribe. This principle creates for society a non-doctrinaire mould of constant awareness, one which stays outside the monopolistic orbit of the priesthood, outside any claims to gnostic secrets by special cults. Interpretation, as it is universally, rests mostly in the hands of such intermediaries but rarely with the dogmatic finality of, for example, Christianity or Islam.[6] Their principal function is to reinforce by observances, rituals and mytho-historical recitals the existing consciousness of cosmic entanglement in the community, and to arbitrate in the sometimes difficult application of such truths to domestic and community undertakings.

One other example, a fortunate blend of myth and history, penetrates even deeper into that area of man's cosmogonic hunger, one which leads him to the profounder forms of art as retrieval vehicles or assertive links with a lost sense of origin. That the play, *Oba Koso*, is also a tragedy is not deliberate but it is of course more than coincidence. Comedy also expresses a world-view, so does melodrama and the other labels of convenience which we attach to drama. But, despite a Molière or a Ben Jonson, even comedies of the archetype must first reduce humanity to the manageable circle of the dramatist's lens. Tragedy dares to thrust it beyond, suggesting areas of unplumbable mysteries in its passage. It is possible to experience or to penetrate the framework of a world perception from tragedy. Sadly, the would-be tragedies which flood the African literary scene display little of this understanding. Their tawdry claims to attention are fulfilled only through momentary frustration at one's inability to refer to available printed plays or to capture, in the literary idiom, that essence of allegory or symbolic drama which so eloquently, in traditional form, consoles mankind for the limitations which hinder it from grasping the kernels of mysteries that constantly litter his awareness.

Oba Koso straddles the modernistic gulf between symbol and expository action and dialogue with the essence of poetry, a perfection of unity rarely encountered on the modern African stage. Written and played in Yoruba, it provides a uniquely apposite reference as it has enjoyed a variety of linguistic audiences all over the world—German, English, Yiddish, Russian, Polish, French, etc.—and nowhere at all has it failed to elicit that profound communal catharsis which is one of the acknowledged ends of tragic action. It constitutes a living instance of the universal roots of the tragic pulse and the transcendental nature of poetry over the medium of transmission—language, music or movement. One must speak again of the preliminary evocation of a hermetic world, autonomous, demonstrably cohesive, neutral to exterior mores and values, a rich and persuasive evocation achieved through the felicitous plurality of the dramatic media, a stylistic and sensual assault both on intimates of that culture and on alienates, equally. A code of meanings is established through the media of rhythm, movement and tonal-specific harmonies which instantly create their own territory of reality. The initiate knows, of course, that even the paraphernalia of the protagonists is endowed with significant meanings, social and myth-referential imports. The alienate senses this with as great certainty and, while he necessarily loses something of the specificity, he is enabled to create with ease a parallel scale of referentials since he views it all in the framework of motion and stylised conflict all obeying a finely regulated rhythm of relationships. He may not, especially if he is tone-deaf and chronically a-rhythmic, appreciate that both rhythm and timbre are also specific and cogent, but his intelligence and sensibility respond to the fact that he is a participant within an integrated matrix of cultural forces, that the tragic unfolding of the reign of Oba Sango is not merely an interesting episode in the annals of a people's history but the spiritual consolidation of the race through immersion in the poetry of origin.

In so far as it is history, the play concerns the machinations of a tyrant, Sango, who aims to immobolise one or both of two increasingly powerful chiefs in his kingdom. He employs the classic trick of despatching them out to keep order on the borders of the kingdom, confident that their matching egos would bring them in fatal conflict with each other. As is usual in these cases, Sango's own councillors and subjects have themselves egged him onto the course. The ruse fails, however. The two warriors meet and fight, but the victor spares the vanquished. They grow individually more and more powerful. Again, at the insistence of his people Sango summons them and organises yet another duel. This time the victor, the same as before, Gbonka, slays his opponent, then turns on the king and demands his throne. The terrified subjects now act in character, begin to abandon their king. In a rage at this betrayal he turns on them and slaughters a few. But the abomination (and the betrayal) drives him out of the city and in despair, he hangs himself. Or rather, he does not hang. For the postscript of the play is his apotheosis and the title of the play, *Oba Koso* means—the king did not hang. Disgusted by human fickleness, history declares, Sango ascended the heavens and joined the other deities of the Yoruba pantheon.

Here now is a sample of Sango's praise-song; it celebrates his intemperate power and ferocity:

> You think the worm is dancing but
> That is merely the way it walks
> You think Sango is fighting you but
> That is merely the way he is.
>
> He dines on pounded yam with the family head
> Then seizes his first-born on the porch
> And slays him
> He cracks the wall, splits the wall
> He splits it wide open and
> Rams two hundred thunderstones in the crack.

But beatitudinal passages of lyricism abound, paving the way for a restorative post-climax of tragedy for the race. The conflict, stylised, drains off the evil energies of excess. Those self-destructive principles embodied in, for example, the above praise-song are purged from the community through the medium of the suffering protagonist. Tragic drama of this nature (and tragic poetry) operates through the homoeo-pathic principle, and it should create no surprise to find the expression 'praise-song' applied to such wanton savagery or to find in performance that the lines are chanted in a non-critical, adulatory and joyous in-volvement. Such passages and their counter are essential to a sense of realistic health in the community; they embody, it should also be remembered, the conjurative aspects of nature-mysteries and the origin of the race. Invocation of nature-munificence is not a passive operation nor can it be effected by mere pietistic rote. The support of the com-munity, its insistent will, is written into the poetry of such tragedy. If the protagonist is their symbolic representative through the abyss of origin—racial but also individual—the simplistic moral selectiveness cannot be applied to what energies may be conjured from nature to aid the emissary. Sango dares the symbolic abyss of transition on behalf of his people, the resources which he calls upon for his passage of terror cannot but be both good and evil. His tragic excess and weakness fulfil the cyclic demand on, and provoke the replenishment of, choric (communal) energies and resilience. It is an eternal strain which can be countered only by an equal dare, so thorough and if necessary so amoral that the protagonist is seen as a reflection of that communal truth with all its mottled origin.

This sense of origin, the coming-in-being of the race, dominates the drama. Thus Timi, one of the manipulated generals, arrives for the first time at his new settlement—yet another paradigm of origin that poetry insinuates into the action—a total stranger, isolated and appre-hensive. He invokes universal aid through his song:

> I come this day to Ede town
> It is the gentle wind that says, blow
> Towards me
> Spirits of teeming termites say, swarm
> Towards me
> Air is the Father of Dew
> Dew is the Father of Showers
> Showers are the Father of the Ocean
> Ocean is Father of long-trodden Earth

and his appeal, while primarily addressed to the as yet unseen inhabitants of Ede are expanded to trigger awake the animal and spirit world and all Nature forces, linking them to him through the sympathetic memory of their own origin. The resulting strength of acceptance that he must derive from a favourable response is an echo of similar beneficence derived by the existing inhabitants; it is also a renewal. His prayer was once their prayer of appeasement to unseen forces on first invading the once virgin soil. The response of the unseen chorus, in whom all denizens of this undemarcated world are now symbolically fused, is therefore emotionally experienced as a re-enactment of their own birth and origin. The tribulations of wandering and settling, of uprooting and displacement, join with this representation of human loneliness and alienation, sensations which lie at the emotional root of tragedy. Timi's song is a summons on man and nature for the remedial aid of acceptance and the key to unlock this source of guarded strength is the mythopoeic evocation of the passage of race.

> I come this day to Ede town
> It is the gentle wind that says, blow towards me
> Spirits of swarming termites say, swarm towards me
> Two hundred rafters support the house
> Two hundred lizards support the wall
> Let all hands be raised to sustain me. . . .

Like the preceding passage, the constant thread is—continuity. Timi's struggle is presented as inseparable from the evidence of Nature at its most domestic. It merges into the larger universe of wind, rain and ocean, growth and regeneration, a humanistic faith and affirmation which is the other face of tragic loss. And so, even this lesser character, no less than Gbonka, no less than the choric compact, no less than Sango himself, is the protagonist of continuity, skirting the rims of that heart of cosmic mysteries into which his leader Sango will shortly plunge.

Located in the poignant moments of the race's coming-in-being, the terrain has nevertheless grown familiar and pertinent even to the alien participant in these tragic rites of origin. This is because *Oba Koso* confidently asserts its own laws of cohesive interiority. It expands thereafter through the jubilant accents of poetry and passion to a retrieval of the enlarged consciousness of being, universal and individual.

Notes

1 The following remarks are based on plays observed *in situ*, that is, on the spot where the performance originates and ends and at its appropriate time of the year, not on itinerant variations on the same theme. The specific play referred to here was a harvest play which took place in a farm clearing some three miles south of Ihiala in the then Eastern Region of Nigeria, 1961.

2 Kola Ogunmola, in his stage adaptations of Amos Tutuola's *Palm-Wine Drinkard*, built on this tradition, one that is still manifested in ancestral mask comedies.

3 George Steiner, *The Death of Tragedy*.

4 Karl Popper, *The Open Society and its Enemies*.

5 This is indeed the unifying rationale of the Ifa (Yoruba Divination) corpus.

6 This accommodating nature, which does not, however, contradict or pollute their true essences, is what makes Sango capable of extending his territory of lightning to embrace electricity in the effective consciousness of his followers. For his part Ogun becomes not merely the god of war but the god of revolution in the most contemporary context—and this is not merely in Africa but in the Americas to where his worship had spread. As the Roman Catholic props of the Batista regime in Cuba discovered when it was too late, they should have worried less about Karl Marx than about Ogun, the rediscovered deity of revolution.